W9-CSC-809

San Jose and Its Cathedral

Saint Joseph
Descendant of the House of David
A humble carpenter
Husband of Mary, mother of Jesus,
Who watched over her son with love and care
Proclaimed by Pope Pius IX patron of the Church
He is the
Patron Saint of the City of San Jose
and the Cathedral of St. Joseph

View looking north of Plaza Park, Fairmont Hotel, San Jose Museum of Art, and St. Joseph's Cathedral (PHOTOGRAPH © ROBERT W. CAMERON)

San Jose
and Its Cathedral

By Marjorie Pierce

Foreword by Bishop Pierre DuMaine

WESTERN TANAGER PRESS · SANTA CRUZ
1990

Copyright © 1990 by Marjorie Pierce

Dustjacket design by Lynn Piquett
Dustjacket painting by Robert Moesle
Text design by Michael S. Gant
Typography by TypaGraphix

Additional Photo Credits: page 31, W. R. Rambo, *History of the Sainte Claire Club*; pages 39–41, courtesy Mirassou Vineyards; pages 42–42, courtesy Paul Masson; pages 49 and 51, courtesy Thomas McEnery; page 64, bottom, and page 72, *San Jose Mercury News*; page 100, Ralph Rambo; page 103, bottom, courtesy the Sainte Claire Club; page 142, courtesy Thomas McEnery.

All rights reserved. No portion of this book may be reproduced without permission in writing, except for quotations in critical articles or reviews.

ISBN: 0-934136-47-5
Library of Congress Card Catalog Number: 90-071209

Printed in the United States

Western Tanager Press
1111 Pacific Avenue
Santa Cruz, CA 95060

In loving memory of Bobbi

Acknowledgements

It would be difficult for me to try to name all those who have been helpful in the writing of this book, but I'll start with my husband, Bob Pierce. Not only was he patient and understanding of the long hours I spent poring over research material and glued to the computer, but he made a major contribution in reproducing most of the old photographs that appear in the book. Next I should thank my editor, Michael Gant, for his patience and then offer a special thanks to Michael Malone for his expert editing of the chapter on Silicon Valley.

History people are always generous in sharing their knowledge. Included among those are San Jose's official historian, Clyde Arbuckle; Brother Thomas Marshall, S.J., archivist California Province + Society of Jesus; Julia O'Keefe, archivist Santa Clara University; Leslie Asunaga, archivist San Jose Historical Museum; Frances and Theron Fox; and Bart Sepúlveda. Helping in special ways were Cecily Kyes, James Purcell, Frank Fiscalini, and Carmencita Cardoza. And a special thank you is due the Most Reverend Bishop Pierre DuMaine.

Contents

Foreword

San Jose is California's oldest city and newest metropolis. St. Joseph of San Jose is California's oldest parish and newest cathedral.

These two historical facts are not just a curious coincidence. They are so tightly interwoven that they constitute the single fabric of the history of Santa Clara Valley. Since 1777 the heart of this valley has been the "pueblo" of San Jose, and since 1803 at the heart of San Jose has been the church of St. Joseph.

With this book, Marjorie Pierce has celebrated the interweaving of these two histories into the single story of our city and our valley. And she has done it in the certain knowledge that history is not merely a matter of important events and extraordinary personages, but of ordinary lives of ordinary people, who occasionally do extraordinary things and together bequeath a heritage of accomplishment and vision. Even if we too often take it for granted, this heritage is important to each new generation.

A journalist who has chronicled the life of our community for nearly thirty years, Marjorie Pierce offers a wonderfully rich array of anecdotes and personalities, wisely letting the reader gradually discern the recurring themes of energy, hope, vision, and diversity that have given this city and valley their special character in every generation, including our own.

The main recurring theme of her story is, of course, St. Joseph parish and church, not just as the site of the baptisms, weddings, and funerals of old families and new immigrants, but as the historical center of the city and the enduring symbol of certain values the community shared and a certain vision it had of itself.

Thus the story of *San Jose and Its Cathedral*, as told by Marjorie Pierce, is not just a family album for nostalgic citizens of the city or faithful members of the church. It is a subtle challenge to the present generation to appreciate our heritage, to weigh it thoughtfully against our

Bishop Pierre DuMaine blesses a child after a confirmation at Our Lady of Guadalupe Church (PHOTOGRAPH © DAVID FLEMATE)

present values and vision, and to hand it on carefully to new generations, in the hope that in another hundred years *San Jose and its Cathedral* will have more stories worth telling and another to tell them with the zeal and affection of a Marjorie Pierce.

BISHOP PIERRE DuMAINE, Diocese of San Jose

ix

Introduction

When Bishop Pierre DuMaine asked me to write a book on the history of St. Joseph's Cathedral, I didn't hesitate. St. Joseph's was our first parish when we came to San Jose in 1948, and it was where our son, Mark, was baptized the following year.

I soon learned in talking with members of the old families that even though most have moved to other parishes, the close bond with St. Joseph's still exists. Everyone had a story to tell. Non-Catholics as well as Catholics now share the joy of seeing it returned to its original glory as the cathedral and the seat of the diocese of San Jose.

As I started my research it became apparent that the history of St. Joseph's and the history of San Jose and the Santa Clara Valley were so intertwined that this book must be about both. It is not intended to be a textbook with footnotes to slow down the reading, but rather the story of the people and the events that made this church and this valley unique.

The story begins with the Spanish explorers coming upon this fertile valley, whose only inhabitants were the Ohlone Indians. They knew immediately that this was where they would build their first civil settlement in Alta California—to act as a buffer against the English, French, and Russians who were casting covetous eyes in this direction and to grow food for the presidios at San Francisco and Monterey.

In November of 1777 Lt. José Joaquín Moraga brought sixty-six settlers to a site he had chosen on the Guadalupe River and raised the red and gold flag of Spain to found the Pueblo de San José de Guadalupe as a smattering of curious Indians looked on. Many of the early settlers' names are still familiar in the valley, such as that of Don Luís María Peralta, who served as *comisionado* for many years and was a devout member of the pueblo church. The Bernals, descendants of the Rancho Santa Teresa grantee, are still much in evidence, as are Sepúlvedas, Pachecos, Alvisos, and others.

There was great joy in the pueblo in 1803 when the cornerstone was laid for the first pueblo church in the plaza (on the site of the current cathedral), less than three miles from Mission Santa Clara. It would become the center of pueblo life. A second adobe church was built in 1835. It was renovated in 1858, but again an earthquake, that enemy of adobes, did irreparable damage in 1868. San Joseans were proud of the Theodore Lenzen–designed frame church, dedicated in 1869. But alas, only six years later, it was to go up in flames. Undaunted, Father Congiato started making plans immediately for the fourth St. Joseph's Church, which was dedicated in 1877. It is this church, restored at great effort and cost, that is now the grand St. Joseph's Cathedral, dedicated November 4, 1990.

With the takeover by Mexico in the 1820s began the period of large land grants. Foreign ships started docking at the Embarcadero de Santa Clara (Alviso). The rancheros bartered hides, called "leather dollars," for merchandise. All this was to change in 1847 with the signing of the Treaty of Guadalupe Hidalgo by the United States and Mexico, signaling the end of the Mexican War and the beginning of the Americanization of the pueblo. The fun-loving Californios, who enjoyed their fandangos and fiestas, and who had extended generous hospitality to visitors, now found themselves involved in legal entanglements to obtain patents to their lands.

The Pueblo de San José de Guadalupe, its name shortened to San Jose, and English the official language, became the first capital of the new state of California in 1850. The Americans were industrious. They planted their farms around the town, opened businesses, and prospered. During the last half of the century came the Irish, the Germans, the Chinese, and the French, who planted grapes and started wineries. At the turn of the century, the Italians and the Japanese arrived in large numbers. The advent of the railroad in 1864 was to make an impact in the shipping of fruit. After World War II, the shift to manufacturing increased, and with the emergence of Silicon Valley, San Jose become the heart of the technology center of the world.

The San Jose of the 1990s, more than 200 years after its founding as a Spanish pueblo, is a city of skyscrapers silhouetted dramatically against the backdrop of the softly rolling eastern foothills.

The heart and soul of this modern metropolis is St. Joseph's Cathedral, standing on the site of the first adobe church of 1803. Its stately presence is a monument to the city's past, present and future.

Ohlone Indians, such as Padre Crespí noted seeing in 1797 (SAN JOSE HISTORICAL MUSEUM)

CHAPTER ONE

In the Beginning

This story begins in a wide valley covered with groves of oak trees, tall grasses, and marshes. Down its center winds a river with wild grapes and clutches of sycamores and willows growing along its banks. To the east are softly rounded foothills that turn a mauve color in the bright afternoon sun—and on the west rises a deep green redwood- and pine-forested range.

It was this scene that attracted the Spanish explorers when they came through over two centuries ago. They called it "Llano de los Robles," meaning "Plain of the Oaks." The Indians called it "Thamien," and later the Americans named it the Santa Clara Valley.

The Indians inhabiting this Garden of Eden were the Ohlones. They lived in little dome-shaped houses made of tules, clustered around a clearing in villages which the Spanish called *rancherías*. Food was plentiful. There were deer, elk, antelope, and rabbit to hunt; the streams bulged with fish and the trees with acorns, which they ground into mush—the staple of their diet.

Roaming the hills and valleys were wild animals such as mountain lions, bobcats, and coyotes. But it was the grizzly bear—lumbering along the streams devouring salmon and steelhead, and feasting on acorns and berries—who was the Indian's enemy.

Gaspar de Portolá headed the first overland expedition for the King of Spain into Alta California in 1769. He was in search of Monterey Bay but passed it by. His party camped near the San Francisquito Creek, beside a giant redwood tree which they called "Palo Alto." This became the name of the city that grew up on this spot and a landmark for explorers and missionaries. On a boulder beneath the tree today is a bronze plaque placed by the Historic Landmarks Commission with an inscription that tells the story. The tree may still be seen by the railroad bridge.

Meanwhile, Portolá's scout, Sgt. Francisco Ortega, made a reconnaissance of the area and returned to tell about seeing a great estuary. Padre Juan Crespí, diarist for the expedition, who had climbed a hill to see for himself, confirmed Ortega's report and said that it could "hold all the navies of Europe." The estuary Ortega discovered is known today as the San Francisco Bay.

Another explorer, Pedro Fages, accompanied by a dozen soldiers, a muleteer, an Indian, and Padre Crespí, came up from Monterey and opened El Camino Reál for seventy-five miles north. As they approached what is now Milpitas, he wrote, "Over the plain we spied seven heathens, shouting as though from joy at seeing us; we left five villages to our right, each of them having six houses of spherical shape with considerable numbers of heathens living in them."

When the zealous president of the Alta California missions, Fray Junípero Serra, read the reports of the large number of "heathens" and of the fertile soil, he immediately started plans for the two new missions. One would be built at Yerba Buena and called San Francisco de Asís, (commonly known as Mission Dolores because of the stream, Arroyo de Dolores, that ran into the lake nearby), and the other Mission Santa Clara de Asís.

The Spanish plan was for the military to protect the land with presidios; the missions to Christianize the heathens and grow food; and the pueblos to colonize.

Mission Santa Clara

Mission Santa Clara was founded in January of 1777 by Padre Tomás de la Peña at a site along the Guadalupe River (named El Río de Nuestra Señora de Guadalupe by Fray Pedro Font on an expedition with Anza the year before), eighteen leagues south of Yerba Buena. After an *enramada* (brushwood shelter), an altar, and a wooden cross were built, the bells rang out for high mass to begin. A scattering of Indians gathered around who, in contrast to the formality of the Spaniards' showy dress,

The Pueblo

Spain's King Carlos III and Viceroy Antonio María Bucareli, meanwhile, had decided they must act quickly to establish civilian settlements in Alta California. The shipping of food supplies from San Blas by sailing ship had become increasingly dangerous and expensive. Neither the presidio at Yerba Buena nor at Monterey had a climate or soil conducive to growing food.

Secondly they feared foreign invasion. The Russians were already at Fort Ross and the English and the French were casting covetous eyes in this direction. Colonization seemed to be the answer. A third reason was the need for good saddle horses. With the nutritious grasses and the mild climate, the horses multiplied so fast that within a short time they had a surplus.

Shortly after Felipe de Neve's appointment as governor of Alta and Baja California (considered by historians to be the finest of Spanish governors), he began searching for a site for a pueblo. On a return trip from the presidio at what was later to be called Yerba Buena, he passed through the ten-mile-wide Llano de Los Robles. Impressed with the flat land for growing grain, the grazing land for livestock, and, most important, a river that could be dammed for irrigation, he knew that he need look no farther. His first order of business on arriving at the presidio was to instruct the *comandante*, Lt. José Moraga, to move ahead with plans to establish a pueblo.

Establishing the Pueblo

In November of 1777 Moraga chose a site two and one-half miles below Mission Santa Clara on the Río Guadalupe where, joined by sixty-six settlers and a few curious Indians, he raised the red-and-gold flag of Spain in the name of King Carlos III. Thus was founded the first civilian settlement in Alta California, the Pueblo de San José de Guadalupe, named for its patron saint, Saint Joseph, and for the nearby Río Guadalupe.

Moraga chose the first settlers, or *pobladores* as they would be called, from the presidios at Monterey and San Francisco. Most had made the arduous 800-mile journey with the Anza expedition the year before from Tubac, Mexico, through searing desert heat and freezing mountain snows. The experiences of the American emigrant trains to California (with the exception of the Donner Party) pale with comparison to the hardships suffered by these people.

They were a motley crew—only José Tiburcio Vásquez,

The Palo Alto tree, a landmark for the Spanish explorers near which the city of Palo Alto grew up (PALO ALTO TIMES)

wore practically nothing at all—an apron of deerskin on the women and a G-string for the men. Little did they suspect that they were the reason for the white men's coming.

King Carlos III decreed that the Indians must come to the mission of their own free will—but that did not deter the padres from offering trinkets and gifts as a means of enticing them to Christianity and, in their minds, at least, a better way of life. They did not anticipate, however, that the Indians lacked immunity to the foreigners' diseases.

Padre Serra visited the mission later that year and several other times. Although he had not yet received formal permission from Rome and the king, and against the orders of Gov. Felipe de Neve, he confirmed 160 Spaniards and Indians in 1779. He came for the last time in 1784, a few months before his death, to dedicate the mission.

a mulatto, could read and write. A hundred years later, one of his descendants became the notorious "Robin Hood" bandit, José Tiburcio Vásquez, who met his death by hanging next to the courthouse. Other settlers included Ignacio Archuleta, a Spaniard, and Manuel Gonzales, an Apache Indian, who acted as scout and translator on the journey.

The soldiers, called *soldados de cuera* (leather-jacket soldiers) because of the sleeveless cuirass of several layers of leather they wore to deflect Indian arrows, were corporal of the guard Valerio Mesa, Gabriel Peralta, whose son Luís was to become one of the pueblo's most respected residents, and Joaquín Castro with his wife María Martina Margarita Botiller. Twelve days after their arrival Martina gave birth to a daughter. The first white child born in the Pueblo de San José de Guadalupe, she was christened María Ysabel at Mission Santa Clara by Padre Murguía with Gabriel Peralta and his wife, Ysabel Berryessa, her godparents. For a baptismal present Padre Junípero Serra sent the infant a medallion that was treasured by the Castro family. Their son José Mariano Castro received Rancho Las Animas, the only rancho in California ever granted by a viceroy.

Building a Pueblo

After the formal founding ceremony, the *pobladores* set about building temporary shelters, called *palisados*, with walls of boughs and mud and tule-covered roofs. Moraga laid out the pueblo around the plaza, dispensing to each *poblador* a *solar* (plot of land) on which to build his house, four pieces of agricultural land, called *suertes*, on which to grow his grain, and the use of the communal grazing lands for his livestock.

In a pastoral form of communism, each father of a family received a salary from the government, livestock, two horses, a saddle, a lance, a gun, farming implements, and tools. All this and clothing, too. The next order of business was to construct a dam and dig an irrigation system of *acequias* (canals) that snaked their way through the pueblo to the separate fields. Moraga indicated on his map building sites on the east side of the plaza for an *iglesia* (church) and for the *juzgado*, a one-story, three-room adobe, built in 1797, that served as the seat of government affairs, an assembly hall, and a jail. It remained at Market and El Dorado (Post) streets until 1850. The red brick Metropole Hotel built on this site in 1902 is a historical landmark.

In 1794 the Spanish government ordered compulsory education. A school was established in the granary with Manuel de Vargas the first teacher, soon succeeded by Ramón Lasso de la Vega. The parents were required to pay two and one-half *reales* a month.

The Indians from the neighboring *rancherías* seemed friendly enough, but they outnumbered the *pobladores* by a ratio of 100 to 1. It behooved Lieutenant Moraga to have Corp. Valerio Mesa set up a night patrol of four soldiers. Spanish law made it clear that the Indians must not be harmed or treated unjustly; that the settlers should not infringe on Indian land; and that if they wanted Indians to work for them, they should make arrangements with the Indian chieftains.

Indians, however, were not allowed to ride horses. The government figured an Indian on foot would be no match for a Spaniard on horseback. This changed, however, with the coming of the Mexican regime. The Indians acquired horses and became daring rustlers.

The *alcaldes* (mayors) were appointed by the governor until 1783, when the *pobladores* took it upon

Capt. Juan Bautista de Anza, who led the expedition from Tubac, Mexico (now Arizona), to San Francisco, an exhausting 1,500-mile journey (SAN JOSE HISTORICAL MUSEUM)

3

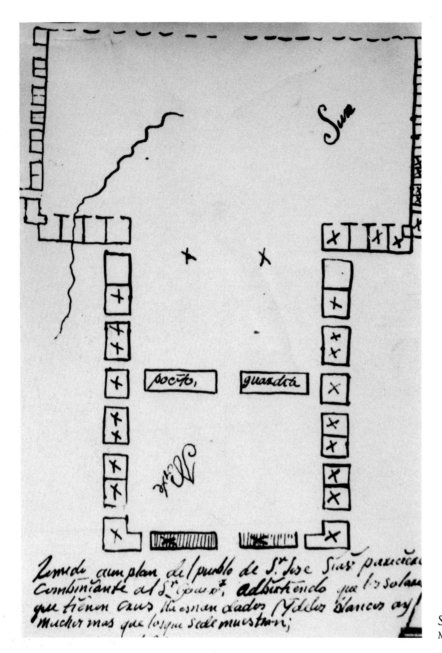

Said to be the first map of the pueblo (SAN JOSE MERCURY NEWS)

themselves to hold their first election. When the choice of Ygnacio Archuleta proved unpopular, the governor named Manuel Gonzales *alcalde*, followed by Ygnacio Vallejo, father of Mariano Vallejo, an officer in the Mexican army who became a large landholder and was responsible for wooing the state's first American civil capital away from San Jose.

Valerio Mesa's descendants married into early settler families. His grandson Juan Prado Mesa, as a reward for fighting the Indians, received the Rancho San Antonio grant in Los Altos where the Los Altos Country Club is now located. Another descendant, Sarah de Quevedo, was active in St. Joseph's Church. Her son, Dr. Albert de Quevedo, a professor at University of Santa Clara,

lived with her in a little adobe house on Park Avenue facing the plaza until it fell victim to redevelopment in 1960.

José Joaquín Higuera, descendant of original settler José Manuel Higuera, received the Rancho Pala grant; another José Higuera relative received the Tularcitos at Warm Springs.

The family of Comisionado Macario Castro grew in size and in landholdings, owning seventy ranchos and controlling 10 percent of the land in the state. His son José Tiburcio was *alcalde* in 1819. Tiburcio's son Gen. José Antonio Castro became governor of California (1835–36) and general of the Mexican forces in California (1845–46). A Castro descendant, Diane Ikeda of

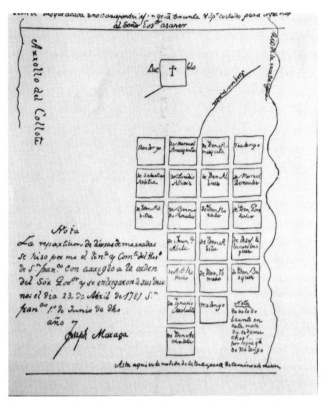

Map of pueblo indicating the allocation of plots for settlers; note the cross indicating the site for a future church

Cupertino, who served on the St. Joseph's restoration committee, says that Macario Castro was a religious man and that he had a crucifix given to him by the revered *presidente* of the missions, Fray Junípero Serra, which he used for administering the oath of office to his men. When Mrs. Ikeda went to Rome in 1988 for the beatification ceremony of Padre Serra, she took with her a family heirloom, an implement for making hosts for Father Serra that belonged to her cousin Ernie Miramonte of San Leandro. Evelyn Martínez, active in historical circles, is a descendant of original settlers José Sinoba, a herdsman, and his wife, María Gertrudis Bojorques.

Second Pueblo

Although the *pobladores* were a fun-loving, lighthearted people, life wasn't always easy. Lieutenant Moraga erred in his choice of sites. The land was too low, and the heavy rains the first year caused the dam to give out. The pueblo and Mother Nature were at odds. The *pobladores* lost all their plantings, and in following years their adobes melted. Permission finally came in 1797 to move the pueblo to higher ground, a mile and a half to the south at the site of the present plaza. The new pueblo's boundaries were from St. John Street to mid-

way between San Carlos Street and Auzerais Avenue on the south, from Market Street on the east to San Pedro Street on the west.

The moving of the town farther away from the mission, with the river the dividing line, helped appease the padres at the mission who complained that the Law of the Indies did not permit locating a pueblo so close to a mission, that while they were trying to teach the Indians to be pious, childlike, and innocent, the *pobladores* were a bad influence. Unfortunately, in most cases the Indians found life in the pueblo to be more appealing than the strict regime of the mission.

The pueblo, surrounded by tall grasses and mustard and with only narrow trails connecting it to Monterey and Alviso, developed slowly. In 1806 Von Langsdorff of the Rezanov party wrote of a night of peril he and his companions spent on their way to Santa Clara, being obliged to defend themselves against wild bulls and bears and scarcely knowing which they feared more.

The pueblo's adobe houses, small, with dirt floors, were the ultimate in simplicity. They were furnished with rawhide chairs, stools cut out of whalebone, and beds made of rawhide and covered with fine linen sheets, linen pillow covers, and padded comforters. On the walls were crudely painted pictures of saints. The houses had no chimneys, so the cooking was done outside. If they

The communion host press used by Junípero Serra (COURTESY DIANE IKEDA)

5

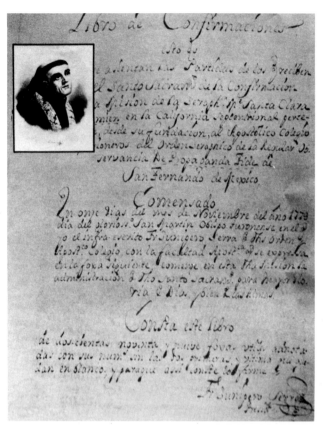

Padre Junípero Serra, president of the California missions
(JUNÍPERO SERRA, DE NEVI AND MOHOLY)

needed heat, they burned charcoal on a small brazier in the center of the room.

Early Visitors

It was their gardens and the warmth of their hospitality that most attracted early visitors to the valley. A Russian explorer, Otto von Kotzebue, wrote, "The houses are pleasant and stand in the midst of orchards and hedges of vines bearing luxuriant clusters of the richest grapes." He added, "The inhabitants came out to meet us and, with much courteousness and with the most ceremonious politeness of the Spaniards, invited us to enter their simple but cleanly kept dwellings."

British sea captain George Vancouver, on a trip around the world in 1792, who rode horseback down from San Francisco, described the orchards and the valley's scenic beauty. "We entered a country I little expected to find in these regions," he said. "For almost twenty minutes it compared to a park which originally had been planted with old English oak."

The Alameda

With no church of their own, the *pobladores* made the three-mile trek to Mission Santa Clara for mass by horseback. The women usually rode in their creaking *carretas*—wooden carts with two wheels made of a section of log, an axle attached with wooden pins, and a wooden frame tied with strips of hide that was pulled by oxen and prodded along by an Indian boy with a sharp stick.

It was not an easy trip. The wild Mexican longhorn cattle that roamed the countryside threatened, as did the treacherous Guadalupe River when it overflowed during wet winters. The *pobladores* also feared unfriendly Indians who might be lurking in the eight-to-ten-foot-tall mustard. They appealed to their beloved Padre Magín de Catalá at the mission, who listened sympathetically. He responded by setting to work to build, with the help of 200 Indians, a *carretera* (roadway) to link the pueblo with the mission. From the beginning it was called The Alameda. For protection from the hot summer sun and as a buffer from the wild animals, they planted willow trees, dug from the thickets along each side and down the center.

When the padres from the mission made sick calls, they must have been an impressive sight as they all walked down The Alameda accompanied by an acolyte who made known to all who passed that the priest was carrying the sacred host. Travelers passing by would bare their heads and in most cases fall to their knees.

When travelers met along The Alameda they always stopped to visit. They talked about the new arrivals in the pueblo, new wells for the cattle, the valor of the vaqueros, the arrival of ships at the Embarcadero de Santa Clara de Asís (Alviso) and, of course, the beauty of the *señoritas*.

CHAPTER TWO

Padre Magín de Catalá

Most loved of all the padres was Fray Magín de Catalá. The stories about this saintly man and his predictions are legendary. In the fifty years following his death so many people wrote letters to Archbishop Alemany about Padre Catalá that, combined with a request from the Jesuits at Santa Clara, the the archbishop ordered an inquiry. In 1884 he brought the petition before the Ecclesiastical Council to have Catalá's name ultimately placed on the Catalogue of Saints. At the archbishop's request, Father Piccardo took great pains to find trustworthy persons who would tell the facts as heard from eyewitnesses. Later that same year the archbishop presided over a tribunal for Padre Catalá's beatification.

In the book *The Holy Man of Santa Clara*, the author, Rev. Zephryn Engelhardt, told of a great drought in 1823 in the valley. There had been no rain the preceding year and the losses were great. As many as 5,000 sheep perished. The Indians begged Father Magín to do something. The good padre responded by asking all the people to join with him in a prayer. After the Holy Mass, during which he had preached fervently, he announced that rain would soon follow.

He then led a procession down The Alameda with an acolyte carrying the crucifix at the head of the procession (it is now in the chapel at Santa Clara) surrounded by the candle bearers. They stopped at each of the fourteen stations to send up their petitions to God.

Don Secundino Robles (of the San Francisquito rancho) testified at the inquiry that they saw a black cloud far away in the mountains to the west. "It grew larger and wider and approached rapidly. When we were about 300 or 600 feet from the church the rain began to fall in torrents and it was accompanied by a heavy wind. The acolytes wondered greatly that the candles we bore were not extinguished by the wind but kept burning. I remember this well, for I was about fourteen years old and was one of the boys that carried candles." The rain, he said, continued falling for seven days.

Another incident was told by María Josefa Berryessa of children cutting grass at the mission to feed the domestic animals when a bear suddenly rushed from the thicket. Padre Catalá happened to be nearby. He walked towards it and told it gently not to harm the girls. As though he understood, "the beast turned and quietly trudged away." These and other miraculous events were testified to under oath by reliable people.

A San Francisco doctor, W. S. Thorne, M.D., told a story about Father Catalá at a meeting in San Francisco

Padre Magín Catalá telling the Indians about the crucifixion in front of an altar in Santa Clara Mission church

7

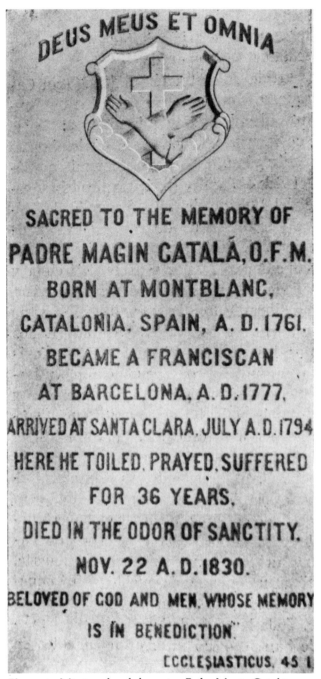

Plaque in Mission church honoring Padre Magín Catalá

in 1906. He said that while he was attending Santa Clara College, a professor White told the class that Padre Magin Catalá, who had the gift of prophesy, had predicted there would be a big earthquake in San Francisco. Three days after Dr. Thorne told the story, the big quake occured.

What transpired after the tribunal sent its report to Rome is hazy. The archbishop was elderly and returned to his native Spain. The witnesses were also along in

years. The process of beatification is long, involved, and expensive. Whether Padre Catalá was a saint was not determined, but there is no doubt that he answered the description of the name given to him by his people, "The Holy Man of Santa Clara." His body rests in the Santa Clara Mission Church near the sanctuary on the gospel side. The Catalá Club, a group of women supporters of Santa Clara University, founded on the 100th anniversary of Catalá's death, honors his memory.

Tales of The Alameda

From the time Padre Magín and his Indians built their *carretera* in 1794, The Alameda has had a long and varied career. On one of several trips to the valley, Capt. Alfred Robinson wrote, "It is frequented on feast days when all the town repairs to the Church at Santa Clara. On Sunday may be seen hundreds of persons of both sexes, gaily attired in silks, mounted on their finest horses and proceeding leisurely up the road.

"No carriages are used and, of course, the scene is divested of all the pomp and splendor which accompanies church-going in the larger places of the republic." Robinson, who later married a Mexican woman of the prominent de la Guerra family in San Diego, added, "Yet in one respect it excels them all, that is in the display of female beauty. No part of Mexico can show such bright eyes, fine teeth, fair proportions and beautiful complexions."

The Californios, great equestrians that they were, found The Alameda an ideal tract for racing their horses and sometimes oxen that they had trained to race. Later The Alameda became a thoroughfare for the stage-coaches running between the pueblo and Yerba Buena. The only other means of travel between these two points before the coming of the railroad in 1864 was by stern-wheeler from Alviso.

In 1862 it became a toll road operated by the Alameda Turnpike Co., and in 1887 it carried electrified cars. Still later it became Highway 101.

In the latter part of the century it developed into an avenue of fine homes. Today most of these have been converted into offices or torn down and replaced with commercial buildings. Still another change: for the first time in almost 150 years The Alameda no longer bisects the University of Santa Clara campus. It has been rerouted, and the school has an impressive new entrance.

CHAPTER THREE

Don Luís María Peralta

Don Luís Peralta, one of the Pueblo de San José de Guadalupe's most respected residents and a legendary figure in the valley's history, lived in the pueblo under the flags of Spain and Mexico, as well as the Bear Flag and the Stars and Stripes. In 1776, at the age of eighteen, Don Luís walked from Tubac in Anza's party with his father, Gabriel Peralta. He enlisted in the army and served with Padre Fermín de Lasuén at Branciforte (Santa Cruz), where he and several soldiers raised the first cross for the Mission Santa Cruz on a hill about half a mile south of the San Lorenzo River. He married María Loreto Alviso, and they became the parents of twenty-five children, seventeen of whom lived.

After retiring from the army in 1807, Peralta was appointed *comisionado* of the pueblo, a post he held until 1822. When Mexico gained its independence from Spain, the position was abolished. In the meantime, he bought the adobe of the Apache Indian Manuel Gonzales on West St. John Street (at that time St. Augustine) that is now the last pueblo adobe in San Jose. A California historical landmark, it is known as the Peralta Adobe.

In 1820, as a reward for his service as a military man and an Indian fighter, the Spanish government granted him the 48,000-acre Rancho San Antonio. One of the finest in California, it covered most of Berkeley, Oakland, Piedmont, and Alameda. Peralta and his wife, however, preferred to live in the adobe while his four sons occupied the rancho. When everyone was rushing off to the gold rush, this gentle and wise man counseled his sons not to go. He said, "God gave the gold to the Americans. If he had wanted the Spaniards to have it he would have let them discover it before now. You can go to the ranch and raise grain. That will be your best gold field, because we all must eat while we live." His advice was well-taken, and his sons profited accordingly.

Peralta planted orchards, mostly pear, around his

Ralph Rambo pen sketch of the restored Luís María Peralta Adobe, which is now a California State Historical Landmark and on the National Register of Historical Places (FRANCES FOX)

9

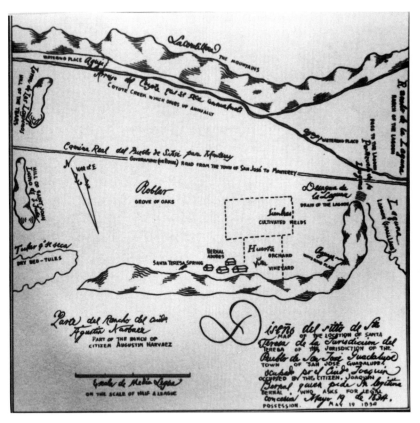

A diseño (map) of Rancho Santa Teresa. This is the type of map the rancheros used to prove their land grants for patent. Indicated are oak trees, lagoons, Coyote Creek and a tule area. (SAN JOSE HISTORICAL MUSEUM)

adobe, which was located on the outskirts of the pueblo extending down to the Guadalupe River. Foreign visitors frequently noted the luxuriance of his gardens. One of the pueblo's most loved residents, Peralta died a wealthy man, leaving an estate of over one million dollars. Although his name lives on in a junior college, a hospital, and several streets, he preferred during his last years to live a simple life in his adobe with two of his daughters.

He never lost his military bearing; when he was in his eighties he would ride to his Rancho San Antonio, sitting erect in his saddle. The great San Antonio spread was to experience many of the same problems of the other ranchos: squatters taking cattle and large legal expenses over patents.

The character of Don Luís is well illustrated by the inscription of his sword, given by his heirs to the de Saisset Museum at Santa Clara University. It reads, "Do not draw me without cause; do not sheath me without honor."

He was a deeply devout man. In her book *Luís María Peralta and His Adobe*, Frances Fox writes, "He was a familiar figure in the pueblo, half blind hobbling to mass at St. Joseph's Church, accompanied by his Indian servant." After his death his two daughters, dedicated members of the church (one is said to have spend half of her inheritance on masses), watched life from the front door of the adobe.

A frequent visitor to the Peralta adobe was the newly arrived Bishop Alemany on the rounds of his large diocese. After Peralta's death in 1851, when a lawsuit was instigated by his married daughters, the bishop wrote a letter stating Peralta was of sound mind when he saw him shortly before his death. Named in the law suit but exonerated was Peralta's good friend Father John Nobili, pastor of St. Joseph's and founder of Santa Clara College (University of Santa Clara), who witnessed the signing of the will.

Despite his wealth, Luís Peralta remained humble in death. He requested in his will that his body "be carried to Mission Santa Clara in the same hearse that is used for my fellow men, the Indians."

The Bernals

The Bernals are a well-known Anza-trek family who came early to the pueblo. Joaquín married María Josefa Sánchez, daughter of Capt. José Sánchez, Anza's top henchman on that overland journey. Figueroa granted him the 10,000-acre parcel known as Rancho Santa Teresa in 1835. Edenvale and the IBM plant are located on the rancho land.

The most productive of the Santa Clara Valley ranchos, the Santa Teresa was listed in 1834 as having four

10

adobes, sixty-eight dependents (the Bernals were a prolific family; in the baptismal registry at St. Joseph's Church almost every third child seemed to be a Bernal), a 1,000-vine vineyard, 100 fruit trees, 2,100 head of cattle, 120 head of lesser stock, 3 bonds of mares, 50 broken horses, and 5 mules. One of the features of this ranch always noted was the Santa Teresa Spring, which still has a small flow.

When patented by the U.S. to Joaquín's son Agustín in 1867, the Santa Teresa was probably the only rancho that received more land than requested. Agustín not only inherited his father's acumen for business but was also a lieutenant of the militia in San Jose in 1841 — and *juez de campo* (judge of the field) in 1846. The Bernals had their share of problems with the Indians. When Captain Fisher of the neighboring Rancho Laguna Seca and Joaquín Bernal lost several hundred horses to marauding Indians in the late 1840s, they formed a patrol. Joaquín's sons Bruno, Agustín, and Juan Pablo fought Indians raiding Mission Santa Clara, and Joaquín's grandson Apolinario, a resident of the pueblo, was killed by Indians trying to save an ambushed priest at Mission San José (which was founded in 1797 in Alameda County).

Agustín's brother Bruno, who acquired Rancho Alisal, helped him run the Santa Teresa. Bruno's descendents include Dr. Robert Bernal, a dentist, whose father, Clement, at the death of his parents, was raised by the Jesuit fathers at St. Joseph's. Paul Bernal, Robert's son, a lawyer who has taken on the task of family historian, estimates there are 10,000 Bernal descendents today.

Two of Joaquín's daughters married especially well: María Dolores to Don Antonio Suñol — the most literate and probably the wealthiest man in the pueblo — and María Pilar to Don Antonio Pico, another successful businessman and a cousin of a governor, Pío Pico.

The sisters, with their brothers Juan Pablo, who had an adobe in the pueblo where the circle of palm trees now stands between the Fairmont Hotel and the San Jose Museum of Art, and the aforementioned Agustín, received the enormous Rancho El Valle de San José grant near Pleasanton. At the end of the war Agustín moved to the rancho, where he built one of the finer adobe homes.

His brother Juan Pablo and his son-in-law John Kottinger built adobe homes nearby. Agustín built a racetrack on the ranch in 1860 — the first in California. It is still used for racing by the Alameda County Fairgrounds in Pleasanton.

In 1943 San Francisco financier Walter Johnson bought Agustín's adobe. Its five-foot-thick walls were in disrepair,

Bruno Bernal of the Rancho Santa Teresa family (COURTESY MARIE MANN AND GEORGE STRICKLER)

but with meticulous care he restored it — expanding it from a six-room house into a fourteen-room showplace.

Agustín's son José Jesús Bernal received the Cañada de Pala grant at Mount Hamilton (later acquired by San Jose lawyer and historian Frederic Hall). Juanita Lennon, daughter of Carlotta Bernal and Daniel O'Brien (also related to the Higueras and Chaboyas), grew up on the Rancho de la Lampe part of Cañada de Pala. She was baptised, made her first communion, confirmed, and married in St. Joseph's Church.

The Sepúlvedas

Although Sebastian Sepúlveda was not one of the original founders, he moved to the pueblo in 1805 with his wife, María Luisa Botiller. Sebastian came from Mexico with the Rivera y Moncada expedition in 1781 and settled in the Pueblo de Los Angeles. Sepúlveda Boulevard, a well-known thoroughfare, is named for this family. The coastal area known as Palos Verdes is on a Sepúlveda rancho.

Sebastian, however, ran into problems with the law, according to his great-great-great-grandson Bartólome Sepúlveda of Milpitas. Strong on the history of San Jose and the Sepúlveda family, he says he believes Sebastian was accused of killing an Indian and that he was transferred to Northern California, where he served with the military at Yerba Buena, Mission Santa Clara, and San Jose. Sebastian's son Juan Bautista Sepúlveda, who married María Francisca Pacheco, built adobes on his two *solares* on the plaza between Market and Balbach streets extending to the river—one for his mother and the other for his own family.

In an interview Father Arthur Spearman, University of Santa Clara historian, did with Frank Berryessa and his wife, Juana Sepúlveda, in 1930, she told of the funeral of her eighty-nine-year-old grandmother in the 1890s in St. Joseph's Church. She said it was a custom then to walk to the church. The men took turns carrying the casket from Keyes Street. According to Juana, who was ninety years old at this time, her grandmother didn't

Juan Crisóstomo Galindo, mayordomo *at Mission Santa Clara for Padre Catalá* (COURTESY BART SEPULVEDA)

want to be set on the stand. She was laid on the floor in the casket in front of the altar. Under her head for a pillow was a piece of adobe from Mission Santa Clara. "Francisca Pacheco de Sepúlveda was my father's mother," Juana said. "She was ninety-eight or ninety-nine when she died."

A romantic episode in the Sepúlveda family as told by Mrs. Fremont Older in a series she wrote for the *Evening News* in the 1920s involved the courtship of Juan

Maria de los Angeles Alviso married, against the objections of her parents, Bartólome Sepúlveda in the adobe church of San Jose de Nuestra Señora de Guadalupe. They spent most of their married life on the Rancho Milpitas. (COURTESY BART SEPULVEDA)

Bautista Sepúlveda's son and the daughter of José María de Jesús Albiso (Albizu) of the Milpitas rancho. The Alvisos, grantees of Rancho Milpitas, disapproved of the marriage of their pretty, "delicately nurtured" daughter María, but her ardent suitor, Bartólome, was not to be denied.

As sometimes happened in those days, the dashing young Bartólome rode to the Rancho Milpitas, swept the lovely María up on his swift horse, and carried her off in the night to the home of his mother. At first, the priest at St. Joseph's would not marry them. Finally, after many exchanges of messages and without Don José María giving an inch, they were married in the adobe church of San Jose. All must have been forgiven afterwards, because the couple spent most of their married life on the family rancho. Eventually they retired to a home on North Eighth Street in San Jose. Their children were married in St. Joseph's Church.

Their grandson John Morgan Sepúlveda, father of Bart

Sepúlveda of Milpitas, lives on the part of Rancho Milpitas that still remains in the family, across the road from the José María Alviso adobe at the corner of Piedmont Road and Calaveras Boulevard, built about 1837.

The Berryessas

That brings us to the Berryessa family. Although the name lives on in the Santa Clara Valley with the Berryessa School District, Berryessa Road, Berryessa Creek, and, in Napa County, Lake Berryessa, the family story is one marked with tragedy. Nicolás Berryessa, who came with the Anza party, married Gertrudis Peralta, sister of Don Luís María Peralta. His son Nicolás II received the Rancho Milpitas land grant from San Jose *alcalde* Antonio Chabolla (Chaboya) in 1834 only to have it declared illegal the following year and granted to José María Alviso. Berryessa's son José de los Reyes, who received Rancho San Vicente, on part of which the noted New Almaden mine was located, was shot in the back by Kit Carson on a trip to Sonoma to visit his son, who had been taken prisoner by Frémont. At Rancho San Vicente, Francisco Berryessa was stabbed to death by a visitor who, for some unexplained reason, hid under his bed. In the pueblo, Nicolás II's son Demesio Berryessa was lynched by the Vigilantes on San Fernando Street, falsely accused, it is generally believed, of a murder. Small wonder that the father went insane.

In 1868 the U.S. patented the San Vicente to José Reyes's widow, María Zacarias Bernal de Berryessa, too late and too little for the Berryessas to benefit from the great wealth accrued from the New Almaden mine. Still bitter over the treatment of the Californios by the

María Francisca Pacheco married Juan Bautista Sepúlveda. He applied for and received two lots in the pueblo where he built two adobes at Market and Balbach streets. One was for his mother, María Botiller Sepúlveda. (COURTESY BART SEPULVEDA)

"gringos," San Joseans Naomi Berryessa and her sister, Mercedes, daughters of Abel Berryessa, referred to the land transfers as "the Watergate of the West," according to an interview in *West Magazine* of 1985 by Frank Vivano.

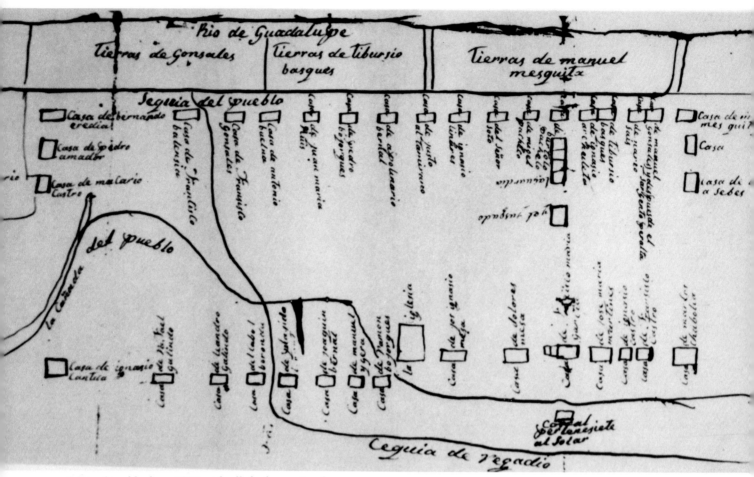

Map of pueblo from 1820 with all the lots assigned (AUSTEN WARBURTON)

CHAPTER FOUR

The Pueblo Gets Its Own Church

All was going well for the *pobladores* in what the Americans were later to call "The Valley of Heart's Delight"—their crops were producing, the livestock increasing—but one thing in the pueblo was missing for the deeply religious Californios—a church of their own. True, they now had the tree-lined Alameda to travel on to the mission, but there was still the danger of being charged by wild cattle. The heat in the summer could be oppressive, and winter rains often caused the Guadalupe to overflow. Their patience worn thin, a group of the townspeople met with the pueblo's top authority, Comisionado Macario Castro. They appealed to him to ask permission from the *comandante* in Monterey, José de la Guerra y Noriega, to build a church in the pueblo.

About this time the government was making changes, so it wasn't until 1802 that the official letter arrived from Monterey granting permission. In his letter of approval, José Joaquín Arrillaga requested that each family tithe by contributing half a *fanega* (bushel) of grain each year towards the cost of the church. "To the willing mind," the governor wrote, "ways and means are easy, and a gift to the church impoverishes no man."

Castro, a sergeant in the army of his native Spain, who came to the pueblo in 1790, immediately set the wheels in motion to start building on the site that Lt. Moraga had proposed on his map, where the cathedral now stands on the corner of Market and San Fernando streets. A year after receiving authorization, the excited townspeople, who now numbered 217, gathered on the feast day of Santa Clara, July 12, 1803, for the laying of the cornerstone.

The *comandante* declined the honor to officiate, calling himself "a man of impiety and unworthy of such an honor" and citing his pressing official duties. In his place he sent José María Estudillo, whom he described as "a most worthy cadet" to join with Padre José Viader and Sgt. Macario Castro in presiding at the ceremony.

With great solemnity the young cadet Estudillo, wearing the traditional presidial officer dress—black hat trimmed with white plumes and gold braid, fitted purple velvet waistcoat, light blue trousers, a gold stripe down the side seam, and black half boots—performed the ceremony. So that its memory would be perpetuated, he placed some coins representing the reigns of several Spanish sovereigns along with a statement of the ceremonies in a sealed box under the cornerstone prepared by the Indians beneath the location of the future altar. Translated from Spanish, the statement read:

In the Pueblo of San José de Guadalupe, the 12th day of July 1803, Señor Don Carlos IV, being King of Spain, Don José Joaquin de Arrillaga, governor 'ad interim' and lieutenant of the royal army; the retired sergeant Macario de Castro, commissioner of the Pueblo, Ignacio Archuleta, ordinary Alcalde; and Bernardo Heredia and Francisco Gonzales Regidores; at 6 o'clock of the evening on said day was made the consecration of the first stone and mortar of the church which was commenced in the said Pueblo dedicated to the Patriarch, Señor San José, and the Virgin of Guadalupe; which ceremony was celebrated with much solemnity by the Rev. Padre Fray José Viader, (acting) minister of the Mission of Santa Clara, Don José María Estudillo, cadet, acting as Godfather by proxy from the Alférez José Antonio de la Guerra y Noriega, commandant at the Presidio of Monterey; who placed in the cornerstone moneys of the several recent sovereigns and a duplicate of this document in a bottle sealed with wax for its preservation in the future; and for all here present we sign it in the same pueblo, the day, month and year aforesaid.

Fray José Viader, José María
Estudillo as Proxy for Alférez
de la Guerra y Noriega
Macario de Castro, Commoner

The whole town now set to work in earnest to build their church. Men, women and children pitched in, including the Indians. Each brick, eighteen inches long, fourteen inches wide, three inches thick, and laced with straw, had to be sun-dried.

In a series Mrs. Fremont Older wrote for the *San Jose Evening News*, she repeated an account given to her by Mrs. Luisa Sepúlveda Mesa, who had heard it from the lips of her mother, Francisca Pacheco Mesa. She told how the women worked on the first church. Mrs. Mesa said that it was not always easy for the Indians to find good soil for making adobe bricks and it was necessary to obtain the permission of the owners of the land to make them. Many, however, were made in the plaza in back of the present church.

In Mrs. Older's story Mrs. Sepúlveda Mesa is quoted as saying, "The Spaniards in San Jose had no race feeling against the Indians, and side by side with the red men they worked, señors, señoras and señoritas. Delicately nurtured women carried the hod. Nothing that they could do was too much."

"At last," Mrs. Older wrote, "after much effort the little church was completed, and it was covered with a thatched roof of tules. It seemed the most beautiful building in the world to those women workers as they knelt on the dirt floor (a few pews were added later) and looked at the simple little pictures on the walls and worshiped and gave prayers of thanks." The little pictures were primitive paintings by the Indians, who extracted the bright colors from the roots of native plants and red cinnabar that was to become a bonanza for the New Almaden mine. A few statues were brought over from Mission Santa Clara. The church's high windows were narrow on the outside and wider inside to admit more light, to resist wind and rain, and to keep the church cool in the summer.

Simple though it was, there was great joy in the pueblo now that they had their own church. It became the center of pueblo life for meetings and fiestas, as well as masses. Holy days were big events and called for the staging of processions around the plaza. For the Feast of Corpus Christi they would parade carrying statues of the saints on platform poles. Father Catalá and Father Viader, the first priests assigned to say mass in the new church, could not come on a regular basis, so news that they were coming to make calls immediately stirred up excitement among the *pobladores*.

The little adobe church had been completed only a short time when, on March 19, as the townspeople celebrated the feast of Saint Joseph, they saw the miracle of the swallow legend unfold as the birds arrived in hordes and started to build their mud nests under the eaves of the church. Every year, according to a story in a historical series in the *San Jose Mercury* by Marion Bailey Kaufman, the swallows returned on Saint Joseph's Day just as they do at Mission San Juan Capistrano.

Life in the Pueblo

Although the adobe houses were small and lacked ventilation, the mild climate was conducive to outdoor cooking and entertaining. That was the birth of what has become a Californian tradition—the barbecue. Weddings inspired a celebration and included the whole community. Following the church ceremony there would be a feast and sometimes another at the home of the bride in late afternoon. At nightfall there would be a fandango at which they danced to the music of guitars, violins, flutes, and sometimes trumpets and drums, performing the lively *jota* and the stately *contradanza* with men and women dancing and retiring in lines and executing maneuvers of an intricate sort. Usually these fandangoes continued for several nights.

Mission Santa Clara during the Spanish regime by Andrew P. Hill (COURTESY CARL ZINK)

16

MARCELO
FROM AN ONLY PHOTO

Marcelo the mission Indian. He became an asset to the mission, supervising construction and later serving as alcalde. *He was granted Rancho Ulistac.* (RALPH RAMBO)

The Californios especially loved picnics, or *meriendas* as they were called. Men and women in *carretas* or on horseback would make their way in a procession to a designated spot where they had their barbecue, played games, and danced. Even wash day was turned into a fiesta. A U.S. Navy officer, Lt. Charles Wilkes, described a visit to the pueblo in 1841. "As we crossed the torturous branches of the Río Guadalupe and had a view of the pueblo it seemed as if it were a gala day and as if everyone were abroad celebrating it on the banks of this river. It turned out to be the general washing day of the village." He went on to describe the long line of dresses, the many colored garments drying on the shrubs and trees, and the crowds of women and children.

What most delighted the Californios were the exhibitions of horsemanship. The bear and bull fights provided another exciting form of entertainment. In those early days the grizzly bear was a common sight on the countryside. As Padre Font described him in his diary, "He was horrible, fierce, large and fat." The Californios would

lasso one of these huge animals and haul him to the site of the *merienda*. The grizzly bear is long gone from the California scene—not a single one remains—but he is remembered for posterity on the white, green, and red flag of California.

Mexico Takes Over

The era of Spain's domination ended in 1822 when Mexico won its independence and took over the control of Alta California. The flag of Spain came down from the *juzgado* and in its place was raised the red, green, and white flag of Mexico. The people had been happy with the Spanish rule, but they had no choice. The *pobladores*, as did all the people of California, swore allegiance to Mexico. The Spanish government subsidies to the *pobladores* ended. The ships from San Blas no longer came with supplies, and no money came to pay the king's officers; the missions were secularized, and the buildings began to deteriorate.

About this time, however, the Mexican government started making large land grants to soldiers. With the proliferation of cattle and the fertility of the soil for raising grain, grapes, and fruit, the rancheros prospered. Fortunately for the people, more and more trading vessels started arriving at the Embarcadero de Santa Clara (Alviso) with requests for otter skins, hides, tallow, and grain. The hides, or "leather dollars," became a medium of trade for manufactured products such as furniture and clothing brought ashore by the sailors. In some cases hides would go to New England to be returned the following year as shoes for the Californios. Richard Henry Dana, in his book *Two Years Before the Mast*, wrote that the embarcaderos on San Francisco Bay "do more business in hides than any in California. Large boats or launches, manned by Indians . . . are attached to the missions and sent down to the vessels with hides and to bring away goods in return." The Spanish galleons from Manila stopped at Monterey for essential fresh food—a means of preventing scurvy with the crew. In turn, they traded spices and silks from the Orient.

There were no fences in early California (the only fence between San Jose and San Francisco was on Commodore Stockton's rancho). The cattle were free to roam the countryside. Once a year, usually in the spring, there would be a roundup at one of the ranchos—it might be the Bernals' Santa Teresa, Martin Murphy's Ojo de Agua de la Coche, Suñol's Los Coches, Fisher's Laguna Seca, or one of many others—for the *matanza* (killing of cattle for hides).

The matanza *usually took place at the same time as the roundup and branding of the cattle. The longhorn steers were killed for hides and tallow, which were used for barter with the merchant ships coming into port at Alviso.*

The vaqueros, with much whooping, hollering, swinging of riatas, and swirling of dust, would drive their cattle to the appointed rancho. With skillful maneuvering of their ponies (the Californios were the finest horsemen in the world and could turn on a dime), each would separate the steers of his ranch for branding. Some of the cattle were then let loose; others killed and their hides stretched out on the ground to dry. The fat was boiled in large iron caldrons for tallow to make soap and candles.

After the *matanza* came the fun time: the races and the games of skill. A favorite was the *carrera del gallo* (the rooster pull)—in which a live rooster would be buried in the ground up to his neck, which they had greased. The horseman would ride by at full gallop and try to snatch the rooster. In another test of equestrian skill, a rider would carry a tray of glasses, filled with wine, at a full gallop without spilling a drop. The big day would wind up with a barbecue.

Hospitality Californio Style

The hospitality of the Californios knew no bounds. They greeted family, friend, or stranger with the familiar *Pase Usted, Señor, mi casa es su casa* (Come in, sir, my house is your house). As there were no hotels in those days, the visitor would be invited to stay as long as he pleased. A saddled and bridled horse was provided and a place at the table and a fresh bed every day. At dinner they called for the saints to protect their guest through the night. In the morning they thanked the saints for the well-being of their guest and made a wish that he would remain another day. At the missions the padres usually greeted guests with refreshments of hot chocolate and fruit and accorded them the same hospitality, offering a room for the night and always sending them off with a fresh horse and their blessings.

Unfortunately, even though they accepted the Californio's hospitality, the visitors sometimes wrote disparagingly of their hosts, considering them indolent and failing to recognize that under Spain's rule they couldn't own any more land and that there was no incentive. Besides, with ample food for his table and grazing land for his livestock, the Californio couldn't understand why one should work hard if it wasn't necessary. In the book the late Professor Edwin Beilharz coauthored with Donald De Mers, *San Jose—California's First City,* he wrote, "Unfortunately there was a cultural miasma which made Anglo-Americans see the worst and overlook the best in Hispanic culture. Anglo-American observers were rarely conscious of the Mexican's innate dignity, the almost complete lack of malice, the strong family bonds, the warm hearts and quick smile which distinguish most of them as people."

Departure of Father Viader and Father Catalá

Life in the pueblo went on pretty much the same as the population slowly increased. Earthquakes did considerable damage to the pueblo, but the church of San José de Guadalupe survived. Eventually, however, the quakes took their toll. In 1818 cracks appeared in the walls, but it was the quake of 1822 that did the severe damage. Although the church was in dire need of repair, with its roof near to collapse, Padres Catalá and Viader continued to say mass for the people.

It was a sad day in 1830 for the parishioners of San José y la Virgen de Guadalupe church when death came to their beloved Padre Magín Catalá, the "Holy man of Santa Clara" who had given so generously of himself to his people. Many believed that through him they were cured by a miracle. His funeral was a near riot as the distraught people tried with scissors to get a piece of his robe. The procession had to be stopped several times and a new robe put on him.

Three years after Padre Magín's passing, when Mexico's Secularization Act of 1833 came into effect, the *pobladores* again had heavy hearts as Padre José Viader, the last of the Spanish Franciscans at the mission and the church of San José de Guadalupe, bade them a touching farewell.

One who probably missed Padre Viader most was Marcelo, the six-foot-two mission Indian (it remains a mystery as to his origin because he was almost twice the size of the Ohlones). Marcelo had appeared at the mission one day with two companions. They decided to beat up on Padre Viader, but the priest was too fast for them. He grabbed them, bumped their heads together, and then said he forgave them. Marcelo was so taken back by Padre Viader's compassion that he became building foreman and served a term as *alcalde* of the mission. Gov. Pío Pico granted to him and another Santa Clara Mission Indian, Cristobal, Rancho Ulistac, now the site of Great America and high-tech firms. Twice a year Marcelo made his way from Alviso to the mission church to say his prayers. Marcelo sold his share to some Americans for $500 but later denied it, saying that he was drunk. He continued to live there until his death in 1875 at Fenton's Indian Mound Ranch. He claimed to be 125 years old, but mission records showed him to be under 100.

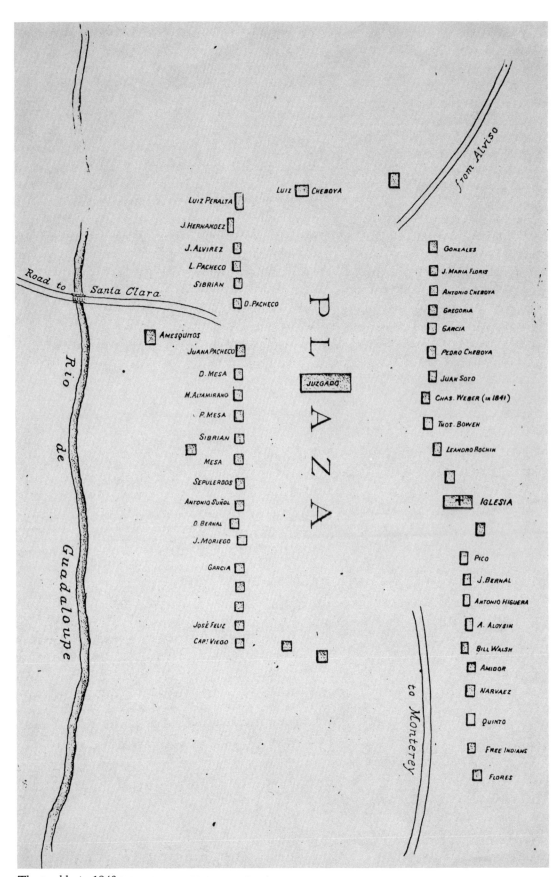

The pueblo in 1840 (SAN JOSE HISTORICAL MUSEUM)

CHAPTER FIVE

A New Era for the Pueblo Church

The departure of the last of the Spanish Franciscans marked the beginning of a new era for the pueblo church. Time and weather had taken its toll—the tule roof leaked and the earthquakes of 1812 and 1818 had been especially damaging.

The first Mexican Franciscan, Padre Rafael Jesús de Moreno, who came from Zacatecas to become pastor of the church of San José de Guadalupe, must have been appalled at what he found, because the year after he arrived he announced to the parishioners that he wanted to build a new church. The people rejoiced at this news. They asked if the tithes (one-half *fanega* of wheat per year) they had originally paid to the king of Spain for whatever church purposes he chose, and had voluntarily continued to pay to the Mexican government, could be applied to the new church. Governor Figueroa not only consented but also gave a personal donation of $30.

One of the pueblo's most prominent citizens, Don Antonio Pico, who was *alcalde* at that time, agreed to take charge of the building of the new church. His brother-in-law, Don Antonio Suñol, the pueblo's most educated and wealthiest citizen, not only agreed to assist him but also gave additonal land for it. Both Pico and Suñol made donations of materials and funds, and Suñol loaned his 150 Indian servants to help to make the bricks. In the archives of the California Province + Society of Jesus in Los Gatos can be seen a sheath of bills personally paid by Suñol. Members of the *ayuntamiento* (town council) offered their support as well. At the death of Padre Moreno in 1849, before the completion of the church, Padre José Pinyero was sent to replace him.

The Pueblo in 1841

The Suñol and Pico adobes were described in a series of articles Mrs. Fremont Older wrote for the *San Jose News* that first appeared in the 1920s taken from interviews Mrs. Older had with early Californians and American pioneers in the early 1900s. In a piece, reprinted in 1941, called "Neighbors in 1841," she takes her readers on a tour of Market Street conducted by an unidentified old California don. She said that he knew all the adobe houses on Market Street between the Southern Pacific Station and San Salvador Street. He had danced in them, he had flirted in them, he was related to their occupants.

As they walked down Market Street, he paused near the Farmer's Union, pointed down San Pedro Street, and said, "Luís Peralta lived here. The Peraltas had the most important land grant in Northern California. His wife was named Loreta." As they turned towards city hall the don said, "Juan Alvírez lived here. The Alvírezes had a ranch near the 12-Mile House (Captain Fisher's Rancho Laguna Seca)." Next to the Alvírez house were two Pacheco houses. They belonged to Luis and his brother, Dolores. "In 1846 Dolores Pacheco was *alcalde*. He tried to arrest Captain Frémont for taking a horse from the Peraltas. Frémont defied the *alcalde*'s summons and said he could pay attention to no such trifles and went on his conquering way."

He pointed out the Louis Altamirano house and, next door, that of Pedro Mesa. "Near the Mesas were the Sepúlvedas. Mesa married a Sepúlveda." As they approached Park Avenue, he showed her the house where Antonio Suñol lived. Proceeding along South Market Street they came to the house of José Noriega (grantee of Rancho Quito and political office holder).

By this time they had reached the outer border of fashionable San Jose in 1841. They paused near the Columbia Hospital. "There across the street was the old *rancheria*," he said. "Not the broncos or wild Indians but the Christian Indians who worked at the mission. They lived in houses built of a double trellis of willows. The trellis was filled with mud. The houses had tile roofs. The Indians wore serapes and blankets which they

Don Antonio Pico, delegate to the Constitutional Convention, alcalde in 1845, and delegate to the convention that nominated Lincoln; he took charge of the building of the second adobe church (CLYDE ARBUCKLE COLLECTION)

bought at the mission where they worked."

They hesitated a moment at the home of Agustín Narváez (grantee of the San Juan Bautista rancho), then in succession passed the houses of Bill Walsh, an Irishman, and those of two well-known families, Antonio Higuera's and Juan Bernal's.

Mrs. Older noted that Don Antonio Pico's house was at the corner of San Fernando and Market streets opposite St. Joseph's Church. "This was probably the most famous residence in San Jose in 1841," she said. "In the rear they had a vineyard where many entertainments were given. The vineyard extended to where the San Jose Hardware on Market Street now stands." After passing St. Joseph's Church, they came to the house of Leandro Rochin, a musician who played often at dances. They passed the houses of Thomas Bowen, a lumberman, and Charles Weber. Weber's Creek during the gold rush was named for him. Before Weber went to Stockton he gave Frank Lightson for whom Lightson Alley was named, all of his San Jose property as a wedding present.

22

In the middle of the street where Market joins Post, not far from Weber's house, stood the *juzgado* (city hall). On the site of the old Wells Fargo Building was the house of Juan Soto, a relative of the great bear fighter.

"During our tour of fashionable San Jose of 1841," she wrote, "the don's eyes brightened, his step quickened, his hat was at a gallant angle. His youth seemed to revive as he pronounced the great names of 1841."

Don Antonio Pico

Don Antonio has been described as an exceedingly handsome man with a commanding presence and courtly manner. A man of merit as well as means, he was a signer of the Treaty of Guadalupe y Hidalgo, a delegate to the Constitutional Convention in Monterey, and later a delegate to the Republican convention that nominated Lincoln. Although he fought with the Californios in the Mexican war, he put together a contingent to join the Union cause in the Civil War. He became the first lieutenant governor of California under Gov. Peter Burnett, and a justice of the Supreme Court of Cali-

Don Antonio Suñol arrived in the pueblo in 1818 after serving as Napoleon's scribe in the Battle of Waterloo. The pueblo's most literate citizen, he was the first postmaster and first banker. (COURTESY MARIE MANN AND GEORGE STRICKLER)

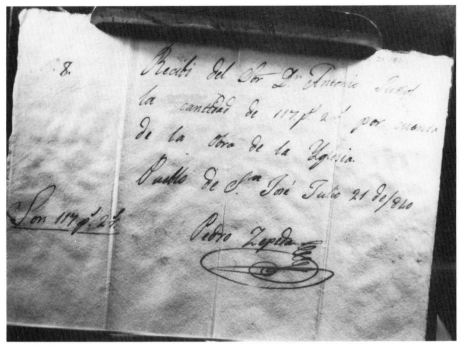

Receipt of bill paid by Don Antonio Sunōl, one of many for the San José de Guadalupe church (ARCHIVES, CALIFORNIA PROVINCE + SOCIETY OF JESUS)

fornia. In appreciation for his support, Lincoln appointed him receiver of public moneys. This meant he had to live in Los Angeles. He missed the Santa Clara Valley and soon resigned to return to the growing city of San Jose.

His cousin Pío Pico, who later became governor, lived in the pueblo in 1821 and had a cantina where he served his own wine in false-bottomed ox-horn tumblers. This innovation didn't make him popular with the *pobladores*, who felt they were shortchanged. Pico soon moved to Southern California, where he went on to bigger things, becoming the last Mexican governor of California.

Antonio Pico and his wife, Doña Pilar Bernal, frequently entertained the Americans in their richly furnished home on the site of the present San Jose Museum of Art. In the diary of Grandma Bascom, an American who came with her family at the time of the gold rush, she tells of attending the wedding of one of the Pico's daughters and of the elegant silk and embroidery gowns on the California women. One of Pilar Pico's descendants, George Strickler, says that when the American flag was raised the first time over the *juzgado* by James Weekes, Doña Pilar was so incensed she chopped the flagpole down.

Don Antonio Suñol

Antonio Suñol, a native of Barcelona, may have lacked the good looks of his brother-in-law, but he made up

for it with French charm and polish, which he probably acquired from his schooling in Bordeaux, France. He arrived at the pueblo in 1818 after serving in the French navy as a scribe to Napoleon. For this service he received a gold medallion from the French government citing him "for meretorious service in the surrender of Waterloo." The whereabouts of this medallion is unknown, but the late Dolores Sainsevain Turek, great-granddaughter of Suñol, who died in 1988 at the age of ninety-three, saw the medal at the home of Dr. Eugene Filipello, son-in-law of Pierre de Saisset, whose wife, María de Jesús, was the widow of Suñol's son, José Antonio.

Following his French navy experience, the adventurous young Antonio Suñol signed for a trip around the world on a sailing ship, the *Bordelaise*. He became ill, however, and left his ship in Yerba Buena in 1817. After being nursed back to health by the padres at Mission Dolores, he made a trip down to the Pueblo de San José de Guadalupe, liked what he saw and, after receiving the stamp of approval of the pueblo's *comisionado*, Don Luís María Peralta, stayed to become the pueblo's first foreign settler.

Suñol started his business career by proving himself a master of marketing techniques. He sold hides from the great Rancho Santa Teresa for Joaquín Bernal to the foreign ships that came to the Embarcadero de Santa Clara. A good match for the shrewd Yankee traders, he soon was able to marry Joaquín Bernal's daughter, María Dolores, and to move into an adobe in the pueblo. He opened a mercantile store and in 1823 added a grog shop, where he sold his own wines, making him the first liquor store owner in Northern California.

A man on the move, Suñol in the 1820s mined for gold and silver at what became the New Almaden mine. Fortunes were made there later from quicksilver. He did, however, strike gold when he mined in the Sierras. While there he observed the price of cattle and started moving his own stock to the gold fields. Back in the pueblo he reopened his mercantile store, where he sold supplies at a nice profit to the prospectors passing through on their way to the mines.

From his appointment as first postmaster of the pueblo in 1826 to his service as a member of the *ayuntamiento* (town council) and as *alcalde*, which added to his strong financial status, he rose to become the most powerful man in the town when he was appointed sub-prefect of the First District, which covered San Francisco, Branciforte (Santa Cruz), and the pueblo of San José. A member of the U.S. Exploration Expedition, Lt. Charles Wilkes, who stopped in San Jose in 1841 and visited Suñol, described him as "short, dapper, (maybe a bit pompous), rosy-cheeked," adding, "he appeared more like a pastry chef than the *alcalde* of San Jose."

Wilkes said Suñol told him that as sub-prefect he had very little trouble, except for the Indians who were stealing horses. In the back of his mind he may have been thinking of a plot that had been perpetrated by an Indian named Xenon with a group of raiders who planned to kill several men including Suñol. What made this more disturbing was that, with the end of the Spanish rule, the pueblo no longer had the military protection of the presidios.

As the town's most successful businessman, he was also the town's first banker. Because people trusted him, they let him keep their cash, something that was in short supply in California at that time, in his strong box.

In 1835 Capt. John Sutter came from New Helvetia to pay him a call that was to be the beginning of a long business arrangement and a friendship that later sadly eroded. As Suñol sent supplies, Sutter got deeper and deeper in debt. One time, to appease Suñol, he sent beaver pelts for payment and another time Indian servants. When the gold rush came, Sutter, successful in his diggings, was able to pay off his debts to Suñol, but their friendship was never the same.

In 1839 after many tries Suñol, with his brothers-in-law Juan Pablo and Agustín Bernal and Antonio Pico, finally received the Rancho del Valle de San José grant. The 64,000-acre spread had provided grazing lands for Mission San José and included the towns of Pleasanton and Sunol, which was named for Don Antonio.

In the late 1840s Suñol, feeling that he needed grazing land for his cattle closer to the pueblo, acquired Rancho Los Coches (Ranch of the Pigs) for $500, the amount owed to him by the grantee, Roberto Ballermino, a Christianized Santa Clara Mission Indian. Suñol added three brick rooms to Roberto's one-room adobe, taking the precaution of extending the bricks two feet below ground level instead of mounting them on a rock base commonly used at that time. Facing Lincoln Avenue in Willow Glen, it is said to be the first brick house in California. It became the summer home of Don Antonio and Doña Dolores, where they entertained in the grand early-California manner. Their guests included members of the first legislature and Bishop Alemany, the first bishop of the diocese, who was from the same province in Spain as Suñol. The Suñols preferred, however, to entertain at their larger house in town across from St. Joseph's, where the Wells Fargo Bank now stands.

In Mary Bowden Carroll's book *Ten Years in Paradise*, published in 1903, the author, a society editor, wrote to

Josephine Sunōl, daughter of Jose Sunōl and Jesusita Sunōl, was a devoted member of St. Joseph's Church. (COURTESY MARIE MANN AND GEORGE STRICKLER)

24

people who lived in the pueblo in the early days, querying them on social life of those times. Mrs. Frances A. Suñol-Angus, daughter of Narciso Suñol, wrote, "I speak of the early '40s, my own father's boyhood days and my grandfather Don Antonio Suñol and his home are a fair picture of the chivalrous host and the warm-hearted hospitality of the times. The guest chamber was seldom untenanted and seven or eight guests together were welcomed and entertained two or three successive weeks." She added that English, Russian, and American trading vessels made periodic visits to San Francisco, and the merchandise was brought overland on pack horses. When time permitted, the supercargo captain and some of his officers would accompany the caravan and for weeks were royally entertained by the Suñols.

"There being 50 to 150 Indian servants in the household, each guest was provided with his special one, who waited upon his every want during the visit." She went on to tell of the horses, silver-mounted saddles, and "a servant to clasp and unclasp each gentleman's spurs, while another led his horse away." She mentioned the homes of Don Salvis Pacheco, Don Dolores Pacheco, and Don José Noriega besides that of her grandfather as generous hosts.

She described the manner in which invitations to a ball were sent. A gay cavalier in holiday costume, mounted on a spirited horse, "pranced and curvetted through the plaza singing (to his own guitar accompaniment) some ditty" and when he had the attention of all he would extend the invitation to rich and poor (wealth had no special status according to Mrs. Suñol-Angus). He then moved on to stop at the door of each house with his daylight serenade and invitation.

Mrs. Coleman Younger, in telling about social life in the 1850s, said that she remembered spending a delightful evening at the home of Don Antonio and Doña Dolores Suñol, whose hospitality was unbounded. She commented on their trained Indian servants and exquisite table linens adorned with Spanish drawnwork.

After the American takeover, despite his prominence and business acumen, Suñol ran into the same problems as other rancheros: the presence of squatters and the difficulty of obtaining title from the U.S. It was a long, expensive fight to obtain Los Coches. Although he didn't suffer the fate of many who were wiped out with the long delay and by the lawyer fees, the ordeal took a toll on his health.

A friend of Santa Clara College, Suñol taught there for a time. The olive trees that he donated to the school still grow along the adobe wall. Cuttings from these trees were planted by Don Ramón Argüello on his Rancho Quito, and the olives were made famous by the next owner, Edward Goodrich.

A great sadness came to the Don when his son José Antonio was killed by a squatter named Wilson on Rancho del Valle, where the young Suñol had a home. Don Antonio was bereft at the loss and bitter that the killer was never apprehended. A stained-glass window on the left side of St. Joseph's Cathedral depicting the Holy Family is dedicated to the memory of José Suñol. His daughter, Josephine, is also remembered in the cathedral by the ornate sanctuary lamp that hangs form the ceiling and burns night and day before the Blessed Sacrament. A gift from the family, it was lit on June 16, 1907, on the first anniversary of Miss Suñol's death.

Antonio Suñol's son Narciso, who was educated at his father's school in France, married Rosaría Palomares, sister of Jesusita, and moved to the Pleasanton ranch after the death of José. Their daughter Josephine married Wilford "Dick" Weller of San Jose. Their grandchildren, John Ernest Weller and his sister, Jean Weller Kolb of San Jose, attended St. Joseph's Church.

Doña Dolores Bernal Suñol died in 1845. In the book of burials is the statement written in Latin by Padre José Jesús y María Gutiérrez stating that in the pueblo church of San José de Guadalupe he gave ecclesiastical burial to Doña Dolores Bernal, wife of Don Antonio Suñol, at the entrance on the epistle side of said church. A few years later Suñol married Dolores Mesa in a ceremony performed by Padre Pinyero, St. Joseph's first pastor after the church became a parish. Their attendants were Magdalena Peralta and Don (José) Fernández.

In 1853 Don Antonio sold fifty acres of Rancho Los Coches and the brick house to a Capt. Stefan Splivalo, who enlarged the building, adding a second floor, and encased it in a wooden frame. Suñol then sold a third of the rancho to Gen. Henry Morris Naglee and deeded one-third to daughter Paula and son-in-law Pierre Sainsevain. It was here that Sainsevain planted his grapevines and later subdivided Sainsevain Villa.

In the 1970s the present owner, businessman John Bruzzone, did extensive restoration to the house, and it is listed on the National Register of Historical Places as the Roberto Adobe.

Second Adobe Church Completed

With the support of the Picos, the Suñols, the Bernals, and other old families, the second adobe church of San José y Nuestra Señora de Guadalupe was finally completed in 1845. It was pretty much an enlarged

Narcisco Sunōl, son of Don Antonio Sunōl
(COURTESY JOHN WELLER)

version of the first adobe, only longer and wider with a tile roof instead of the tule roof that had leaked for so many years.

The year before, when bishop of California Francisco García Diego visited, Suñol had told the bishop of the church's poverty and asked for help. The bishop answered that same day. He bestowed upon St. Joseph's all the images and pictures not already placed in the sacristy of the Mission Santa Clara: two sets of vestments (one black and one violet) and six large wooden candlesticks, all donated in perpetuity.

In the papers of Father John D. Walshe, S.J., pastor of St. Joseph's from 1905 to 1908, he relates a story told to him by Joaquina Gubiotti Pozzo, who worshiped in the second adobe church as a child of six to eight years of age. She said that when Father John Nobili, S.J., came from Santa Clara for Sunday Mass, he would breakfast afterwards at her family's home.

Joaquina described how the devout and handsomely dressed Mexican ladies came to church accompanied by their Indian girl servants carrying the *petate* (palm leaf mats) to lay on the adobe floor for kneeling.

Kentucky writer Edwin Bryant, who passed through the pueblo in 1846, noted, "The church, which sits near the center of town exteriorly resembles a huge Dutch barn." He also took note of Don Antonio Suñol's garden. "The grapevines were were bowed to the ground with the luxuriance and weight of the yield, and more delicious fruit I never tasted."

On this trip Bryant visited a public place where he said both men and women were engaged "promiscuously" in a game of monte. He commented cynically on the contrast between the Californios and the Americans. He said that the Californios conducted themselves with great propriety, but that "the loud swearing and other turbulent demonstrations generally proceeded from the unsuccessful foreigners. I could not but observe the contrast between the two races in this regard. One (the Californio) bore his losses with stoical composure and indifference—the other (the American) announced each unsuccessful bid with profane imprecation and maledictions." Bryant added, "Excitement prompted the hazards of the former and avarice the latter."

American Arrivals

In the late 1820s and '30s more and more foreigners began to arrive. John Burton from Provincetown, Massachusetts, master of a ship that crashed on the rocks in San Diego, found his way to the pueblo. He also found a wife in Juana Galindo, whose father, Juan Galindo, was *mayordomo* of Mission Santa Clara and whose mother was Jacoba Bernal, daughter of Joaquín Bernal and Josefa Sanchez.

Fluent in Spanish, Burton was popular with the Californios, who called him El Capitan Viejo (the old captain). When he became the first mayor of the pueblo after the American flag was raised, he was helpful to the *pobladores* during that difficult period. Dolores Pacheco, first *alcalde*, and Pedro Chabolla, second *alcalde* at the time of the flag raising, had chosen not to continue at their posts.

James Alexander Forbes, a Scotsman who came by way

26

of South America in 1833, married in Mission Santa Clara another of Juan Galindo's daughters, Ana María Galindo. An educated man, fluent in Spanish, he, too, fit into the pueblo scene. Under John Burton, he was the first *juez de paz* (justice of the peace).

Forbes built the stone flour mill on Los Gatos Creek, which he called the "Santa Rosa." It now houses the Forbes Mill museum, which can be seen from Highway 17. It was not far from the trail taken by Padre Lasuén when traveling between Santa Clara Mission and the Santa Cruz Mission at Branciforte, and later taken by Frémont. Competition from Campbell's Mill near Saratoga was too much for Forbes and he declared bankruptcy.

Grantee of Rancho El Potrero de Santa Clara, Forbes sold the property, located at an angle of the Guadalupe and The Alameda to Commodore Robert Field Stockton. Stockton later discovered that the acreage was considerably less than indicated by Forbes. Stockton, who had served in the War of 1812, was sent West in command of a squadron in 1845 and appointed military governor in 1847. He subdivided the property and had prefabricated houses shipped from the East. He also brought B. F. Fox out from the East with plants to landscape the property. Fox's nursery and home were showplaces. Returning to New Jersey, Stockton served as United States Senator for that state from 1851 to 1853.

The first non-Hispanic to arrive was a Scotsman named John Gilroy (originally John Cameron), who skipped ship at Monterey and made his way to the pueblo. He married María Clara Ortega (granddaughter of the scout Francisco Ortega) and settled on Rancho San Ysidro. His name lives on in the city of Gilroy.

Two years later, in 1816, Thomas Doak, a whaler, arrived on an American ship. He changed his name to Felipe Santiago, headed for the Santa Clara Valley, married a daughter of José Mariano Castro's, and settled on Rancho Las Animas. William Gulnac came in 1833 and married María Ceseña, sister-in-law of Capt. William Fisher. With Isaac Branham he built the first mill on Los Gatos Creek.

Martin Murphy, Sr., patriarch of the Murphy clan, which he brought from Ireland to Quebec province, then to Missouri and, finally, over the Sierras by wagon train to the Santa Clara Valley.

CHAPTER SIX

The 1840s

In the 1840s the sleepy little Spanish town began to awaken from its slumber. A gradual infusion of Americans and Europeans injected new blood into the pueblo and its adobe church. Many of the new arrivals overland included the Martin Murphy clan, the Charles Whites, the James Reeds, the Thomas Kells, and James Enright. From Baja California by sea came Captain Fisher, Julian Hanks, and Ramon Ceseña with their families—all members of the adobe church.

The year 1844 marked the arrival of Martin Murphy, Sr., and his large family of twenty with the Stephens-Murphy-Townsend party. Their Conestoga-type wagons with multispoked wheels were the first that most of the Californios, familiar only with the solid oak wheels of thir carretas, had ever seen.

This was not only the first wagon train to cross the Sierras and the first to bring cattle, but also the first to open a direct route across the country to the coast. It was this route that the transcontinental railroad followed in the 1860s and, one hundred years later, the parallel highway we know as Interstate 80.

Elisha Stephens was the pathfinder, joined by Caleb Greenwood and his two half-breed sons by his Crow Indian wife. Stephens homesteaded 160 acres in the Cupertino area which he called Blackberry Farm. Today a golf course and club by the same name occupy part of his property. Stevens Creek Boulevard, the dam, and the park are named for Stephens, but obviously someone goofed in the spelling. He and Greenwood resented John Frémont being called the "pathfinder"—but it apparently was not a title claimed by Frémont.

Dr. Townsend of this party was the first medical doctor to settle in the pueblo, and he founded the first Masonic lodge. He and his wife died during the cholera epidemic of 1850. Moses Shallenberger, eighteen-year-old brother of Mrs. Townsend, who assumed guardianship of their three-year-old son, John, first took him with his Indian nursemaid to stay with the nuns at Notre Dame Academy and then to the padres at Mission Santa Clara. When he was grown and serving in the state assembly, he visited Notre Dame with his wife, an alumnus. He recalled his early days with the sisters.

Martin Murphy

Martin Murphy, the senior member of the party, had migrated from Ireland to the Quebec area of Canada, in search of freedom of religion and education. (The English, at that time, forbade the Irish from attending any kind of school.) From there he moved his family to Missouri, where his wife and a grandchild died of malaria. Father Hoecken, a Belgian Jesuit missionary priest who cared for the sick members of his family and other victims of the disease, told Murphy about the California climate, and that the established religion there was Catholic. Never having been there himself, the priest could only tell him that it was west of Missouri on the shores of the Pacific. That was enought to light a fire in Murphy.

Although almost sixty years of age, Murphy did not hesitate to join Elisha Stephens and Dr. and Mrs. John Townsend with nineteen members of his family on the overland wagon train journey. They passed hostile Indian tribes without incident. In fact, it was an Indian, named "Truckee," who, communicating with signs, directed them to Donner Lake (originally called Truckee Lake), which was to be named for the ill-fated party that two years later spent a freezing winter there.

Part of the Murphy party went ahead. When they reached Sutter's Fort, they learned of efforts to depose Governor Micheltorena; if this happened, they might be driven from the country. Martin Senior and Junior took off with Sutter, returning after the battle of Charevengo.

This was to be the beginning of the saga of the

CAPT. STEPHENS POSES FOR HIS ONE AND ONLY PICTURE

Capt. Elisha Stephens, who led the first wagon train across the Sierras: the Stephens-Murphy-Townsend party. He purchased land in the Cupertino area and called it Blackberry Farm. Stevens Creek Road is named (and misspelled) for him. (CLYDE ARBUCKLE COLLECTION)

Murphys in California. With a seemingly unquenchable thirst for land, Martin Murphy started acquiring ranchos until he and his sons had more than ten million acres. Not even Henry Miller, the Cattle King, who arrived in California five years later and made his headquarters at Gilroy, could exceed that figure.

Rancho La Coche

Murphy first purchased the 9,000-acre Rancho Ojo de Agua de la Coche (Pig Spring) from Juan María Hernández. He moved with his four unmarried sons and daughters into the Hernández adobe at what is today the intersection of Las Llagas Road and Hale Avenue. Before long he added the Las Llagas, the Las Uvas, and parts of the Las Animas rancho. Murphy chose a site on the Coche rancho with a view of Murphy's Peak (now called El Toro Peak) to build an adobe home of his own. The Kentucky journalist Bayard Taylor, on his way by foot to Monterey to cover the Constitutional Conven-

tion in 1849, wrote in his much-quoted book *El Dorado* that he was greeted at the door by Martin Murphy's daughter, Ellen, that she introduced him to Murphy and several houseguests, and that "his cottage is a well-known resting place to all the Americans in the country."

He described it as commanding a splendid prospect: "Beyond the house and across a little valley rose the conical peak, an isolated land mountain that served as a landmark from San Jose to Monterey." After dinner Murphy provided Taylor with a horse and invited him to join him on a ride up the mountain.

The next day, on his way to San Juan Bautista, as Taylor crossed over Rancho Las Animas (most of it later acquired by Henry Miller, who built a summer home and family compound on Mt. Madonna), he met one of Mariano Castro's sons. An outgoing, friendly fellow, the young Castro invited him to share his meal.

Martin Murphy, known as a shrewd but kindly and generous businessman who had purchased his land legally, was deeply religious. Although well into his sixties, he thought nothing of riding horseback twenty miles to the pueblo church of San José de Guadalupe to attend mass. He built a chapel on his rancho which he named San Martin for his patron saint, Saint Martin of Tours. The town that grew up around it owes its name, San Martin, to this man and his chapel. He died in 1865 at the Almaden home of his daughter, Margaret Kell.

Diana Murphy and Morgan Hill

The nearby town of Morgan Hill was named not for a "hill," as many people thought, but for the husband of Murphy's granddaughter Diana Murphy. One story is that train passengers on their way to visit Diana and Morgan would ask to get off at Morgan Hill's. Another is that when Hill subdivided his wife's rancho, he gave it his name. Diana's father, Daniel, was the largest land owner of the Murphys, with ranches in Nevada, Ariona, and Mexico, as well as California, covering three and one-half million acres. After his death, Diana's mother, Maria Fisher, daughter of Capt. William Fisher of the neighboring Rancho Laguna Seca, married Peter Colombet. They had a large home in San Jose at Fifth and William streets.

Despite Diana's great beauty, inherited from her Spanish grandmother, and her wealth, inherited from the Murphys, her life was not a happy one. After her husband's sister, Sarah Althea Hill, became involved in a scandal with Senator Sharon they were snubbed by San Francisco society. Their daughter Dianne made what

The Martin Murphy, Jr., home was shipped around the Horn and reassembled on Rancho Pastoria de Borregas in what is now Sunnyvale.

appeared to be a good marriage to Baron de Reinach-Worth, but on her honeymoon, she suffered a breakdown and a few months later took her own life. Diana and Morgan Hill were divorced. He died in 1913 at the Nevada Ranch. He was buried in the family plot with his father-in-law, who, ironically, had opposed Morgan's marriage to his daughter. Diana moved to London, where, still beautiful at the age of sixty-one, she married Sir George Rhodes, brother of Sir Cecil Rhodes, for whom Rhodesia was named.

The *Jenny Lind*

Martin Murphy's daughter, Margaret, and her husband, an Englishman named Thomas Kell, followed her family to California in 1846. Thomas purchased property on the Almaden Road where he planted grain. Active members of St. Joseph's Church, the Kells gave land for a cemetery near where the Baptist Church now stands. The state appropriated the land for Highway 85, and the bodies were moved to Calvary Cemetery. When the Kells' son, Bernard, died in the explosion of the *Jenny Lind* in 1853, Bishop Alemany wrote a warm personal, but direct, letter to Margaret, telling her, in essence, that she must stop grieving and get on with her life.

The *Jenny Lind*, a side-wheel steamboat that plied the waters between Alviso and San Francisco—leaving at night and arriving at its destination the next morning—was the only means of transportation between the pueblo and Yerba Buena. One hundred and fifty people were aboard when, at a point just north of Dumbarton Bridge and the Leslie Salt Flats, the steamer's boiler exploded, killing thirty-four people, and horribly scalding others.

For Martin Murphy, Sr., the explosion of the *Jenny Lind* was a double tragedy. He lost not only his grandson but also his own son, Bernard. The elder Bernard had met and married Catherine O'Toole on a trip to Quebec to bring his sister, Johanna, to California. Bernard and Catherine settled in his prefabricated tin house, which had been shipped by way of Panama and assembled on his Rancho La Polka.

Catherine Dunne

Catherine was again to know sorrow when her only son, a student at Georgetown University, was stricken with a strange malady and died. Martin Murphy was ready to step in and run the ranch for his daughter-in-law, but Catherine put her dainty foot down and said she was quite capable of handling her own affairs, which, as it turned out, she did and did so very well. In addition to Rancho La Polka, she inherited her son's portion of Martin Murphy's Rancho Uvas. In 1862 she married James Dunne, owner of Rancho San Felipe and part of Rancho San Lorenzo (better known as the Topo). Dunne died in 1874, leaving Catherine with three children: Peter, who married Josephine Masten (their son, Peter Dunne, became a prominent Jesuit priest who sometimes came to the parish where he grew up, St. Joseph's, to say mass and give retreats); Mary Phileta, who marred Joseph Rucker of the San Jose real estate family; and Bridget Catherine, who married Ralph Hersey.

In the 1895 edition of *Sunshine, Fruit and Flowers* is a story on the progress of the valley in which it says of Rancho Uvas "the great Catherine Dunne ranch of

18,000 acres is being sold in lots of five, ten, twenty and forty acres." Prices ranged from $25 to $125 per acre.

Catherine always said she planned to live to be a hundred, but she missed by three years. She died in 1925 at the age of ninety-seven at the Santa Barbara home of her daughter, Catherine Hersey. Her name is remembered in Morgan Hill with Dunne Avenue and St. Catherine's Church.

Martin Murphy, Jr.

More visible than his father, Martin Murphy, Jr., and his wife, Mary Bulger, lived a much grander life style on their Rancho Pastoria de las Borregas in what was called Murphy's Station and is now known as Sunnyvale. It is said they entertained every important person who came to this part of California.

They came overland from Missouri with his father's party in 1844, after losing a child in the malaria epidemic. On the way, Mary Murphy gave birth to a daughter named Elizabeth, who almost drowned during a crossing of the Yuba River tied to the pummel of her father's saddle. In relief and half laughing, he gave her the middle name "Yuba." Elizabeth Yuba Murphy married a San Franciscan, William Taafe, and for a wedding present her father bought half of Rancho La Purísima Concepción from Juana Briones Miranda. They built their home on the site of the Foothill College.

Their son, Martin Taafe I, married Rose Hoffman, daughter of María Timotea Bernal and Charles Hoffman, superintendant of the New Almaden mine. Members of St. Joseph's, the family owned a home on Fourth Street. Elizabeth died at the age of thirty, leaving four children, and William died a few years later. Mrs. Martin Murphy, Jr., raised the children. Another son, James, died while a student at Santa Clara College. He is buried in the Santa Clara Mission—his headstone can be seen on the right side of the entrance. A great-grandson, James Taafe, still lives with his family on a part of the original family rancho in Los Altos Hills.

Martin and Mary settled first along the Cosumnes River, where he was the first to raise grain in the Sacramento Valley. Of historical note: General Castro had his horses in the Murphy corrals at the start of the war between the U.S. and Mexico.

In 1850 Martin, Jr., decided to move to the Santa Clara Valley so his children could attend school. He bought 5,000 acres of Rancho Pastoria de las Borregas from Mariano Castro for $12,000 in gold and put on it a house he had already ordered precut and milled to his specifications in the East—and had shipped around the Horn.

The thirty-room house, put together with pegs and leather straps, became a showplace surrounded by gardens and lawns. Murphy family members lived in the house for over 100 years.

The El Camino ran between their house and the bay, and when the house was first built, they could see from their front porch the steamers on the bay passing on their way to and from Yerba Buena and Alviso.

They had their own railroad car for traveling back and forth to San Francisco and their own train stop, called Murphy's Station. Travelers up the peninsula were welcomed to pass the night, and a room was always kept ready for their friend Archbishop Joseph Sadoc Alemany when making his rounds to visit churches between San Francisco and Monterey.

The Party of the Century

There probably has never been a fiftieth wedding anniversary party to equal that of Martin and Mary Bulger Murphy on July 18, 1881—said to be the biggest bash in the history of California. No one knows for sure, but various accounts range from 3,500 to 10,000 guests. The Murphys alone would have made a crowd. The banks in San Francisco closed (business was at a standstill), and special trains, engaged by the hosts, brought partygoers from San Francisco, including such familiar names as the James Phelans, with their son, who became Senator James D. Phelan, and Archbishop Alemany. Others came by carriage, wagon, or horseback, including the Arques family, the Fentons, the James Enrights, and the Halfords.

Issac Branham supervised the barbecue of the finest beef, lamb, and pigs from the rancho's herds in a pit 115 feet long, 4 feet wide and 4 feet deep. Besides the barbecue there was a wagonload of hams, and another of roasting chickens. Lemonade was served to the teetotalers; barrels of lager, kegs of whiskey, and a freight car of champagne were provided for those with stronger tastes. California's first senator, William Gwin, led off the toasts, followed by wealthy railroad man Col. Peter Donahue and, among others, Judge C. T. Ryland, who paid special tribute to Mary Bulger Murphy. He told of her feeding the squatters on the ranch unbeknownst to her husband, who at the same time was trying to have them evicted.

Murphy's health started to fail after the celebration. He and his wife moved into town to a house on Market Street to be near St. Joseph's Church. Four years later he was buried from this church with Archbishop Alemany celebrating a solemn requiem mass. In her book *Martin Murphy, Jr., California Pioneer 1844–1884*, Sister

Gabrielle Sullivan said that "the day was one of mourning for the community of San Jose; flags were flown at half-mast, the city hall and business houses were closed. On the way to the cemetery in Santa Clara where another large group of friends awaited, the cortege of 200 stopped at the Convent of Notre Dame where an honor guard of sisters and students paid their last tribute to the friend and patron of the Academy."

The pallbearers represented the who's who of San Jose, including Judge David Belden, F. E. Spencer, T. W. Spring, Mariano Malarin, B. P. Rankin, Edward McLaughlin, Pedro de Saisset, James Enright, C. T. Ryland, and William Dunphy.

The Murphy home, with its gardens, gnarled pepper and fig trees, and Canary Island palms, met its demise to bulldozers in 1961 despite the efforts of the Sunnyvale Historical Society and others to preserve it. All that remains is the brass plaque designating it as a state historical landmark.

This much-admired man, who left an estate estimated to be in excess of five million dollars, could, ironically, only sign his marriage certificate with an "X."

James Enright

Undoubtedly, the Murphys' oldest friends attending their fiftieth wedding anniversary celebration were their neighbors James and Mary Enright. Following the same path as his old friends, Jim Enright had come from Ireland and farmed first in Canada along the St. Lawrence River. He then moved to St. Joseph, Missouri, and two years later to California on the same wagon train with Thomas and Margaret Murphy Kell. He bought a 900-acre parcel—referred to on the patent simply as the Enright Tract—adjoining the Murphys' Pastoria de las Borregas. Enright married Margaret Mary Duncan, a native of Scotland who came via South America by sailing ship. Her father was a furniture maker and worked in Valparaiso with James Lick. According to her grandson Austin Enright, when the Duncans arrived at Moneterey in 1846, the ship's captain saw a flag flying that he didn't recognize. "He told my great-grandfather Duncan to take the boat and go ashore and find out about the flag. It was, of course, the Stars and Stripes of the United States, which had been raised two days before.

"My grandfather was a successful man. He owned property in San Francisco around the Palace Hotel—had several ranches here. In the earthquake of 1906 the house where I was born at Seventh and Reed streets was destroyed. My father lost everything and had to start over again. I remember going to my grandmother's house on Williams Street to stay with her. She had fifty or sixty acres of orchards."

Enright's grandfather A. L. Kellogg, a Methodist minister who had been advised by his doctor to go West for his health, came to Santa Clara in 1845. Finding a population of mostly Indians, he had to figure out something else to do. He planted a garden where the P. M. Mill was later located. When he saw the size of the seeds he decided to go into the seed business. He became a partner of C. C. Morse's, and together they became the largest seed growers west of Mississippi, leasing 1,400 acres of land from Martin Murphy, Jr., estate in Sunnyvale; from the Sargent Ranch in Gilroy; and in the San Juan Bautista valley, which used to be a sea of color in the spring. Kellogg sold out to Morse, whose son, Lester, merged with D. M. Ferry Company, and the name became Ferry-Morse Seed Company. Austin's grandmother Margaret Enright was active in St. Joseph's Church. In the cathedral is a semicircular stained-glass window over one of the doors in her memory. Another window is dedicated to George Enright, a relative from Limerick. Jim Enright, whose land dealings extended to Santa Cruz, is remembered in a stained-glass window in Holy Cross Church there.

Another Enright named Joseph made a name for himself in 1864 with his Enright's Patent Strawburning Portable Engine for powering thrashing machines. A boiler and smoke stack on wagon wheels, it was advertised as the "most perfect of its kind."

Austin Enright's wife, Marie Kaiser Enright, who was married first to her husband's good friend, the late Dr. Cletus Sullivan, attended St. Joseph's Church. She has quite a family history. Her great-great-great-grandfather was Capt. José Antonio Sánchez, an army captain in the Anza Expedition who received the extensive Buri Buri land grant in San Mateo County (now the site of the Crystal Springs reservoir). His son Francisco led the Battle of Santa Clara. Marie Enright's mother, Phoebe Isabel Gould, born at Lawrence Station near Alviso, was the second youngest of fifteen children. She married William C. Kaiser, who came from Germany and ran the Ross Hotel on First Street near the Montgomery Hotel. She died on Christmas Day, 1987, at the age of 105.

Captain William Fisher

One of the early non-Spanish members of St. Joseph's in the 1940s, Capt. William Fisher lived with his large family in the Alvírez adobe on Rancho Laguna Seca in

33

The Fisher family of Rancho Laguna Seca in front of Fiacro Fisher's home (COURTESY ROBERT FISHER)

the Coyote area. A native of England, Fisher, as a nineteen-year-old seaman, sailed from Boston on a clipper ship bound for California to trade in hides and tallow. He left ship at San José del Cabo, near Cabo San Lucas, at the tip of Baja California. There he married a Spanish girl, Liberata Ceseña.

Skipper of his own ship, the *María Teresa*, Fisher sailed up the coast carrying goods from Mexico to early-California settlers. On a trip to Monterey in 1845 Fisher, who had become attracted to the land south of San Jose, attended a land auction. He outbid Charles Weber and John Gilroy, among others, by paying $6,000 for the 20,000-acre Rancho Laguna Seca of Juan Alvírez, former pueblo *alcalde*. It stretched from a mile north of Coyote to Morgan Hill.

Merchant men in those days were couriers of news—both written and by word of mouth. In the Larkin papers is a letter from Santa Barbara dated May 23, 1845, to Thomas Oliver Larkin that reads in part, "Mexico has declared war against the U.S. This news comes by Mr. Fisher from the cape. Mr. Fisher received this news from a gentleman of his acquaintance direct from Mazatlan."

While Fisher was on a trip to Baja to bring his family up to his newly acquired rancho, Capt. John C. Frémont, leader of the Bear Flag Rebellion against Mexico, occupied the Alvírez adobe. In his memoirs Frémont wrote,

wrote, "By February of 1846 we were reunited in the Valley of San Jose about 13 miles south of the village of that name on the main road leading to Monterey which was about 160 miles distant. The place which we had selected for rest and refitting was a vacant rancho called the Laguna belonging to a Mr. Fisher." Frémont was the second military leader to make use of the Laguna Seca. Just before Fisher purchased it, Governor Micheltorena camped there with the 150-man army.

On the trip back from Mexico on board the *María Teresa*, the Fisher family was joined by Liberata's brother, Ramón Ceseña, his wife, María, and children, and by Fisher's partner in the shipping business, a fellow New Englander, Julian Hanks, who had also married a Baja California girl, Isabel Montoya.

Robert Fisher of San Jose, a great-great-grandson of Fisher's who researched the family history, writes that every Saturday the family rode to St. Joseph's to attend mass in his double-seated carriage which Captain Fisher had ordered shipped from the East, one of the first in California. Before returning on Sunday afternoon, they would visit the Ceseñas and the William Gulnacs (she was a Ceseña) and the Julian Hankses. A story is told that when Captain Fisher went to Yerba Buena to take delivery of his carriage, he was accompanied by his daughter, María, who refused to get into it. Compared

34

to the heavy wooden-wheeled *carretas*, it seemed to her like some sort of skeleton affair. Mary, as she was called, married Daniel Murphy, the largest land owner of the Murphys. Some time after she was widowed, she married Peter Colombet.

In addition to raising cattle (traders from merchant ships came to buy his stock) aand growing grain and grapes on the ranch, Fisher had an adobe in the pueblo where he ran a mercantile business. Fisher, a member of the first city council under American rule, lived only five years after he came to the valley. He is buried in Mission Santa Clara cemetery. Liberata outlived two other husbands, Dr. George Bull and Caeser Piatti.

Julian Hanks

Captain Fisher's old friend and business partner, Julian Hanks, who also served on the first city council and as a delegate to the Constitutional Convention in Monterey, built the first sawmill on Los Gatos Creek with Charles Weber. During the American occupation, Hanks was one of the group selected to govern San Jose.

In naming the streets in the pueblo, usually the last name of the person so honored was selected. In Hanks' case, however, the powers that be chose his first name. Perhaps it was because in Spanish the "H" is silent and the letter "J" is pronounced like "H." So, Julian Hanks in Spanish was pronounced "Hoolian Anks." The locals apparently preferred the sound of "Hoolian" to "Anks."

In the 1860s Hanks set off on a sailing trip down the coast of Mexico with a shipload of ammunition to aid Emperor Maximilian, who was having his problems in Mexico. The worst fears of his wife, Isabel, who always worried about her husband when he went to sea, apparently were realized, because he was never seen or heard from again. It is believed his ship was sunk by the British.

Sixty descendants of William and Liberata Fisher and of Julian and Isabel Hanks (the two families intermarried) gather regularly for a family reunion at the Laguna Seca ranch. The classic 100-year-old American house was built by the captain's youngest son, Fiacro Fisher, for his wife, Gertrude Hanks, who was in poor health and couldn't tolerate the dampness of the Alvírez adobe. It is now occupied by the Verl Lybberts, who are active in horse circles and use it for square dances, hay rides, and horse training.

Grandsons of Fiacro and Gertrude attending the 1989 picnic were Robert Fisher of San Jose with his wife, Beverly, and family and Douglas Pinard of Los Altos with his family. Captain Fisher had twin sons, Thomas and

Liberata Ceseña Fisher, wife of Capt. William Fisher of Rancho Laguna Seca (COURTESY ROBERT FISHER)

Cipriano, who were born in Mexico and came up in the boat with the family. They returned to Cabo San Lucas, Mexico, while still in their teens to run some of the family ranchos. Daniel Fisher, a descendant of Cipriano's, came from Ensenada for the reunion, and from La Paz came Blanca Fisher Aramburo and her brother, Arturo Fisher. Thomas (the other twin) married Anna Hanks. Their grandson George Fisher came from Galt for the family reunion. His sister, Diana Fisher Stewart, lives in San Jose.

Charles Weber

Although Charles Weber, a native of Prussia, was overbid by Captain Fisher for Rancho Laguna Seca, he received patent to Rancho Cañada de San Felipe y las Animas, better known as the Weber Ranch, in 1866. Weber came to the valley in 1841 and married Ellen Murphy, the daughter of his neighbor Martin Murphy. A prosperous merchant in San Jose, he is better known for his part in the Mexican war and as founder of Stockton.

In the early 1920s Weber Ranch (also known as Coyote

The Coyote Post Office at Rancho Laguna Seca is now at the San Jose Historical Museum. (COURTESY ROBERT FISHER)

Ranch because of its location on Coyote Creek) became the property of the five O'Connell brothers, Elmer, Daniel, Maurice, Charles, and Franklin (sons of Thomas and Julia O'Connell), who had a hay, wood, and coal business at Sixth and St. James streets.

A grandson, Kenneth O'Connell of Saratoga, tells a story of how they financed the purchase with a loan of $125,000 from Bank of Italy (Bank of America) even though they didn't have $125 between them. He says, "The bank's president, A. P. Giannini, had a different way of making loans. He'd look a man over and if he liked what he saw, he would loan him the money." The O'Connell brothers proved A. P.'s judgement to be right.

Franklin O'Connell sold out his share of the ranch early in the game and bought Rancho San Felipe, also known as Dunne Ranch. Fenton O'Connell, his son, is still ranching on the Rancho Lomerias Muertas land which he and his wife, Pat, call El Rancho San Benito. It is located on the Bolsa Road between San Juan Bautista and Hollister.

According to Maureen Tiernan of San Jose, daughter of Daniel O'Connell, the Coyote has diminished in size over the years. The county took over a large portion for Anderson Dam in 1950. United Technology bought another large chunk of acreage in the mid-1950s.

Pala, which he is said to have bought from the grantee, José Higuera, for song. Added to that he had 2,000 acres of Rancho Rincón de Los Esteros and a number of city lots.

In a letter White wrote about the pueblo to his parish priest in Missouri (the letter is in the California Room of the San Jose City Library), he told of horse thieves and runaway sailors. "Very little ground is fenced . . . posts and rails cost $100 a thousand. I have set out some 1,500 vines and 200 fruit trees, but little farming is done." He failed to note that there were practically no roads, so that fences would have impeded travel, which was mostly by horseback.

"The natives go out in the spring with their families," he continued, "and build houses of mustard stocks, remain a few months until the crops are safe and then return to their houses (in the pueblo). There are two seasons, spring and summer. Mines of coal, gold and quicksilver have been found. Land has doubled in value since last spring."

The bright, energetic young White, *alcalde* of the pueblo, was to live only until the age of thirty. He was a passenger on the ill-fated steamboat *Jenny Lind* when it exploded en route from Alviso to San Francisco in 1853.

Charles White

Charles White came from Missouri in 1846 with his wife, Ellen, and two children. They joined the pueblo church and entered into the life of the community. A shrewd businessman, White invested in real estate. "White Road," named for him, runs through Rancho

James Frazier Reed

James Frazier Reed crossed the Sierras, with his family in the tragic Reed-Donner party that was snowbound at Donner Lake (originally called Truckee Lake) in the winter of 1846–47. Reed, like his compatriot Charles White, was prominent in civic affairs, as well as a wagon-maker. He was one of nineteen men who signed to put up money for the first capital and one of the founders of the Masonic Order in San Jose. Active in real estate, he named the streets in his first subdivision (Reed Reservation) for family members: Margaret for his wife (who actually spelled it "Margret"); Virginia and Martha (who was called "Patty") for his daughters; Charley for his infant son; Keyes for his mother-in-law, who died on the trip to California; and Bestor for the surveyor who laid out the subdivision.

According to Reed's great-grandson Frazier Reed of San Jose, "My grandfather Charles Cadden Reed was born across the street from St. Joseph's. I remember my grandfather and my Aunt Patty telling about life in the pueblo and of the parties that went on for days and days."

He said that Patty's sister, his Aunt Virginia, married John Murphy, son of Martin Murphy, Sr., in St. Joseph's. "Virginia," he continued, "spent a lot of time with the Patrick Breen family during that winter they were snowbound in the Sierras. She was impressed with the way the Breens, who were Catholic, gave thanks for everything. She vowed that if she ever got out of the Sierras she was going to become a Catholic." After her marriage she became an active member of St. Joseph's Church, and her name appeared frequently in stories of the church's events. John Murphy, like his father-in-law, James Reed, became active in public affairs and was elected councilman in the first election in 1849 and later sheriff.

Frazier Reed said his father, Frazier Reed, Sr., was married in the early 1900s to Josephine Vollmer of Campbell in St. Joseph's Church by Father Gleason, adding, "My brother and I were baptized and confirmed there."

Paul Masson Mountain Vineyard, photo by Ansel Adams (COURTESY PAUL MASSON)

CHAPTER SEVEN

The French

French became the third language in the pueblo in the late 1840s and early 1850s as the migration from France increased. The sisters of Notre Dame were Belgian and emphasized French in their school, and St. Joseph's first pastor, Padre Pinyero, had lived in France and spoke the langue fluently, making them feel at home in the adobe church.

The mild climate, rich soil, and availability of water reminded the newcomers of their native France, so they lost no time setting out orchards and vineyards. With their knowledge of winemaking, they soon began importing cuttings of wine grapes from France.

The Pelliers

Louis Pellier came from France to dig for gold but gained everlasting fame as the "Father of the Prune." During the wet winter of '49 in the Sierras, he made a trip to the pueblo. Impressed with the valley's agricultural potential, he decided to stay and persuaded his brother, Pierre, to join him. He bought twenty or so acres on North San Pedro Street and Chaboya Alley, where he developed his City Gardens nursery and picnic grounds.

All was going so well that the brothers decided that Pierre should go to France to get scions of the petit d'Agen prune and select wine grapes. Louis would stay home to prepare the soil. The trip was doubly successful, because he also found a wife. On the trip back all was not smooth sailing. Rounding the Cape of Good Hope, the ship ran into severe storms that delayed passage, giving Pierre no end of concern over the survival of the prized petit d'Agen. He solved his problem by talking the cook into selling him some potatoes in which to insert his cuttings. This kept them moist until the ship reached California. Thus was saved the prune that was to make the Santa Clara Valley famous and a lot of men wealthy. Even today 90 percent of the prunes in this country

are descended from Pellier's petit d'Agen. Despite the difference in life style and living accommodations, Pierre's French wife, Henriette, adapted well to the pueblo scene and became an active member of St. Joseph's Church, as did their children and grandchildren.

Louis grafted the petit d'Agen to wild plum stock and offered them for sale in his nursery. But there were few takers. San Joseans had been "sold" on a larger, but inferior, prune for drying. It was J. Q. A. Ballou who started Pellier's prune on its road to success when he

Peter and Justine Mirassou on their wedding day, 1912

Pierre Mirassou (center) with his two brothers-in-law, Philippe Prudhomme (left) and Alfred Renaud (right), circa 1888

drafted them to domestic plums. The yield was impressive and the reception by the public enthusiastic. The credit for marketing it, however, goes to a native of Germany named John Rock. Within ten years the valley was producing one-third of the world's prunes. In the spring of the year, from Palo Alto to Gilroy and from Alum Rock Canyon to Saratoga and Los Gatos, the valley was a carpet of white blossoms.

Happiness somehow eluded the kindly Louis Pellier. Although he loved children (he used to invite the sisters and children from Notre Dame convent next door to come over and pick fruit), his marriage in St. Joseph's Church by Father Goetz to a woman named Constance Bache was a fiasco. He was so deeply depressed when she returned to France after purportedly trying to poison him that he suffered a nervous breakdown and died in 1872 in Stockton. He was buried in Kell Cemetery (land donated by Thomas and Margaret Kell) in the Almaden area that was confiscated for Highway 85. San Jose's historian, Clyde Arbuckle, walking over the property one day discovered Louis's tombstone. It is now at the San Jose Historical Museum.

Pellier Park, in the area of San Pedro and St. James streets on part of the former City Gardens Nursery property, is a tribute to the memory of Louis Pellier, who made San Jose the "Prune Capital of the World." It is a miniature fruit orchard planted with the petit d'Agen

prune, d'Anjou pears, and five varieties of grapes. Through the efforts of history buffs Leonard McKay and Jim Arbuckle, children and future generations will be able to see the kinds of trees and grape vines that once covered the valley. Many of the over 250 Pellier descendants attended the dedication ceremony in 1977.

The Pellier brothers, according to Pierre's great-grandson Norbert Mirassou, got into wine production by accident. "They had grapes that didn't sell and decided to make wine in a building alongside the nursery. They would put a barrel of it in the picnic area so the workmen could have a glass with lunch. They still had a surplus, so they decided to sell it."

Pierre pursued the wine operation on 300 acres of Antonio Chabolla's (Chaboya) Rancho Yerba Buena in the foothills of Mount Hamilton that Louis had purchased. He planted his vine cuttings from France and dug an underground cellar to keep the wines cool.

A daughter of Pierre's named for her mother, Henriette, married a new arrival from France, Pierre Mirassou. They moved up on her father's ranch and joined in the production of wines that would eventually bear Mirassou's name. Originally, Norbert said, they sold most of their wine wholesale to brokers in San Francisco. "There was no requirement to register labels at that time." When Mirassou was only thirty-three years of age, he died, leaving Henriette with five young children. The following year she married Thomas Castalegno, a workman on the ranch. They carried on the wine operation, and it is said that Henriette, who worked with her father in the vineyards and in the winery, learned so much that she became the first woman winemaker in California.

Pierre and Henriette Mirassou had three sons, Peter, Herman, and John, and two daughters, who were married in a double wedding ceremony in St. Joseph's: Marie Helen to Philippe Prudhomme and Elsie to Alfred Renaud. Herman and Mary Mirassou were also married in St. Joseph's in 1909, according to a granddaughter, Nadine McDonnell of Monte Sereno. John Mirassou married Eulalie Flory in Porterville. His son, Don, is the last Pellier still growing prunes on his ranch at Madrone. He and his wife, Joyce Kuamme, were married at St. Patrick's Church, but because it was contrary to church regulations to have a nuptial mass on Sunday, they attended mass that morning at St. Joseph's.

Peter Mirassou married Justine Schrieber, who came with her parents from France as a small child in the 1890s and grew up on a neighboring Mount Hamilton ranch. Their three sons bought land at Quimby and White roads which they planted in grapes, a parcel on Aborn Road (still headquarters of Mirassou wines), and two

The Mirassou vineyards on Aborn Road in 1860

others which they planted in orchards. During Prohibition they shipped 80 percent of their grapes to Boston, New York, and Chicago for Italian families to make their own wine.

Right after World War II the brothers decided to separate and divide the properties. John took the ranch on McLaughlin Road. Herman took the orchards that became the Cambrian golf course in the Los Gatos area and were subsequently subdivided for research and development and industrial sites. Peter took the vineyards on Aborn Road. In 1924 he and Justine built the Spanish-style house that still stands next door to the stone winery.

Their sons, Norbert and Edmund, grew up in that house and attended St. Joseph's High School. Their daughter, Mary Bernice (Mrs. Sal Piazza), who now lives in Boulder Creek, attended Notre Dame High School, as did most of her cousins. On Sundays the family drove into town together to attend mass at St. Joseph's.

A few years after the repeal of Prohibition, Edmund and Norbert resumed wine making at the Aborn Road plant. Around 1945 they designed the first Mirassou label. Although the name remains the same, the logo has been redesigned many times—"like practically every

other day," says Norb kiddingly. With the population influx in the 1950s, the Mirassous purchased ranches near Soledad where they planted grapes. Most of their vineyards today are in Monterey County.

Norb and Ed, who brought the Mirassou wines into prominence, are still in charge of production. Ed's three sons, Daniel, James, and Peter, who are fifth generation in the family business, handle sales. Dan Mirassou is president. Norb's son, Steve, left the company a few years ago to start his own wine busines under the name Juan Tomas. Norbert and Edmund have nineteen grandchildren between them—the sixth generation in California—so there seems no question that Mirassou, the oldest family-owned wine business in the United States, will live on.

Charles Lefranc

Until the secularization of the missions, the padres at Mission Santa Clara produced all the wine used in the valley except for individual families who made wine for their own consumption. The first Frenchman to come,

Peter Mirassou and Herman Spadafore transporting barrels to railroad cars for shipping, circa 1913

in 1842, was a farmer from Bordeaux named Etienne Thee. He bought Rancho San Juan Bautista land from José Agustín Narváez on what is now Blossom Hill Road and planted mission grapes along the banks of the Guadalupe. He called his winery, which was the oldest commercial winery in Northern California, "The Sweet Grape Vineyard."

Along came Charles Lefranc, a tailor from Passy, France. A meeting between Lefranc and Thee at a gathering of French people in San Jose resulted in their joining forces. Lefranc, who was the more agressive, bought additional land and imported European stock (Pinot,

Paul Masson wearing his trademark cut-away coat and pince-nez glasses

Savignon, Cabernet, and Grenache), which he grafted on to mission root stock. He lined the thick adobe walls of their winery with great oaken casks that, like their wine cuttings, had rounded the Horn from France in four-masted sailing ships. Within a decade Lefranc's wines ranked with the best in the West, winning many prizes. Not only was the quality high, but the winery produced 100,000 gallons a year — an auspicious beginning for Almaden Wines.

Along the way Lefranc had cemented relationships with Thee by marrying his daughter, Adele. The young woman must have had quite an interest in wines herself. According to R. V. Garrod in his book *Saratoga Story*, Adele carried on horseback to the Almaden homestead from Rancho Cañada de Raimundo in San Mateo County cuttings of a white grape given to her by a Spanish nobleman.

In the courtyard of Lefranc's home in the Almaden Vineyards, surrounded by lovely gardens, the short, rotund, meticulously dressed man, who sported a heavy moustache and pointed goatee, played host to celebrities. Many were on their way to the New Almaden mine, a few miles to the south, including Admiral Farragut of Civil War fame, (at the time commandant of the Mare Island Navy Yard), Generals W. Tecumseh Sherman and Ulysses S. Grant (before he became president), and Henry Halleck, superintendent of the mines and builder of the outstanding Casa Grande residence there and the Montgomery Block in San Francisco. As the genial host poured wine for his visitors in the courtyard between the house and the winery, he pointed with pride to his olive trees flourishing along the terrace, to the pepper trees with their gracefully hanging branches, and to the flowering oleanders.

Ironically, it was here that Lefranc's life abruptly ended. He was supervising the unloading of grapes from a two-horse spring wagon when suddenly a workman lost control of a crate. It slipped from his fingers, struck a wheel, and crashed to the ground. The unexpected commotion frightened the horses, and the petrified animals reared, sending a dozen or more crates crashing to the ground. Apparently hoping to prevent the horses from bolting, Lefranc brandished his cane and was trampled by their flashing hooves — a violent end for a man who had so enjoyed the good life.

Charles and Adele had three children: Henry, who, with his wife Louise Delmas, was killed in an accident when their runabout collided with an electric trolley at Race Street and The Alameda (their small daughter, Nelty, was thrown free and raised in San Jose by her aunt and uncle Celine and Joseph Delmas); Marie, who re-

The stone winery building at Paul Masson Mountain Winery (now called the Mountain Winery) forms a backdrop for the summer concert series in the amphitheatre. The portal is from St. Patrick's Church in San Jose, which was destroyed in the earthquake of 1906.

mained single; and Louise, who married a young man from the Burgundy district of France named Paul Masson.

Paul Masson

Paul Masson, who had been attending the Sorbonne in Paris, was shipped off to California in 1878 by his father, a doctor in Lyon, to enroll in the University of the Pacific. A story is told that because of his partisan political stand at the Sorbonne he was not accepted at Santa Clara College. According to the late Nelty Lefranc Horney, in an interview with this writer in 1974, Paul Masson's father considered him a ne'er-do-well and asked his old friend Joseph Delmas of San Jose if he could give him something to do. Delmas didn't have anything at the time, but his friend Charles Lefranc said that Masson could have a job sweeping out the winery. That didn't last long. Mrs. Horney said that Masson soon graduated

to working in the office and, following the example of Lefranc, married the boss's daughter.

The good doctor obviously misread his son. Although Masson never got around to attending the University of the Pacific, he became a partner of Lefranc's and was recognized worldwide in his own name. Having grown up in the Cote d'Or, or Burgundy, area of France, he already knew something about viticulture. Lefranc and Masson had an office in San Jose. With the death of Henry Lefranc, Masson took over the complete operation of Lefranc wines, opened new offices, and dropped the Lefranc name from the letterhead. His cellar and wine business, the Paul Masson Champagne Company, was located in the Lefranc Building on West Santa Clara Street.

After Louise and Paul's marriage in 1888, the couple went to France on their honeymoon. Masson had been considering the possibilities of producing champagne and took advantage of the opportunity to secure cuttings of champagne grapes. He found the perfect location for his

43

vineyard on the slopes of the Saratoga foothills, where the annual rainfall of thirty inches is twice that of the valley. The absence of fog, the morning sunlight, the way the sun's rays fall at an angle rather than directly, and the chalky soil all made it an ideal location for his petit pinot vines. After purchasing the land from a man named Allessandro Rondoni, he hired Chinese labor to clear the ground of rubble, manzanita, scrub oak, and wild holly. He was ready to plant his "Little Vineyard in the Sky," as he affectionately called it, although it was officially named La Cresta Vineyard. Much later it became known as the Paul Masson Mountain Vineyard. With its backdrop of tall stately redwoods and view of the Santa Clara Valley all the way to the Golden Gate, the setting was nonpareil.

His champagne operation was in full swing in the 1890s, and by 1914 his champagne won the Gran Prix in Saint Louis—the first awarded to an American champagne. When Prohibition came Masson, without missing a beat, secured permission to produce sacramental and medicinal wines as well as selling his grapes for juice.

He also built a chateau in his mountain vineyard. Patterned after an old country place in his native Burgundy, it had a walk-in fireplace with seats at each end, wrought-iron chandeliers, and beams two or three feet in diameter. Here he entertained his friends and celebrities with great flair. A bon vivant who lived life to the hilt, Masson wore a trademark silk waistcoat and pince-nez glasses with flowing ribbon. Unrivaled as a host, before dinner he would spread pâté generously on great slabs of French bread but had to be pressed to pour even a thimbleful of sherry. "It will ruin your meal," he would caution, "the palate was not made for such punishment." After icy champagne with dinner, he served port with fruit and cheese. Although Masson was a generous host, both gracious and charming, he was also an astute businessman and kept a close look at the books.

When San Jose's exclusive Sainte Claire Club held its "Roll Call" meeting in a dell on the property, Masson always told members to bring their own demi-johns if they were planning to take any wine down with them. They responded by bringing gallon jugs. Dorothy Farrington of San Jose tells a story about Masson. He took her father, Bill Bogen, Sainte Claire Club member and Campbell orchard owner, crawdad fishing. Not unusual for those days, both were formally attired in suits with high stiff-winged collars and pearl stick pins. Masson slipped and fell into the creek. Lying flat on his back, he looked up at Bogen and said imperiously, "I may lose my equilibrium but never my dignity."

In the early 1900s Paul and Louise had a home on

Pierre Sainsevain, delegate to the first Constitutional Convention in Monterey, sold his hotel on Market Street for the first capitol.
(COURTESY MARIE MANN AND GEORGE STRICKLER)

Balbach Street. Patricia Carroll Cadogan, who grew up nearby, played with their daughter, Adele. She remembers the elaborate dollhouses, swings, and toys which Adele generously shared. From Balbach the Massons moved to a house designed by architect Bernard Maybeck on South Thirteenth Street in the exclusive Naglee Park district. It subsequently became a San Jose State fraternity house.

So far as anyone knows, Louise never visited her husband's vineyard in the sky. She had seen all the social life and met all the celebrities she cared about at her father's home. Deeply religious, she devoted her time and efforts to St. Joseph's Church. Paul and Louise, nevertheless, appeared to have had a solid marriage. After she died in 1932, Masson wrote to a friend in Beaune, France, about "the loss of my wife of forty years to whom I owe my material success, my joys and my enviable youth."

The earthquake and fire of 1906 wrought heavy damage in San Jose and sent thousands of bottles hurling from the racks of Paul Masson's wine cellars. St. Patrick's Church in San Jose was destroyed, but its impressive Romanesque portal, brought around the Cape from Spain, remained intact. With a generous donation to the church's building fund, Masson acquired it for the face of the stone winery building that is recessed into the hillside and topped with a champagne glass. The winery facade forms the backdrop for the stage of a natural amphitheatre that became the setting for the highly successful "Music at the Vineyards" concerts that were started in the late 1950s by Hannah Fromm, wife of Paul Masson Vineyards president Alfred Fromm, and his brother, Norman Fromm. With new management they branched into popular music with such artists as Mel Torme, George Shearing, and Harry Belafonte and into jazz and rock.

In 1988 when Ray Collishaw and Bill Marocco bought the Masson property, which they call the Mountain Winery, they announced that they would continue with the popular summer series. In a conversation with Ray Collishaw, he said, regarding the development of the property, that they have submitted a request to the Saratoga Planning Commission to divide the bottom seventy-five acres into ten lots. "We may just leave the rest open."

Antoine Delmas

Another Frenchman who arrived mid-nineteenth century and went into grape growing was Antoine Delmas. He planted 14,000 mission grape vines in his French Gardens before deciding to import 10,000 shoots of 80 French varieties. Before sending for his family in France, he arranged for a home south of Santa Clara Street between the Guadalupe River and Los Gatos Creek. The name, Delmas Avenue, came after Isaac Byrd, a hops grower in the "Willows," as Willow Glen was then called, requested a street be built to connect his property to town.

Delmas sent for his sons, Joseph and Delphin. Although Delmas's grape growing went well, he became financially successful in real estate. His home was always a gathering place for the French colony.

His son Delphin, after receiving his master's degree from Santa Clara College and law degree from Yale University, went on to become a nationally famous lawyer. Less was known about his 500-acre ranch, Casa Delmas, in Mountain View. In 1880 he built a summer home for his wife, Pauline, and their four children. He planted vineyards, and his winery was the largest independent winery in Santa Clara Valley, with a capacity of a half million gallons.

Pierre Sainsevain

Pierre Sainsevain, who came to California by sailing ship from Bordeaux, France, was a man for all occasions. He went first to Los Angeles where he learned about wine making from his illustrious viniculturist uncle, Jean Louis de Vignes. After he came to the pueblo he married Don Antonio Suñol's daughter Paula, and putting to use the knowledge he learned from his uncle, he produced the first quality champagne. His great-grandson George Strickler of San Jose has silver goblets awarded to the "Sainsevain brothers Pierre and Jean Louis by the California State Agricultural Society for best champagne"; another for "best native white wine" by the

Paula Sunōl Sainsevain, daughter of Don Antonio Sunōl who married Pierre Sainsevain (COURTESY MARIE MANN AND GEORGE STRICKLER)

California Horticultural Society; and yet another for "Sparkling native wine" by the California Horticultural Society.

Never known for inactivity, Sainsevain built the first flour mill on the Guadalupe River near San Fernando Street in 1844. He was a shipbuilder and a manufacturer of soap, which he sold to Thomas Oliver Larkin, the only U.S. consul in California. On his Rancho Rincón

The Sainsevain wine label (COURTESY GEORGE STRICKLER)

del Río de San Lorenzo land grant in Santa Cruz County he built a sawmill. This rancho is now the site of Henry Cowell Redwoods State Park.

Bitten by the gold bug, he headed for the gold fields with his father-in-law, Don Antonio Suñol, José Amador, and twenty-five Indians. They mined first at Weber's Creek, where they enjoyed a phenomenal run of success, then moved to the Tuolomne River, where Sainsevain found gold in a bar on the river. A *Sacramento Bee* story tells of a tent and shack camp sprouting there overnight that became known as "Don Pedro Bar" for Sainsevain, whose name in Spanish is Pedro. The story goes on to say that in the 1980s this town gave way to what is now known as Don Pedro Dam.

When Sainsevain and his wife, Paula, received one-third of Rancho de Los Coches in part of what is now called Willow Glen from her father, Don Antonio Suñol, they planted fruit trees, grapes, and hops.

During a heavy storm that became a deluge in 1866, the Los Gatos Creek that crossed the property ran rampant, changed its course, and cut through five miles of ranching land. Concerned for his vines, Pierre and his son Carlos dug a ditch to protect their vineyard. With the force of the water, it became part of a new creek channel. This creek later became Dry Creek Road, which runs

between Hicks and Union avenues in Willow Glen. Pierre subdivided most of the 116 acres. Carlos handled the sales of the lots in what was called Villa Sainsevain.

In the sixties Pierre and his father-in-law, Antonio Suñol, built Live Oak Park with picnic tables and a bandstand under spreading oak trees. In his *History of Santa Clara County, California* Eugene Sawyer wrote, "Here on moonlight nights in the early evening the soothing strains of a Spanish lover as he sang and played while his dark-eyed sweetheart raptly listened and softly sighed." They danced the mazurka, waltz, schottische, and other dances of the time, and there was "boating on a pool near the banks of the Guadalupe."

When the first legislature was about to meet in San Jose and James Reed and Charles White's plans for a state capital fall through, Sainsevain sold the hotel he and a man named Zephryn Rochon were building. This transaction ended in the loss column for Sainsevain. His partner absconded with Sainsevain's share, which he was supposed to bank for him in France. Rochon was never heard from again.

Pierre Sainsevain never cut his ties to his homeland. His wife, Paula, took their sons Carlos and Michael to Bordeaux to study at the same school their father had attended. While there her son Paul was born. Several years later when it came time for Paul to board the ship for France to attend school with his brothers, he disappeared, hiding in the sand dunes until after the ship sailed. Apparently none the worse for missing the French schooling, he became the city engineer and a prominent citizen. He made his home on part of his father's Sainsevain Villa. After Paula Sainsevain died in 1883 and was buried from St. Joseph's Church, Pierre returned to France, where he lived until his death, in 1904.

Amable Normandin

From Montreal in 1870 came Amable (always called Amos) Normandin. He skipped the wine business to found the Pacific Carriage Factory with David Hatman, a native of Germany, on Santa Clara Street between Orchard (now known as Almaden Avenue) and Vine Street. Normandin was the craftsman and Hatman the salesman. The latter's daughter, Anna, married Louis Oneal, prominent San Jose attorney, state senator, and political boss. The company later became Normandin-Campen and finally Normandin became the sole owner. In 1882 Normandin built a surrey for Clement Colombet, which was completed in time for the Fourth of July celebration. Some years later Mrs. Colombet gave it to Normandin's son, Louis, who put it on top of their building. It became their trademark. Louis, born in San Jose, was baptized and married in St. Joseph's Church. His wife, Estelle Pinard, was a member of the McAbee mousetrap family of Los Gatos.

Of the town's carriage makers, Normandin was the only one to make the transition from horses to combustion engines. In 1911 he went into the automobile business with a Hudson-Essex dealership. Louis bought out his partner in 1933 and in 1940 made his son Irving a partner. Irving and his brother, Clare, were baptized in St. Joseph's Church and attended its grammar school. Irv stayed on for the high school and Clare went to Bellarmine. Irv married Viginia Caprice, who attended Notre Dame High School. Their son, Lon, named for his grandfather Louis O. Normandin but always called by his initials, followed in the footpath of his two grandfathers and his father by attending Santa Clara University. Lon married Peggy Gretz and three of their children have graduated from the university. Following a family tradition, Lon is a Plymouth-Chrysler dealer.

Pedro de Saisset

Pedro de Saisset seems to be one of the few Frenchmen who never got involved in grape growing or wine making. Little has been written about his origins. He seems to be best known as prime mover in the building of San Jose's electric tower in 1881. Over the door to his tomb at the Santa Clara Mission Cemetary is the emblem of the French consul to San Jose.

According to a descendant of Antonio Suñol's, Pedro was a dairyman hauling produce back and forth from Alviso when he met María Jesús (Jesusita) Suñol, widow of José Suñol, son of Don Antonio Suñol.

After the couple's wedding in St. Joseph's Church, Pedro built a stylish three-story Victorian home on Guadalupe Street next to José Suñol's adobe. It was torn down in recent times to make room for the parking lot for the civic auditorium. De Saisset owned considerable business property, including the Century Block, where the Wardrobe is now located at Second and Santa Clara streets. Dr. Filipello, who married Henrietta de Saisset, told Dolores Turek that de Saisset was the son of Pedro Segundo, the emperor of Brazil. At any rate, pictures of the emperor hung in the de Saisset home, and he was always called the "Brasileiro."

He held a tight reign over his wife's daughters, Josepha and Lola (Dolores), by her previous marriage to José Suñol. One suitor, A. Zicovich, a vintner, whom he

Hatman & Normandin's Carriage Factory on Second Street in San Jose was the only local carriage maker to switch from horses to combustion engines. Lou Normandin, his great-grandson, owns Normandin Chrysler-Plymouth.

turned away, got even with de Saisset when he put up a building next door high enough to block de Saisset's view. According to a Suñol descendant, Marie Mann Strickler, the sisters each left one million dollars to St. Joseph's Church. The de Saissets, parents of two daughters, Henrietta and Isabel, and a son, Ernest, were active in St. Joseph's Church and had a pew in front. Isabel, the last surviving member of the family, gave money to Santa Clara University to build the de Saisset Museum to house her brother's collection of paintings.

Clement Colombet

Clement Colombet came from Nice, France, by way of Buenos Aires, where he spent a year before continuing around the Cape, making stops at Chile, Peru, and

Pedro de Saisset, the French consul, and his daughter Isabel (COURTESY MARIE MANN AND GEORGE STRICKLER)

Henrietta de Saisset, wife of Dr. Eugene Filipello (COURTESY MARIE MANN AND GEORGE STRICKLER)

Bolivia, and finally disembarking at Monterey in 1844. He seemed to have had unlimited energy. Starting out as a tanner, he worked his way to success as a cattleman, driving his stock to Sacramento and to the mines. In 1849, just in time to catch the gold rush business, he had a store in San Jose. In 1851 Clement and Ann Kell, granddaughter of Martin Murphy, were married by Father Nobili in St. Joseph's Church. They moved to Mission San Jose, where Clement planted grapes and became a successful vintner. In 1856 at the annual fair of the California State Agricultural Society, he was awarded the premium prize for his claret wine—the first to a Californian.

Apparently deciding to expand, Colombet bought part of Fulgencia Higuera's Rancho Agua Caliente that had several warm springs on the property and built the Warm Springs Hotel. It was described as the Del Monte Hotel of its day. According to an *Oakland Tribune* story of 1956, "The fashionable and the wealthy from all Bay Area points came, by carriage and stage to partake of its 98 degree baths . . . and to patronize Warm Springs Hotel's saloon, dining hall and gaming tables." It all ended with the disastrous earthquake of 1868. Colombet sold the property to A. A. Cohen, who in turn sold it to Sen. Leland Stanford and his brother, Josiah. They planted vineyards and built a stone winery.

Victor Cauhape

Another Frenchman who, like Colombet, made his success in the cattle business was Victor Cauhape. But the comparison ends there. Cauhape was involved strictly in cattle and meat. Son of a prosperous French family, he eschewed the education they planned for him to come to California in time to experience the terrible earthquake of 1868. He went to San Juan Bautista, where he worked as a cowboy to learn about cattle—an apprenticeship that served him well as he would eventually have cattle and meat businesses in Mexico, New Mexico, Nevada, and Arizona.

He married María Landry of Baja California and they had seven children. The eldest, Francois, married Henrietta Beatty, daughter of Liberty Amusement Co. president and builder of the Liberty Theater, James Beatty. Daughters Blanche and Bertrande were musical and often listed on the programs of St. Joseph's functions.

48

CHAPTER EIGHT

The Mexican War

In 1846 war with the states was brewing. On June 10 a group of Americans in Sonoma raised the Bear Flag and started the Bear Flag Revolt, unaware that the U.S. had declared war against Mexico on May 13. Meanwhile, Commodore John Drake Sloat, who steamed into Monterey Bay with two warships, raised the Stars and Stripes on July 7. Capt. John Montgomery followed on July 9 in San Francisco, as did Lt. Joseph Revere in Sonoma and Captain Frémont at Sutter's Fort.

This was all "Captain" Thomas Fallon in Santa Cruz, who had been with Frémont on one of his expeditions on his way to California and was itching to get into the action, needed to hear. Gathering together some twenty men, and with the sanction of Captain Montgomery, who sent him a flag, he headed for the pueblo of San José. Wary about a report that Castro was in the pueblo, they spent the night at Grove Cooke's rancho three miles south of San Jose. When they received the "all clear" signal the next day they rode into town to raise the Stars and Stripes over the *juzgado* on July 14.

Castro, who had received no word from his scouts (they had been killed by Kit Carson), decided to head south and join forces with Pico, taking with him Captain Weber. After the raising of the flag, the pueblo was a military camp. Weber, who had been freed in the south, was made military *comandante*, with John Murphy his lieutenant. They camped with their soldiers in an adobe on Lightstone Alley.

The Battle of Santa Clara

The war was a disruptive, disturbing time for the *pobladores*, who considered themselves neither Spaniards nor Mexicans but Californios. Although they didn't oppose the possibility of a U.S. takeover (their numbers were too small for that), they did expect to be treated justly and with respect. Unfortunately, this was not always the case. The military forces under Frémont (Weber was the worst offender) confiscated their cattle, horses, saddles, and equipment, causing distrust between the two factions. Antonio Suñol wrote to Capt. John Montgomery protesting their actions. Unfortunately, Montgomery misread Suñol's intentions and put the blame on the Californios. Their frustration triggered the Battle of Santa Clara in January of 1847 — the only battle of the Mexican War fought in Northern California.

In the clash, sometimes called the "Battle of the Mustard Stalks," the Californios, led by Francisco Sán-

Capt. Thomas Fallon was famed for raising the American flag over the juzgado *in the pueblo and served as mayor in 1859.*

chez with an army made up of recruits from the local ranchos, fought in mustard stalks head high the American forces of Charles Weber and John Murphy. The battleground was located at Lawrence Station and Milliken Corners. The action, which has been described as a comic opera, was observed by the locals from the rooftops at Mission Santa Clara. At a safe distance the Americans fired their canons, which soon mired down; Sánchez replied with a few musket shots, but when Captain Aram moved on them from the rear, the Californios retreated into the Los Gatos mountains. This marked the end of the war between Mexico and the United States. The toll was one dead horse and two slightly injured Americans.

Living at the mission in the flea-ridden adobes were American families, under the protection of Joseph Aram, who had sought refuge at Sutter's Fort and were directed to the mission by Frémont. While there, one of the women, Olive Mann Isbell, a niece of educator Horace Mann, started the first American school with pencils, notebooks, and the *McGuffy's Reader* she had brought with her. Her husband, Dr. Isaac Isbell, with John Murphy and Charles Weber, made a treaty with the Indians that was the start of Stockton.

The Stars and Stripes

It wasn't until the signing of the Treaty of Guadalupe Hidalgo at Chapultepec Castle outside Mexico City in 1848 that Mexico officially ceded California to the United States. The government tried to make the transition as easy as possible for the Californios by forming a committee of prominent local politicians and landowners to oversee the process. Some of the men chosen included Antonio Suñol, Dolores Pacheco (immediate past *alcalde*), Felix Buelna, José Fernández, José Noriega, Salvador Castro, William Fisher, Charles White, Capt. Julian Hanks, and James Weekes. The instructions for the group read, "The above individuals are called upon to form a committee in the Pueblo de San José de Guadalupe, on the sixth day of December, 1846, for to sit and decide if anything that may be required for the benefit of said pueblo. They perform as the sole ruling body maintaining the laws for the occupation and later incorporation into the city of San Jose."

John Burton was appointed *alcalde* and James Stokes *juez de paz*. Burton, called El Capitan Viejo (the old captain) by the Californios, married to Juana Galindo, and fluent in Spanish, was an excellent choice. He helped smooth some of the rough spots of the difficult transition for the defeated Californios.

Carmelita Lodge Fallon divorced Capt. Thomas Fallon on grounds of infidelity. Her mother, Martina Castro Lodge, was the grantee of Rancho Soquel and Rancho Soquel Augmentación. (COURTESY THOMAS McENERY)

Thomas Fallon

At the end of the war Thomas Fallon, a native of Ireland, returned to Branciforte (Santa Cruz), where he married the half-Spanish (her mother was a Castro) and half-Irish Carmelita Lodge, daughter of a large landowner. Fallon, joined by Carmelita, soon headed for the Mother Lode country. They returned with enough gold to build a large home facing the plaza in Santa Cruz. Ever restless, Fallon soon sold the house to Santa Cruz County for its courthouse and took off with his family to Texas.

After the tragic loss of their three children, the Fallons moved to San Jose. A sharp real estate investor, he became one of the richest men in town. Less successful politically, his only elected office was mayor of San Jose in 1859. A Protestant Irishman, he was a vestryman in

Capt. Thomas Fallon's residence

Trinity Episcopal Church and a Mason.

The home he built on the corner of San Pedro and San Augustine (now St. John Street) was a showplace of the town with its parklike landscaping and orchards. His neighbors in the area of the old *acequia* were the Peraltas, from whom he bought the orchards, the Chaboyas, the Pelliers, and Notre Dame Academy.

Wealth and a beautiful home were not enough to bring happiness to the Fallons. Carmelita hired D. M. Delmas to represent her in suing her husband for divorce, charging adultery, and moved to Santa Cruz. Fallon countered by accusing her of assault with a deadly weapon (hitting him over the head with a pipe) with intention to kill. He next married the much younger Samanthe Steinhoff in the First Presbyterian Church. After seven years, he instituted divorce proceedings against her. His next romantic disaster was a breach of promise suit which he lost.

Although unlucky in love, Fallon's handsome appearance, ready wit, and pleasing manner seemed to charm all. Noted for his hospitality, Fallon held open house at his San Jose spread for many years. His daughter Annie by Carmelita, considered one of the beauties of San Jose, was baptized in St. Joseph's Church. She married John T. Malone, a lawyer who became prominent on the stage. Fallon's house became a popular restaurant among the press and politicians known as Manny's Cellar. In 1989 it was declared a historical landmark with plans by the city to make it into a museum.

In death even Annie turned against Fallon. In a *San Francisco Call* story of 1886 covering court litigation over his will, she testified that her father broke into rages, that he threatened to kill her, and that he liked to drink. "He wished to be always drinking," she said. Apparently she was fond of her grandmother. Hanging in the San Jose Historical Museum is a painting she did of Martina Castro Lodge.

The Gold Rush

Just about the time things were beginning to calm down in the pueblo after the Mexican War, the news flashed on the scene like a thunderbolt that gold had been discovered at Coloma on the banks of the American River near Sutter's Fort. That was January 24, 1848. The real push began when the first mail ship arrived at San Francisco a year later. Soon the bay was filled with sailing ships carrying men hopeful of making a big bonanza.

Time stopped, business ceased, the pueblo was all but evacuated; in some cases merchants left their doors open so people could help themselves. The town was practically devoid of men. Young and old, short and tall, they all headed for the gold country. The fields had just been planted with grain, but when harvest time came there was no one to do the harvesting. The hogs roaming the land had a feast. Flour came from Chile and sold at exorbitant prices, as did all foodstuff.

Charles White, the pueblo's *alcalde* in 1848, soon learned it was not the best of times to be holding a political position. The town was beset with intrigues; his predecessor was removed from office by the people; and his rapport with the *pobladores*, who accused him of favoring the foreigners, was tense. He decided to chuck it all and go for the gold, leaving Sheriff Harry Bee with

The raising of the flag at the juzgado *in the pueblo plaza, 1846* (COURTESY CLYDE ARBUCKLE)

ten prisoners—all Indians, including some suspected murderers. When Bee asked the departing mayor what he should do with the prisoners he was holding in the calaboose, White tossed the question off with a "Do as you please."

Bee did just that. He took the Indians to the mines to work for him—which they did and with success. After a few months, however, Bee sensed a rebellion in the making. The miners started stirring the Indians up—telling them they should keep the gold themselves—but worst of all they gave the Indians the one thing that was their downfall, "fire water." Heeding his instincts, Bee wisely headed back to San Jose with his loot.

John Murphy, son of Martin, Sr., operated on a larger scale. He employed 150 Indians from Mission Santa Clara to pan for gold for him at Calaveras, with great success. He and his brother, Jim, were noted coming back through the town of Murphys (named for them) leading sixteen burros loaded with kegs of gold. San Jose attorney Frederick Hall, in his *History of San Jose*, said

of Murphy, ". . . generous and benevolent, had he kept his fortune he would have been one of the wealthiest men in the nation."

Josiah Belden

Another San Jose merchant, a Connecticut Yankee named Josiah Belden, arrived with the Bidwell-Bartleson party in 1841. After being taken prisoner by a suspicious General Castro (as he came over the Livermore Pass) and spending five days in the *juzgado* in the pueblo, he was rescued by the British consul, James Alexander Forbes. Belden became a naturalized Mexican citizen and ran a general merchandise store in Santa Cruz for Oliver Larkin. In 1847 he moved to the pueblo, where he opened a merchandise store at Market and San Antonio streets. A canny businessman, he made a fortune selling supplies to the miners on their way to the gold fields. He married Maggie Jones and, in 1850, became the first elected mayor of the incorporated city of San Jose.

CHAPTER NINE

St. Joseph's Becomes a Parish

As the pueblo was changing, the church of San Jose and the Virgin of Guadalupe was changing along with it. Padre José María Pinyero, under the administration of Padre José María Gonzalez Rubio, became the first resident priest of the pueblo church in May of 1849. His parish, which he had to cover by horseback, extended from Morgan Hill to Half Moon Bay. The term "residence" was a misnomer. The priest's living quarters were pretty meager—a small adobe

After serving as Dominican provincial to the United States, Archbishop Sadoc Alemany was appointed by the pope to be Bishop of Monterey and California. A Spaniard, he arrived in San Francisco by way of the Isthmus of Panama on December 6, 1850. (SANTA CLARA UNIVERSITY ARCHIVES)

building on the outskirts of town. On the day he arrived he baptized the daughter of Don José Castro and Doña Petra Castro.

As Americans moved in increasing numbers, and with the shortage of priests, Father Rubio appealed to Bishop Blanchet in Oregon for help. Two Italian Jesuit priests, Father John Nobili and Father Michael Accolti, were sent from Willamette, Oregon. Father Nobili, who spoke English, was assigned to assist at St. Joseph's. Father Nobili's first official act was to baptize an Indian baby whom he named Archangel Gabriel. The relationship between Father Nobili and Padre Pinyero was not a happy one. Although Padre Pinyero was well liked, he was prejudiced against Jesuits (even though he had never met one) and apparently resented Father Nobili.

Father Nobili was among the priests sent from the Jesuit headquarters in St. Louis with Father Peter De Smet, the frontier priest who knew the northwest territory well, to the missions in Oregon. The hard life there affected his health—at one point he was reduced to eating moss. Nevertheless, when the cholera epidemic broke out in San Jose in 1850, he worked tirelessly caring for the victims. At the invitation of Don Luís Peralta, he stayed in the Peralta adobe. The devout don and the intellectual priest became close friends.

After the arrival of Bishop Alemany (appointed archbishop in 1853), Nobili was assigned to start a college at Mission Santa Clara and Father Anthony Goetz was assigned pastor of St. Joseph's. In the meantime Padre Pinyero had returned to Mexico.

A Visitor From Chile

After an unsuccessful effort to dig for gold in the Sierras, Chilean writer, and native of France, Pierre Combet stopped in the pueblo on his way back to Chile. He described his impressions in *Memories in California,*

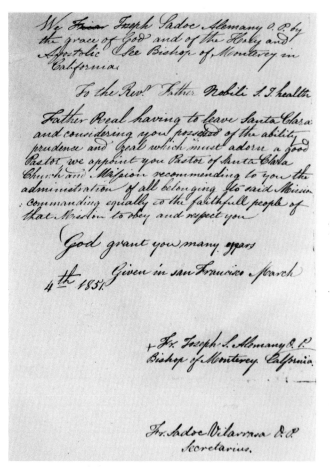

A letter from Bishop Alemany to Father John Nobili appointing him to pastor of the mission and of St. Joseph's (SANTA CLARA UNIVERSITY ARCHIVES)

published in El Museo de Santiago in 1853 and locally in a collection of stories written by Chileans in the book *We Were 49ers* by Edwin A. Beilharz and Carlos U. Lopez.

"It was Sunday," wrote Combet. "Our entry was anything but a triumphal procession. My costume was a red wool undershirt . . . a Mexican sombrero as big as an umbrella and capable of shading a hay wagon."

He said it was time for mass when they reached the plaza and the bells were calling the faithful to church. "We had a chance, therefore, to see many Californios of both sexes, a people we had hardly seen at all on our arrival in San Francisco. Everything seemed to radiate a feeling of happiness. The people had become rich at selling building lots at the rate of one thousand pesos a block."

He described the men's dress—serapes of velvet trimmed with gold embroidery—and added, "But what most caught our attention, naturally, were the women who, if not usually very pretty, nevertheless had all the grace of Andalusian women. Their dresses were all of yellow, green or white silk, and on their shoes were designs of birds, flaming hearts." He went on to write that they wore the classic mantilla the women of Spain and Lima still wear, and with the same grace and coquetry.

"It was a high mass," he wrote, "and the subchanters were three of my compatriots. A fourth man, who accompanied them on the bass viol, I recognized at once; he was Adolfo Beauvoison. I had met him in the mines and we used to sing and play music together every evening. He had just spotted me, and at his signal I took my place in front of the choir stand and lent my voice to the celebration of the mass." The intervals between singing, he said, were filled in by six Mexican musicians. Their instruments were harps, flutes, guitars, and violincellos, and they harmonized perfectly.

Combet was impressed by this congregation of so many different peoples—South Americans, Frenchmen, Italians, Spaniards, and Irishmen. "This assembly of men of many races, wearing the same kind of clothes and worshipping the same God," he said, "did affect me deeply . . . a descendant of the Normans rubbing elbows with an Indian from Sonora." He was impressed by the priest, Padre Pinyero, who, in clear simple terms, advised, "a devotion to work as the source of wealth and recommended a tolerance such as the very Americans themselves practiced."

After mass Combet's friend Beauvoison introduced him to the priest, who thanked him for having sung the divine office and, when he learned that Combet had sung in the cathedral at Santiago, suggested he stay in San Jose to teach seven or eight boys to sing and also to help out in church services. Combet accepted and the following day was made chapel master and first tenor in the church of San Jose.

Father Pinyero had a fan in Combet, who wrote that he was "a man who understood the human heart—in everything frank, ingenuous and trustful. Whenever I read the story of a good priest, the name of Don José Pinyero comes to mind."

Combet couldn't make ends meet on the fees from the church, so he took a job building adobe houses, which were much in need because of the first legislative session in the pueblo. He soon learned that as a construction man, he was a good musician. He was hired to sing at a highly touted concert staged by a pair of four-flushing entrepreneurs. When it flopped, artistically and financially, Combet took this as a signal that it was time for him to return to Valparaiso.

54

CHAPTER TEN

The Constitutional Convention

Following the signing of the Treaty of Guadalupe Hidalgo that ended the war, the Constitutional Convention was scheduled to meet in Colton Hall, Monterey. During the Spanish and Mexican periods Monterey was the capital of Alta California. Henry Halleck was of firm conviction that under U.S. rule the capital should remain there. San Jose's *alcalde*, Kimball Dimmick, presented a strong argument against Monterey and in favor of San Jose. San Josean Joseph Aram agreed with Dimmick. The other San Jose District delegates were probably in favor, but Don Antonio Pico, Jacob Hoppe, Julian Hanks, Pierre Sainsevain, and Elam Brown were not so vocal. After considerable deliberation on the part of the delegates and a major effort by two men, Charles White and James Reed, who promised an impressive capitol building in Washington Square and accommodations for the members, the delegates voted to make San Jose the capital. By a large majority the delegates elected Peter Hardeman Burnett, a San Jose resident, to be California's first governor.

Peter Hardeman Burnett

Peter Hardeman Burnett, a Tennessee native raised in Missouri, had gone to Oregon in 1843. There he served in the Oregon Territorial legislature and was elected a supreme court justice. He practiced some law but mostly farmed. All his endeavors were less than lucrative. Consequently, when he learned of Marshall's discovery of gold, he lost no time in organizing a 150-wagon train and headed for California. Only mildly successful in the diggings, he decided he could do better practicing law. His first clients were Capt. John Sutter and his estate, New Helvetia. One of his early assignments was setting up the sale of lots for Sacramento City—now the city of Sacramento and the state's capital.

At last he was able to send for his wife, Harriet, and family to come to California. They moved first to San Jose, into a house on Second Street near San Carlos, and then to Alviso, which he believed was destined to become an important port. Later, apparently thinking better of that investment, he, with the help of his two sons, dismantled the Alviso house and reassembled it on North First Street.

With unintentional good timing, Governor Burnett was in San Francisco on his way to San Jose from Sacramento on October 18, 1850, the day the mail steamer *Oregon* arrived with the big news that the United States Congress had voted statehood for California. After joining the celebration in Portsmouth Square that night, he left the next morning for the capital in San Jose. The usually circumspect governor, wearing his top hat and frock coat, could not restrain his enthusiasm. As he rode up front with the celebrated stage man Jared Crandall, they raced two other stagecoaches to San Jose with the news. The great stagecoach race was on. Burnett waved his hat and shouted to the people that flocked along the roadside, "California's admitted."

The governor was a devout member of St. Joseph's Church. He had converted to Catholicism while in Oregon. After reading a discourse between a Catholic bishop and a Protestant clergyman, he became interested in the church and read extensively about it. Eighteen months later he went to Oregon City, where, according to his memoirs, *Confessions of an Old Pioneer*, "I found the heroic and saintly Father De Vos, who had spent one or more years with the Flathead Indians. He received me into the church." The friendship was resumed when De Vos was sent to St. Joseph's Church.

Burnett's son, John, the second graduate of Santa Clara College in 1857, became a lawyer, as did his grandson David Burnett, his great-grandson John Burnett (well remembered for his ability to speak both in and out of the courtroom), who died in 1985, and his great-great-granddaughter Francisca Burnett Allen of Los Gatos.

A replica of the State House, California's first capitol building (SAN JOSE HISTORICAL MUSEUM)

Francisca is the fifth generation of Burnetts to practice law in San Jose and the fourth generation to graduate from Santa Clara University Law School.

After Peter Burnett was appointed supreme court justice he spent his last years with his wife, Harriet, in San Francisco. He was buried in Santa Clara Mission Cemetery.

The Meeting of the Legislature

When White and Reed were unable to produce the capitol building they had promised, they compromised by forming a group of nineteen men to sign a note for $34,000 to purchase a nearly completed hotel on the plaza (now the site of the Fairmont Hotel) that was being built by Don Antonio Suñol's son-in-law Pierre Sainsevain and Zephryn Rochon. Until its completion, meetings temporarily took place in the home on the plaza of Isaac Branham. The San Jose delegates were also overly optimistic in their offer of accommodations for the delegates. Tents had to be set up and basic frame structures and adobes hastily thrown together to furnish less than adequate rooms for the delegates.

The scribe Bayard Taylor, in his book *El Dorado,* wrote of the dusty streets thronged with people; goods for lack of storage room standing in large piles beside the doors; the incessant sound of hammers and the rattling of laden carts. Hotels were springing up in all quarters, and French restaurateurs hung out their signs on little one-story shanties. Displaying the deep-rooted prejudice of Americans against Asians, he wrote, "The shrewd celestials [Chinese] had already planted themselves here, and summoned men to meals by the sound of their barbaric gongs." The first Chinatown had sprung up in part of the plaza. Cattle and horses roamed the streets. With the heavy rains there was so much water at First and Santa Clara streets that a little boy drowned.

The undesirables moving in from the gold fields were a drinking, brawling lot—bull fights and gambling took place in the plaza. Opposed by most of the residents and by the padres at the adobe church, the bulls and the matadors were given their marching papers and outlawed by the city council.

Although the first legislature, working under the most adverse of conditions, earned high marks for its judicial writing of laws, it is better remembered for being called the "Legislature of a Thousand Drinks," an epithet that facetiously evolved from the speaker's habit of saying at the end of a day's session, "Let's go have a drink, boys, let's have a thousand of them!"

After the wet, miserable winter of 1850, there was a movement afoot by outside interests to move the capital. White and Reed both made generous offers of land, joined by Dr. John Townsend. But they soon came to realize that they couldn't compete with the clout of Gen. Mariano Vallejo, who offered 156 acres of his vast land holdings in the Sonoma District plus $375,000 in cash to pay for construction of the capital. The third legislature convened only to find out that Vallejo was unable to produce the promised accommodations. They moved to Benicia, and when efforts to move back to San Jose failed, Sacramento became the permanent capital.

56

Anna Maria "Grandma" Bascom ran a boarding house called "Flapjack Hall" during the meeting of the first legislature. The story of her experiences was printed in the Atlantic Monthly *of May 1887.* (COURTESY RALPH RAMBO)

Grandma Bascom

One of the better places to stay during the meeting of the first legislature was "Flapjack Hall," the boarding house of Anna Maria "Grandma" Bascom at Second and San Fernando streets in a house her husband had rented. It was probably the best available but not the style to which this perky, Kentucky-born and -bred woman was accustomed. In an interview in the 1887 issue of the *Overland Monthly*, Mrs. Bascom reminisced about that first year. She told of coming with her husband, Dr. Lewis Hazelton Bascom, and children by boat from Sacramento. There was another doctor in town, so doctoring was not too remunerative, and they were a little short of cash. The ultimate optimist, the plucky little woman made the best of it. She said, "People began to ask if they couldn't stay with us till they found some other home and then, somehow, they stayed on. . . . The first thing I knew I had thirteen boarders—senators, representatives, ministers, and teachers. We got a reputation on batter cakes and our house was dubbed 'Flapjack Hall' by my boy, Al. It stuck to us. I used to go to the legislature and enjoy the fun there as much as the members enjoyed my housekeeping.

"Oh, did I tell you I built the first church [Protestant] and the first schoolhouse in San Jose? I did. I built it

all with my own hands and the only tool I had was a good stout needle. It was the famous 'Blue Tent' you have heard of." A Presbyterian minister she had met on the boat from San Francisco to Alviso, Mr. Blakeslee, asked her to make it. He bought blue jean cloth and cut it out, and Grandma sewed it. He held church services in it and during the winter it served as a school room.

Grandma Bascom also enjoyed the social life. "We had a great deal of party-going and gave entertainment just as if we had elegant houses and all the conveniences. Some of the Spanish people were very stylish. The ladies had dresses rich as silk and embroidery could make them, and in their long, low adobe houses were rich carpets and silk curtains trimmed with gold lace." She told of going to the grand wedding of Miss Pico and a Mr. Campbell at the home of Antonio Pico, but added, "The odd dresses and dishes upset my gravity more than once."

She also described her own party. Mrs. Branham had given her six eggs and she baked an "elegant" cake. "I began by passing it to one of the Spanish ladies and she took the whole cake at one swoop, wrapped it up in the skirt of her gorgeous silk dress and said, 'Muchas gracias.' I was never so surprised in my life, but there was nothing I could say." (The dear lady had no idea she was out of line. It was typical of the Californio hospitality to give generously to a guest.)

The Bascoms had a piano shipped by way of the Isthmus—the first in San Jose. She said, "The Indians and Spanish used to crowd around the doors and windows to hear the wonderful music and many a white man lingered and listened, because it reminded him of home. We moved to a better house in the spring very near where the Methodist Church South afterward stood." In telling about the people in town for the meeting, she said, "Of course you know General Fré-

Notre Dame College was founded in 1851 on Santa Clara Street, which was considered out in the country. In 1868 it became the first chartered women's college in the West. The college moved to Belmont in 1923.

57

mont and his wife were here that winter and I knew them both." Their fortunes changed, and in 1852 the Bascoms built a home. Bascom Avenue was named for the doctor. At Anna Maria Bascom's burial service in 1896, a Methodist minister and a Roman Catholic priest presided.

The Washington Birth-Night Ball

The social life during the meeting of the legislature was described in Mary Bowden Carroll's book *Ten Years in Paradise*, published in 1903. Mrs. Carroll, who wrote society columns in the nineties for the *Mercury*, and the *Morning Times* and *Herald*, interviewed some of the residents of that period. One of those who responded by letter was a Joseph H. Scull, who wrote that during the first legislature "every house was an inn where all were welcome and feasted" and that all through the session not an evening passed without a large party at some home.

"There were very few American women here in those early days," he continued, "and they were mostly married so far as I can remember; and balls being the chief amusement in vogue, consisting of quadrilles, *contra-danzas*, waltzes and Virginia reels and, for variety's sake, occasionally an 'Irish breakdown,' especially when some Celtic fellow citizens were present."

The home of Mr. and Mrs. James F. Reed, parents of Mrs. John Murphy and Mrs. Mattie Lewis, was always the scene of social gatherings and at one of their large dinner parties it was said that Mrs. Reed paid $16 apiece for turkeys and bought all there were to be had.

"Of course, the State Ball at the close," Scull said, "was the big event in San Jose's history." The white satin invitation that was coveted and kept for years to come, read:

Washington Birth-Night Ball
Your company is respectfully solicited at a Ball
to be given at the Capitol
on the evening of the 22d instant
at 7½ o'clock p.m.
Being the 118th Anniversary of the Father of Our Country

The comittee included Don Antonio Suñol, who, with his wife, Doña Dolores (Mesa), gave several parties, Hon. John McDougal, who followed Burnett as governor (he and his wife entertained at their adobe house in the pueblo), Don Andréas Pico, Don Antonio María Pico, and Joseph Aram. Scull listed among the "belles and beauties" on that "memorable night" the governor's

daughters, Miss Rea Burnett, who married Judge William T. Wallace (later Supreme Court Justice), and Letitia Burnett, who became Mrs. C. T. Ryland; Miss Juanita Soto; Mrs. John Murphy (Virginia Reed); and Maggie Jones, who become Mrs. Josiah Belden. Governor Burnett greeted the guests. Although women were few and far between in those days, those present represented the beauty of central Calforia. Some even came by Lilliputian steamboat from distant Benicia in a drenching rain.

Colleges

Education in San Jose took a big step forward in 1851. Santa Clara College, Notre Dame College, and the University of the Pacific were founded that year. Bishop Joseph Sadoc Alemany, who had arrived in San Francisco the year before to take over his post as Bishop of Monterey and California, announced that the Jesuits would take over St. Joseph's and Mission Santa Clara and that Father John Nobili was going to establish a Jesuit college at the mission. After seventy-five years the Franciscans departed for Mexico. Santa Clara started its classes that year, but didn't apply for its charter until 1855, probably because Father Nobili was faced with what seemed to be an insurmountable task.

After the secularization of the missions there was no financial support. Mission Santa Clara, once considered the most beautiful and wealthiest of the missions, had fallen into a sad state of disrepair. There were problems with squatters and intricate legal battles. Padre Suares de Real, the black sheep of the fine flock of Franciscans, who had previously been in charge of the mission, not only lived openly with a woman but sold off parcels of the land for his own benefit.

Padre Nobili, however, who had been sent to California because of poor health resulting from the strenuous life in the Oregon Territory, and who had nursed the sick during the cholera epidemic of 1850 in San Jose, lacked neither courage nor optimism. After five years he finally won title to the mission properties—much of which he obtained by quitclaim deeds.

The following year three Jesuit priests were sent from Oregon to assist him. In the first class were the sons of Governor Burnett, Antonio Suñol, and James Alexander Forbes; both Suñol and Forbes taught some classes. Also in the school was Martin Murphy, Jr.'s son, James, who died in 1852 and was buried inside the church. His tombstone can be seen on the right hand side of the entrance.

Santa Clara College became the University of Santa

Santa Clara University campus in the 1930s. It was called the University of Santa Clara then. The double row of palm trees leads to Mission Santa Clara. (SANTA CLARA UNIVERSITY ARCHIVES)

Clara in 1912, and in 1985 Santa Clara University. From its shaky beginning with a mere handful of students, it has grown to a student body of over 7,000 men and women, with graduate schools in law and business. The school was well on its way in 1856 when Father Nobili stepped on a rusty nail and died of lockjaw.

In 1926 the Santa Clara College prep school moved to the former campus of the University of the Pacific with the new name Bellarmine Preparatory School.

Notre Dame Sisters

When the Belgian Sisters of Notre Dame de Namur arrived by carriage one spring day in 1851 to start their school, they faced no less of a challenge than the Jesuits. Sister Loyola and Sister Marie Catherine approached the pueblo by way of the tree-lined Alameda—yellow fields of mustard that had been planted by the early Franciscan Padres grew eight to ten feet high on either side. Just after they passed the Luís Peralta adobe with its beautiful orchards, they caught sight of the pueblo—a cluster of adobe and wooden houses huddled together, with cattle wandering the muddy streets. No one could have blamed them if they had turned around and headed back to San Francisco.

Even the enthusiasm of Mrs. Martin Murphy, Jr., as they drove around the pueblo in the Murphy carriage,

could do little to lift their spirits. Her husband, Martin Murphy, Jr., of Rancho Pastoria de Las Borregas, a man who could neither read nor write, had made an eloquent plea to Bishop Alemany for a school for his daughters. The sisters, who made comments to each other in French about the pueblo, experienced an embarrassing moment when they learned that their host had lived in Quebec and understood French.

The next morning the sisters had breakfast with Father John Nobili, who was working on plans for Santa Clara College. It was a reunion for the three, who had made a perilous, seven-month voyage on a two-masted brig from Antwerp to Willamette Valley seven years before. Father Nobili must have said the right things, because that same day the sisters announced they would stay: they would meet the challenge.

Martin Murphy, Jr., and a group of supporters who called themselves the "Senators" helped the sisters select some property along the *acequia* on Santa Clara Street near the Peralta property, which was considered out of town at that time. The sisters were hospitably received by the St. Joseph's parishioners. Thomas and Margaret Kell invited them to stay at their home on Almaden Road. When it became too much of a trip into town, the Charles Whites invited them to stay at their place. An invitation from Don Antonio and Doña María Suñol followed. At the Suñol house Sister Marie Catherine gave lessons until the school was opened.

Isabel Argüello, granddaughter of Gov. Luis Argüello and grandmother of Austen Warburton. (COURTESY SISTERS OF NOTRE DAME)

Meanwhile, Father Nobili arranged with a fellow countryman of the sisters from Belgium, Dr. Peter Van Carneghan, for the sisters, including four others who had just arrived from Belgium, to stay in a little hospital that was vacant at the time until their quarters were completed. Attorney Alexander Yoell, whose daughters were later to be stellar students at the school, vacated his office to give them more space.

The school opened that August with daughters of the Suñols, the Murphys, the Whites, and others enrolled. It grew in size and prestige. The students represented a long line of distinguished families, including the daughters of Governors Peter Burnett and John McDougal; descendants of the first Mexican governor (Argüello); and many from prominent Central American and Asian families. Sister Joseph Marie Petar of Saratoga, who was principal of St. Joseph's School in the late 1930s, recalls

that her best friend in her 1921 class at Notre Dame was Princess Kapiolani of Hawaii, and that her sister, Princess Liliukaolani, was also in school. Their mother, Abigail Campbell (class of 1900), who had married Prince David Kawananakoa, was a daughter of Kuaihilani Maipinepine, descended from a long line of warriors, and of James Campbell, an adventurous Irishman.

The sisters taught the children of St. Joseph's the first four grades. When St. Joseph's School was built, they taught the girls, and the Marianist Brothers taught the boys. After the college moved to the Ralston estate in Belmont, Notre Dame High School moved into the Myles O'Connor mansion on Second Street, which had been operating as an orphan asylum.

In a *Harper's New Monthly Magazine*, a writer on a trip from Oakland to the New Almaden mine described San Jose as it looked then—its agriculture, its families of refinement and education residing there—and added, "Here is the celebrated Catholic Female Academy, the oldest and wealthiest educational institution in the state."

When President McKinley visited San Jose in 1903 he and his entourage, while on a drive through the city, paused at Notre Dame College to greet the students lined up in front of the school and to receive the rosebuds presented on behalf of the school by Bertrande Cauhape, daughter of Mr. and Mrs. Victor Cauhape. In 1927 Notre Dame College moved to the Ralston estate in Belmont. Today it is a coeducational fine arts college.

The University of the Pacific

A third school, California Wesleyan College, soon after called the University of the Pacific, was started by a Methodist minister, Edward Bannister, although it was not under the authority of the Methodist Church. The superintendent of the Methodist Church in California, however, gave his approval. The name was changed to the College of the Pacific, and it moved to Stockton. In 1961 the name was changed back to the University of the Pacific.

A contributor to the founding of the school was George Major Hanson, who crossed the plains from Illinois with his family in 1849 and preached in the Methodist Church in San Jose in 1850. According to his son David Mark Hanson, in his book *Recollections of a Pioneer*, his father wanted his children, who were attending school in Santa Cruz, to be able to attend an English-speaking school. George Major Hanson founded the *Gilroy Advocate* as well as several other newspapers in California and, at the Republican convention of 1856,

The University of the Pacific in College Park between San Jose and Santa Clara was chartered in 1851, and the classes started in 1854. It later moved to Stockton. (THOMPSON & WEST ATLAS, 1876)

put the name of his friend Abraham Lincoln in token nomination for the vice-presidency. Hanson's great-great- grandson Mark Hanson Pierce practices law in San Jose a few blocks from the college his family helped to found.

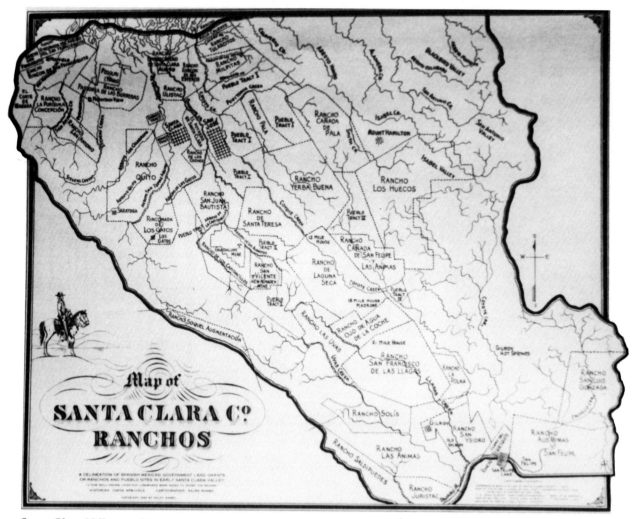

Santa Clara Valley ranchos (RALPH RAMBO)

CHAPTER ELEVEN

The Ranchos

After the United States takeover, the Californios entered a difficult period of transition. With the signing of the Treaty of Guadalupe Hildalgo stating that the Californios should be given title to their land, the U.S. Land Commission was established to settle their claims. The catch for the "land poor" Californios (one that eventually made the Americans "land rich") was the long delay in obtaining patents. The burden of proof of ownership rested with the claimants. They were dealing in a foreign tongue; most had little education; and they had practically no tangible money. Their monetary exchange was the "leather dollar," as hides were called. As a result they had to pay the legal fees and other expenses with parcels of land. This meant that in most cases their large spreads were severely dissipated.

To prove the boundaries of their ranchos wasn't easy. Most often the designations were indicated on the *diseño* (map) by such landmarks as a creek, a gully, a pile of rocks, or an oak tree. In many cases the *diseños* were lost. Some of the rancheros—as in the case of the Berryessa family—claimed hanky-panky in the disappearance of their papers.

On the other hand, the Americans accused the Californios of trying to claim land that wasn't theirs. In some cases this was true, too. According to Clyde Arbuckle, Carlos Galindo sold land along Bascom and Hamilton avenues that was not his. During the long wait, however, squatters (in some cases thinking it was available) settled on the land, took their fruit, and appropriated their cattle.

Rancho Yerba Buena
(Good Herb)

Rancho Yerba Buena was an example of the squatter problem that plagued the Californios. Antonio Chaboya

(Chabolla) had more than his share on his 25,000-acre rancho granted to him by Governor Figueroa in 1833. It was a beautiful piece of land, bordered by the Evergreen foothills, Tully and Metcalf roads, and Coyote Creek. Before the U.S. issued a patent to Chaboya in 1859, squatters, probably thinking it was in public domain, had settled on the land. Many even paid taxes. Benjamin Harrison Gordon, grandfather of Clyde Arbuckle, had to buy his land twice.

Chaboya's efforts at evicting the squatters met with opposition that resulted in the Settler's War of 1861. The squatters armed themselves with sidearms, scythes, and a small cannon (a relic of the Mexican War) and, joined by neighbors and friends, created quite a scene as they marched into town and through the streets. Chaboya enlisted the support of Sheriff John Murphy, who tried to enforce the law with a posse. He should have known better, because no American would go against his neighbor. In time, after the dust settled, Chaboya and his lawyers were able to work out a peaceful settlement.

The Chaboyas had played a role in the pueblo government. In 1797 it was Marcos Chaboya who wrote to Borica requesting permission to move the pueblo. Pedro Chaboya had served as *juez de campo* with Francisco Palomares in 1846 and was second *alcalde* when Fallon raised the U.S. flag. Chaboya Road that runs through the property was named for him.

The family continued to live on the rancho after his death in 1908. Patricia Loomis writes in her book *Signposts II* that one of the descendants, Ramón Chaboya, while plowing his field hit a heavy box. When he opened it he found a hidden treasure of gold. He tried to keep it a secret, hoping to explore further, but word got out and it hit the San Jose newspapers. Unfortunately, no more gold was found and its origin remains a mystery.

By the time of Chaboya's death, his rancho was reduced to 2,000 acres. The area known as Evergreen went to a lawyer for legal fees. In 1887 a German

Vineyards on Rancho Yerba Buena in the eastern foothills

immigrant, William Wehner, purchased 718 acres on which he planted his Loma Azules vineyard and built his showplace residence of wood and stone, quarried in the nearby hills, with six bedrooms and six baths—most unusual for that day. Other German winemakers who had become highly productive in the 1880s included John Cilker, who, with his Cooperative Wine Company of Los Gatos, planted 28,000 vines, and Stefan Splivalo, who bought part of Don Antonio Suñol's Rancho Coches in the Willow Glen area. Albert Haentze, first president of the Wine Advisory Board, bought the Wehner estate in 1915, and the Cribari winery family bought it in 1941. Today it is part of the Villages, a con-

dominium development with a golf course and other amenities.

Part of the Yerba Buena was purchased in the mid-1980s by Syntex, for research and development, from the late Charles Kuhn, whose father, Albert C. Kuhn, an early trustee of the Garden City Bank (forerunner of First National Bank) had bought it in 1910. He planted it in walnuts, prunes, and apricots. His son, Charles, lived and operated the ranch for many years. Charles willed the property to his daughter, Peggy Kuhn Thompson, with life estate of the house and garden to his widow, Jean, now Mrs. Morris Doyle of San Francisco. The Kuhn's neighbors, Robert "Red" Wool of the pioneer

Rancho Pala with the City Reservation (Alum Rock Park) above to the right

64

fruit-packing family and his wife, Felicia, who have lived on the ranch for fifty years, sold their ranch to Syntex. The sale included a provision that they could stay for their lifetimes in the 120-year-old house that was once a haven for bootleggers.

Pala Rancho
(Shovel)

Pala Rancho grant, which extended from Capitol Avenue to the hills and front Penitencia Creek to Norwood Avenue in the Eastern Foothills, was granted to José Joaquín Higuera, descendant of Manuel Higuera, one of the original settlers of the Pueblo de San José. Higuera wasn't able to keep the Pala long enough to go through the patent process. Most of it passed to Charles White in 1850 — many believed by questionable means. Higuera's heirs, who lived on a remaining portion, say White got his "just desserts" when he lost his life on the *Jenny Lind*.

Before his death in 1846 Higuera bequeathed to each of his eleven children 133 cattle, eighty-eight vines and ten fruit trees. The Higueras continued to live on the rancho. His daughter Lydia Higuera married Carlos Sainsevain, grandson of Antonio Suñol. Before her death, in 1988, Dolores Turek, Carlos and Lydia's daughter, passed on to her children, George and Les Strickler and Marie Strickler Mann, family stories of her grandfather Pierre Sainsevain and great-grandfather Don Antonio Suñol and of life in the early days. She said White would push the boundary lines farther and farther into the Higuera property. Higuera would then push the lines back — a see-saw game that White eventually won. The U.S. patented the major portion to the widow of Charles White in 1866.

Rancho Milpitas
(Corn Patch)

When Pedro Chaboya was *alcalde* of the pueblo in 1834, he granted to Nicolás Berryessa II Rancho Milpitas, from Calaveras Road to Cropley Avenue and eastward from Milpitas Road to the hills beyond Piedmont Road. The following year Gen. José Castro declared that transaction illegal and granted the Milpitas to José María Alviso. The Berryessas of today, Mercedes and her sister, Naomi, still harbor ill feelings over the loss of that land.

The U.S. Land Commission made the grant to the Alviso heirs official in 1871. Alviso, who married Juana Galindo, was the son of an Anza colonist and built a fine adobe in 1837 — to which a second story was added later. The adobe still stands at the corner of Piedmont Road and Calaveras Boulevard. Alviso's daughter María de los Angeles and her husband, Bartólome Sepúlveda, spent most of their married life on Rancho Milpitas before moving into San Jose to a home on North First Street. Bartolome's grandson John Morgan Sepúlveda, father of California historian Bart Sepúlveda, still lives on the remaining piece of the family's land, across the street from the Alviso adobe that is scheduled to be restored by the city of Milpitas.

Rancho Rincon de los Esteros
(Corner of the Estuaries)

The Berryessas may have missed out on the Milpitas, but Francisca Berryessa, daughter of Dolores Alviso and Guadalupe Berryessa, did get a piece of Rancho Rincón de los Esteros that adjoined the Milpitas. Dolores's grandfather Juan Ygnacio Alviso, who came as a small child with his family in the Anza party at the age of three, received from Governor Alvardo the Rincón de los Esteros grant of 65,000 acres, extending from the bay highlands to what is now Alviso.

When the time came to go through the procedure to obtain the patent to the rancho from the United States, Don Ygnacio, in need of cash, sold one-third of the rancho to the ubiquitous Charles White, whose widow received the patent for his share. In the will Don Ygnacio made four days before he died, he left one-third of the rancho to his daughter María Dolores Alviso Berryessa and one-third to the children of his son José Domingo Alviso, who had predeceased him. He had already pre-arranged for another son, Manuel, to have Rancho Quito with a life estate to his wife.

Don Ygnacio's grandchildren, who divided the one-third share, were Rafael, in whose name the patent was issued; María Jesús Alviso, whose husband, Andréas Malovos, built a home and a nursery and planted orchards; Estefana, who married Charles Wade (they started Strawberry Ranch next to the Malovoses); and María Josefa, who married Agustín Dias and later a man named Lowe.

Don Ygnacio played an important role at the Mission Santa Clara, where he was *mayordomo*. In 1818 when an earthquake inflicted severe damage, a third mission church was built with Padre Viader the supervisor of construction and Don Ygnacio the foreman. An artist, Agustín Dávalos, was brought up from Mexico to do

Lydia Bartola Higuera of Rancho Pala was married to Carlos Sainsevain (COURTESY MARIE MANN AND GEORGE STRICKLER)

the decorations. He used cinnabar—extracting the juice from bark and roots—for his paintings. One of the unique features of Dávalos's painting was the ceiling of the sanctuary. According to church regulations, the artist should never portray the Holy Spirit as a person, but in his painting of the Holy Trinity, Dávalos did. When the present mission church was built, a picture of the ceiling was found and reproduced. He is buried beneath the chapel of the mission.

James Enright Tract

James Enright, an Irishman who came overland in 1846 from Missouri with the Donner Party and was with the group that split and went to San Francisco, acquired an 800-acre piece of land between Santa Clara and Lawrence Station that had been a Mexican grant to Francisco García in 1845. Enright solved the problem of getting a U.S. patent for his land, which was called simply the James Enright Tract, by sending his own representative by horseback to Washington.

Rancho Quito

Rancho Quito, whose 13,000 acres spread over parts of Saratoga, Campbell, and Cupertino, was no exception to ownership problems. As was the case with many early settlers who had bought their farms from squatters, Daniel Gardner bought his ranch on Fruitvale Avenue in Saratoga a second time from José Ramón Argüello and his wife, Soledad Ortega, in 1861. Gardner's descendants lived continuously on the land for over 100 years until it was sold to West Valley College in 1960. The rancho was first granted in 1841 by Govenor Alvardo to two active members of the pueblo of San José's *ayuntamiento*: José Noriega and José Zenon Fernández. Fernández, a highly regarded teacher who came with the Híjar colonists in 1834, served as *juez de paz* and was secretary of the *ayuntamiento* at the time of the grant. Noriega had served as *alcalde* and was elected one of six *regidores* to help another *alcalde*, James Weekes. He also was appointed to the first *ayuntamiento* of twelve men to govern the pueblo under American rule. Noriega was one of the few Californios who mixed socially with the Americans.

Noriega and Fernández sold the rancho to Ygnacio Alviso, who gave it to his son Manuel, with tenancy to his wife. The Fernández heirs and Manuel Alviso obtained the patent in 1866. Manuel sold to S. M. Mezes, Octavius F. Cipriani, and José Ramón Argüello, who started the rancho on its road to fame for its olives. Don Ramón, son of California's first Mexican govenor, José Darío Argüello, and grandson of its last Spanish govenor, had a spacious home in Santa Clara at Santa Clara and Washington streets and built another home near the intersection of Quito Road and Saratoga Avenue. His mother, who had the large Rancho de las Pulgas in San Mateo County and a home in Santa Clara, came to live with him. He planted orchards, a small vineyard, and seedlings from Mission Santa Clara olive trees given to him by Mrs. Samuel Blythe (Serena Cox, heir of Daniel Gardner). The olive trees were originally given to the mission padres by Don Antonio Suñol.

These olive trees, which still can be seen on Quito Road and Saratoga Avenue, led to the rancho's fame as the Quito Olive Farm. In 1883 Edward Goodrich, an Easterner, acquired the rancho and planted more trees and grapevines between the rows. His El Quito Olive Oil won many prizes, including first place in the New Orleans Exhibition in 1885. The Quito olive gained further distinction in 1939 when 200 of these trees were transplanted on Treasure Island for the Golden Gate International Exhibition.

Lydia Higuera and her husband, Carlos Sainsevain, with daughters Pauline and Lillie (seated on her father's lap) (COURTESY MARIE MANN AND GEORGE STRICKLER)

Rancho San Juan Bautista
(St. John the Baptist)

José Agustín Narváez never regretted his decision to come to Alta California in 1797 as a colonist. His alternative was to go to jail as a juvenile deliquent in Guadalajara. After spending a few years in Branciforte, he became a soldier at the Presidio de San Francisco. His youthful problems behind him, in 1817 he moved to the Pueblo de San José de Guadalupe with his wife, Josefa Higuera of the Rancho Pala family, and became the father of thirteen children, all of whom attended St. Joseph's. He was *alcalde* in 1821 and a member of the *ayuntamiento* in 1827. Governor Micheltorena, in 1844, granted him the almost 9,000-acre rancho, which he named for his favorite saint, San Juan Bautista. Within its boundaries were the Hillsdale, Robertsville, and Willow Glen areas.

The U.S. issued a patent to Narváez in 1865. By this time he was eighty-three years of age and sold off a good portion of the land to American farmers and a Frenchman, Etienne Thee, who came in late 1840s and planted wine grapes. Thee's son-in-law-to-be, Charles Lefranc, went into wine production, which marked the beginning of the Almaden Wines. In 1989 Dividend Construction Company bought the winery property on Blossom Hill Road for a housing project.

Every year on his saint's day, Narváez, dressed in his best, would take a painting of Saint John the Baptist on horseback to Mission Santa Clara to a special mass. Afterwards he would celebrate his birthday with his large family, who included such prominent early-California names as Ortega, Berryessa, Sepúlveda, Alviso, and Chaboya. His daughter Modesta Cantua presented the painting to the de Saisset Gallery at Santa Clara University.

Carl Fisher, a descendant of Narváez's, not only was baptized in St. Joseph's and attended St. Joseph's School, but his grandmother Innocencia Narváez was married in St. Joseph's to Jean Joseph Roberts (of the Robertsville family), and his mother, Carmen Roberts, who was born in the José María Alviso adobe on Rancho Milpitas, was baptized and married to Carl Joseph Palmer in St. Joseph's.

Rancho los Huecos
(Rolling Hills and Valleys)

Rancho Los Huecos, granted by Governor Pico in 1846 to Luís Arenas and John Roland, had a long litigation process. In 1876 it was finally patented to John Roland and J. L. Hornsby. In the meantime Henry Willard Coe had to buy his part of Los Huecos, which he called Rancho San Felipe, several times—first from Samuel Crockett Young and, finally, from Gen. Henry Naglee. Coe, who came West from New Hampshire by prairie schooner in 1847, experienced the Indian wars in Oregon before making his way the next year to San Francisco and ultimately to San Jose.

He bought property in "The Willows" (Coe Avenue is named for him), cleared off the willow trees, planted fruit, and grew hops. During the Civil War he exported hops to Germany. Coe suffered a financial setback from his mining interests, sold his Willows land for $750 an acre, and retired to the quiet of the San Felipe Valley. His son, Henry W. "Harry" Coe, and his grandson, Henry Sutcliffe Coe, enlarged the ranch, which is better known as the Coe Ranch, from 479 acres to 4,000.

Dolores Sainsevain Strickler Turek, daughter of Lydia Higuera and Carlos Sainsevain, died in 1988 at the age of 93. (COURTESY MARIE MANN AND GEORGE STRICKLER)

Henry Sutcliffe sold a piece of the Coe Ranch to his neighbors William Hewlett and David Packard when they bought the adjoining Morrow Ranch, which they called the San Felipe Ranch. Robert Fulton Morrow, whose ranch property covered a territory larger than the city of San Francisco, founded the horse-drawn Sutter Street Railroad that later became the cable car line and ultimately the municipal railroad.

Most of the Coe Ranch was sold in December of 1989 to Huntington Properties, who at present run cattle on it. Henry Sutcliffe Coe's daughters, Winifred Coe Verbica and Nancy Coe, retained an equity in the property. Winifred and her husband, Robert Verbica, are staying on in their home on the ranch. Nancy has redecorated the old family home for herself and is calling it "El Encanto."

The picturesque 11,280-acre Isabel Valley Ranch on Los Huecos escaped litigation. It was part of the Joseph Grant holdings inherited by his daughter, the late Josephine Grant McCreary, who lived on the Mount Hamilton Road ranch, part of the Rancho de Pala grant that is now the Grant Ranch Park. The family always referred to the Isabel as "the back forty." James "Jimmy" Rolf III told his good friend Duncan Oneal that the property was going to be put up for sale and suggested they ride their horses down to see it. According to Duncan Oneal's grandson Jim Oneal, "Pops was taken with the open space, and wildlife, but when he spotted a big buck, that did it."

Oneal bought the Isabel with James Hait and Victor McDonald as partners. They built houses for themselves and developed lakes, which they stocked with bass. Upon the deaths of Duncan and Patty Oneal, their sons, Lou and Dan, became owners of their share, and Dick McDonald, who runs cattle on it, inherited his family's share. Jim and Ruth Hait sold theirs (except for a small portion held for their son, Paul Hait) to builder Barry Swenson, grandson of Carl N. Swenson, founder of the construction company that was headed for many years by Barry's father, Cliff Swenson. Adding to the wildlife, elk and antelope, who used to live on the ranch, have returned, drifting down from Hewlett and Packard's San Felipe Ranch.

The San Vicente and Los Capitancillos
(St. Vincent and the Little Captains)

The New Almaden mine in the Capitancillo Hills twelve miles south of San Jose became one of the wealthiest and most famous quicksilver mines in the world. The mine was located on the Los Capitancillos (Little Captains) rancho of Justo Larios and the San Vicente of José de los Reyes Berryessa. Neither benefited from its tremendous wealth.

Larios sold most of his rancho to an opportunist named Grove Cook, who had come with the Bidwell-Bartleson Company in 1841, for $300 in silver and $25 in merchandise. It was said of Cook that "he was the gentlest soul who ever drew a bead on an Indian." There was so much land in those days that it was of little value unless, of course, there was a rich quicksilver mine on it. Larios went to the gold fields, where he hit it rich, but he soon dissipated most of his wealth. He spent the remainder of his life in Gilroy.

José de los Reyes Berryessa was fatally shot by Kit Carson at the Embarcadero de Mission San Rafael in 1846. After years of litigation, the title to the San Vicente was finally granted to Berryessa's widow, María Zacarias Bernal, in 1868.

CHAPTER TWELVE

The New Almaden Mine

The New Almaden mine was within the boundaries of St. Joseph's parish. Father Juan Bosco used to ride horseback to care for his flock — the Mexican mine workers. In 1856 Archbishop Alemany joined him there to give confirmation to eighteen children. On the Feast of the Holy Cross, May 3, 1884, Father Bosco's successor, Padre Benito, as the Mexicans affectionately called Father Piccard, who occasionally had the luxury of a carriage, took Bishop Riordan to New Almaden to consecrate its new St. Anthony's Church. By this time there were 500 men working in the mines.

A visitor to the mine in 1856, Charles McGettigan, owner of the Star Bakery, told of seeing a shrine with a statue of their patron saint, Nuestra Señora de Guadalupe, in a niche which the miners had carved with care out of a rock in a cave at the mouth of the mine. She was dressed in a white gown with red morocco slippers and an elaborately ornamented headdress. He described seeing the Mexican people offer prayers before going down into the mine and lighting their candles from the candles that burned continuously at the shrine.

There was time for work, and that work was not only strenuous but dangerous, and a time for play. They had their fiestas and their fandangos on the saint's day in the little village. An Easterner who visited New Almaden wrote a story that appeared in *Harper's New Monthly Magazine*, February 1878, in which he told of the social life at the mine.

"A ball was given in Spanish Town by the Mexicans upon the anniversary of their independence. We went up to see the dancing, which was very beautiful. The Mexican girls have exquisite forms — especially when in motion; their dancing was like inspiration." He went on to describe the people of all nations, predominantly the Mexicans and the Cornish people, who came when England was depressed, also the Chileans and the Chinese. Cellos, violins, brasses, and flutes played the Mexican national hymn to open the ball.

Another visitor to New Almaden mine, William H. Brewer, who was making a geological survey of the state, wrote in his *Up and Down California in 1860–1864* about a stay at the New Almaden mine and of a horseback ride. He described the graceful horsemanship of the women: "I wish you could see these Mexican ladies ride, you would say you never seen riding before. I never saw ladies in the East who could approach the poorest of these Spanish ladies whom I have yet seen ride. I cannot convey an adequate conception of the way they went galloping over the fields — squirrel holes, ditches or logs are no cause of stopping — jumping a fence or gulch if one was in the way."

The New Almaden mine, named for the famous Almaden mine in Spain, was originally known as La Mina Santa Clara. Secundino Robles, a dashing and

Don Secundino Robles, mayordomo *at the Mission Santa Clara, showed Andrés Castillero, a Mexican government mining engineer, samples of cinnabar. Castillero determined that it was quicksilver and filed a claim with Alcalde Pedro Chaboya. This was the beginning of the New Almaden mine.*

The Catholic church built at the New Alamaden mine in 1884. Father Benito Piccard of St. Joseph's and Archbishop Riordan presided at the dedication of the church.

handsome don who served as *mayordomo* of Mission Santa Clara, was the first to learn that the valley Indians used cinnabar (a mercury ore) to paint their bodies and to make their crude decorations for the Mission Santa Clara chapel. In the early 1820s he and his brother Teodoro, Don Antonio Suñol, and Luís Chaboya mined the silver there. Unfortunately, they were seeking the wrong kind of silver. They should have been looking for quicksilver (sulphuret of mercury), which is valuable in the reduction of gold ore.

Twenty years later Robles showed samples of the ore to a Mexican government mining engineer, a Capt. Andrés Castillero, who was visiting Padre Real at Mission Santa Clara. Castillero made some tests and determined it was quicksilver. After giving shares to the Robles

brothers and Padre Real he filed a claim with Alcalde Pedro Chaboya. For some reason he did not include José de los Reyes Berryessa, grantee of Rancho San Vicente, on which the mine was located. In need of financial backing, Castilleros went back to Mexico. There he found the Mexican government so involved with the pending war with the U.S. that he received no support nor was he able to return to California. Consequently, he sold his interest to Barron, Forbes Company of Tepic, Mexico. Had he known that gold would be discovered at Sutter's Mill, it might have been another story—a multimillion-dollar story. During their few years of ownership, Barron, Forbes gained over 15 million dollars and in 1863 when they sold to the Quicksilver Mining Co. of New York they received $1,750,000.

Hacienda on Rancho Rincon de San Francisquito where Secundino Robles lived with his wife and twenty-nine children. Unfortunately, Robles sold off portions of the land until it was all gone. (PALO ALTO HISTORICAL ASSOCIATION)

70

Justo Larios, whose Rancho Los Capitancillos covered the Guadalupe Mines and New Almaden. Unfortunately, he sold too soon and for too little to Grove Cook. (CLYDE ARBUCKLE COLLECTION)

This picture is captioned "The Field Party of 1864." Seated is William H. Brewer, author of Up and Down California in 1860–1864, *in which he described a stay at New Almaden.*

They brought in the capable Henry Halleck to manage the mine. Halleck built the Casa Grande in 1852, an imposing three-story mansion that somewhat overwhelmed the little village of adobe and brick houses along a creek. Halleck and his wife, Elizabeth Hamilton (Alexander Hamilton's granddaughter), held forth here when not at their home in San Francisco. In the mid-sixties Samuel Butterworth, the Quicksilver Mining Co.'s new manager, moved in with his wife. He was succeeded in 1870 by James Randol, who stayed until he retired, in 1890. The Casa has survived the years well. The Opry House, where melodramas have been performed for many years, occupies one part; the upstairs have been converted into office space; and the basement now houses a restaurant.

San Jose in 1858

CHAPTER THIRTEEN

The Fifties

With American rule, the second half of the century found English the official language; the Pueblo de San José de Guadalupe the city of San Jose; the *alcalde* the mayor; and the *ayuntamiento* the city council. The *juzgado* was torn down and replaced with new buildings on Market Street. Jacob Hoppe used the adobe bricks that had been hand molded by the Indians and early settlers to build a store and residence. The courts temporarily convened in the Bella Union saloon.

In their *History of San Jose* George McMurry and William James wrote that in 1847 the streets were cow trails with the possible exception of Market and El Dorado, that there were no buildings yet on First Street, and that life centered around the old plaza from San Carlos to Santa Clara streets.

The San Francisco stage, drawn by six mustangs, clattered down the tree-lined Alameda—occasionally a creaking *carreta* passed, and a few wagons hauling quicksilver from the New Almaden mine to Alviso or ox teams hauling lumber from the Santa Cruz Mountains.

The influx of foreigners brought new energies and new attitudes. Although still called the pueblo, it became increasingly more American in its manners and mores. Agriculture made strides, vineyards increased, and the number of fruit trees grew from 18,000 in 1852 to over 100,000 in 1856. Wheat production advanced technically in 1854 from the crude method of using wild horses to separate the wheat from the chaff to a harvester and thresher that had to be pulled by twenty horses.

James Lick, who accumulated an immense fortune in San Francisco real estate, bought a mill near Agnew in 1850. A master carpenter, he paneled his mill with mahogany and later built a mansion nearby. Julian Hanks and Pierre Sainsevain had already built mills. Louis Prevost planted thirty mulberry trees to introduce silk culture; he did well at first but ended up losing all, including his beautiful Prevost Gardens along the Guadalupe.

Even the street bearing his name was changed in 1989 to "Woz Way" for computer wizard and philanthropist Steve Wozniak.

Later in the decade San Jose got its first macadam street between San Fernando and Santa Clara on First Street. Horace Greeley followed his own advice in 1857 and came West to give a lecture in San Jose. He was followed the next year by traveler and writer Bayard Taylor, who was the first to call San Jose "The Garden City."

Men of Prophesy

With Bayard Taylor, it was a case of "love at first sight" when he viewed the valley of Santa Clara on his way to Monterey to cover the Constitutional Convention for the press. He proved to be a visionary. He wrote in his book *Eldorado or Adventures in the Path of Empire* that he had a dream. "It will not be long, I thought—I may live to see it before my prime is over—until San Jose is but five days' journey from New York. Cars, which shall be, in fact, traveling hotels, will speed on an unknown line of rail from Mississippi to the Pacific."

Then he told of another grander dream. "One hundred years had now passed, and I saw the valley, not as now, only partially tamed and reveling in the wild magnificence of nature, but, from river bed to mountain summit humming with human life. I saw the same oaks and sycamores, but their shadows fell on mansions fair as temples with their white fronts and long colonnades. I saw gardens refreshed with gleaming fountains, statues peeping from the bloom of laurel bowers; palaces built to enshrine the new Art, which will then have blossomed here." He ended with "Was it all only a dream?"

An earlier man of prophesy—but with a more somber view—was Padre Magín Catalá, "the holy man of Santa Clara," who, with the Indians, built The Alameda and

San Jose's City Hall in 1855 on what is now North Market Street. Levi Goodrich's turret roof design was a radical change from the adobe. When it was destroyed by the earthquake of 1906, it was serving as a firehouse. (SAN JOSE MERCURY NEWS)

planted the trees. The last year of his life, in 1830, as he gave his homily seated in from of the altar, he predicted, "People will come from almost all the nations of the earth. Another flag will come from the East and the people that follow it will speak a different language altogether and have a different religion. These people will take possession of the country and of the lands." He predicted that the Californios would lose their land and become poor. "The Indians will be dispersed . . . and they will be like sheep running wild." Although he knew he wouldn't live to see this, others then alive would. "There will be no Franciscans here then, but other priests [the Jesuits] will arrive."

The Stock Family

The prophesies of both men came true with the influx of Americans, Irish, French, Germans, Chileans, and, a short time later, Italians. Heading the list of German arrivals was Frank Stock. "He probably bought his way out of the army there," (a common custom in those days) said one of his descendants. Anyway, Stock went first to Chicago in 1845 and from there by way of the Isthmus of Panama to San Francisco, where he sold pans and hardware to the miners. He moved to San Jose in 1852 in time to contribute to the building boom. A tinsmith, he opened a shop on Market Street. In a couple of years, his brother, John, joined him, and they soon moved to South First Street where Woolworth Store and Pellerano Drug Store were later located. They were said to have built most of the tin roofs in San Jose. In 1859 Frank Stock planted a vineyard of Johannesburg Riesling, Zinfandel, and other German varieties at the corner of

Coleman Younger, successful cattleman and St. Joseph's Church member, brought his wife, Augusta, overland from Missouri in the 1850s.

74

The jovial fellow on the right is A. H. Marten, whose wife, Clara Stock, is second from the left in the back. The picture was taken during a celebration at their Alameda home, circa 1900. In the front row are Charles Fay, Jr. (of the San Fracisco Fays), Hortense Lion, Lazard Lion (Lion & Sons furniture), and his daughter, Stella Lion Fay. (COURTESY MARGERY MARTEN RICHARD)

Eighth and William streets. When he discontinued the vineyard, he gave his cutting to Etienne Thee. Frank retired in 1861.

John carried on the business in his own name. Later, when his three sons joined him, the busines became known as John Stock & Sons. Frank, who studied at Santa Clara College, became the first president of Security State & Savings Bank of San Jose and one of the organizers of the Board of Trade. He married Juanita Hinkelbein, a native San Josean.

Peter Stock, the youngest son, who married Elizabeth O'Brien in St. Joseph's Church, became sole proprietor of the business in 1919. Their daughter, Clara, married James Melehan, also in St. Josephs's, and their son, James Stock Melehan, married Patricia Perucci in St. Joseph's Church in 1950—almost 100 years after the first Stock came to San Jose. Their reception in the Sainte Claire Hotel was attended by 600 guests. Jim Melehan is president of Mayfair Packing Co., founded by Pat's father, Joseph Perucci. Pat and her sisters, the late Carmel Vaudagna and Jo'Ann, whose husband belongs to the well-known O'Connell ranching family, grew up in the family home on Losse Court where the entrance to the old Vendome Hotel used to be. Jim Melehan's great-grandparents John and Susan Stock are remembered in St. Joseph's with a stained-glass window depicting Saint Mark the Evangelist.

John Stock's daughter, Clara, married A. H. Marten, a dry goods merchant, whom she met at a Vendome Hotel party. They first lived at Second and Santa Clara streets before building a home on The Alameda. Their son, Frank, married Mary Twohy of Spokane of the

northwest railroad builder's family. They built the Twohy building, now called El Paseo, on South First Street. The Martens' daughter Mavis and her husband, George Parrish, live in Gilroy; daughter Margery and her husband, Henry, in Pasatiempo; and son John F. Marten lives in Los Angeles.

Coleman Younger

Another family who arrived in the early fifties and became prominent members of the community and active members of St. Joseph's were Coleman and Augusta Younger. Younger was to distinguish himself as a leading cattleman and one of the founders of the Agricultural Society. A Missourian who, after hearing of the fertile land and beauty of the Santa Clara Valley, decided to see for himself, came by clipper ship to Monterey, where, for the sum of $150, he hired a Mexican cart driver to take him and his manservant to San Jose. Impressed with what he saw, Younger purchased a choice 210-acre piece of land on Alviso Road before heading back to Liberty, Missouri, to marry Augusta Inskip. Together they came to California overland in a five-wagon immigrant train, bringing with them 500 head of cattle.

In the late fifties Younger imported the finest herd of Durham cows obtainable from Kentucky. They become famous and sold all over the U.S., Central America, British Columbia, and Japan. For their estate, "Forest Home Farm," he had the house precut in the East and shipped around the Horn; planted orchards; and landscaped with ornamental trees. Mary Bowden Carroll's social column noted, "Needless to say that as soon as it [the house] arrived, with true Southern hospitality, it was thrown open and a large party was given." Augusta, a leading hostess, entertained with taste. Her guest lists frequently included Gov. Peter Burnett and his wife, Harriet; their daughters, Rhea, who married William Wallace, and Letitia, with her husband, C. T. Ryland; Don Antonio Pico with his wife, Doña Pilar; Don Antonio Suñol and his wife, Doña Dolores; and Maj. and Mrs. Samuel Hensley. The Youngers converted to Catholicism. At their baptism in St. Joseph's Church Governor

María Jesús Alviso Malovos, granddaughter of Ygnacio Alviso, grantee of Rancho de los Esteros (COURTESY KENNETH MALOVOS)

Burnett was their sponsor and C. T. and Letitia Ryland were the godparents of their daughters.

Lighthouse Farm

Not far from the Youngers on Alviso Road, Andréas Malovos developed another showplace — "Lighthouse Farm" — on part of Rancho Rincón de los Esteros, inherited by his wife, María Jesús Alviso. Malovos, born on the island of Ragusa off the Dalmatian coast of what was

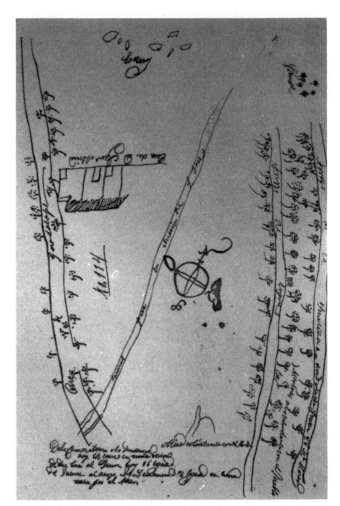

Rancho de los Esteros of Ygnacio Alviso. Note the crude sketch of the adobe where his granddaughter, María Jesús Alviso Malovos, was born, where her sister was married to Charles Wade, and where Henry Richard, Sr. and Jr. were born. (COURTESY KENNETH MALOVOS)

then Austria (now Yugoslavia), left his native land to go to sea in the 1860s. He became involved in his countryman Emperor Maximilian's problems in Mexico. Engaged in commerce with five small schooners, he carried equipment, ammunition, and supplies from ships lying off the Río Grande at Matamoros inland, on waterways too shallow for larger ships, to the emperor's army.

Ultimately his travels brought him to San Jose, where he met the vivacious Jesusita, daughter of Domingo Alviso and granddaughter of Juan Ygnacio Alviso, grantee of Rancho Rincón de los Esteros from Governor Alvarado. That was the end of Andréas's career at sea.

The couple was married in 1870 in the newly completed Theodore Lenzen–designed St. Joseph's Church that was to go up in flames only five years later. They raised their ten children at Lighthouse Farm in the handsome sixteen-room house surrounded by flower gardens and orchards. According to *Sunshine, Fruit and Flowers*, published in 1895 by the *San Jose Mercury* and republished by the San Jose Historical Museum, Malovos, a successful orchardist, planted 22,000 prune trees, 3,000 each of peach and apricot, and 2,500 cherry trees, all watered from four artesian wells and through a system of canals. Sixty acres were devoted profitably to asparagus and twenty-five acres put in pasture for horses and cows. Besides that he had a sixty-acre nursery which he operated with a partner, Henry Martin. The asparagus and other produce were hauled to Alviso and from there shipped by boat to San Francisco.

Three generations of Malovoses were married in St. Joseph's Church: besides María Jesús and Andréas, their son, Andréas Malovos, Jr., married Edith Carolyn Luhrman, a native of Germany, in the church in 1905, and their son, Kenneth Malovos, wed Madelyn Chargin there in 1940.

In Calvary Cemetery a monument marks the graves of Andréas and María Jesús Malovos, of Andréas, Jr., with his wife, Edith, and their son, Andrew III, who was born at Lighthouse Farm.

After Andréas died in 1910 Jesusita moved with her family into a house on Twelfth Street. Kenneth Malovos remembers his grandmother fondly and says there was always a houseful of people at her home. "She was vivacious, musical, played the guitar, and had everyone singing. Her sister, Estefana, and husband, Charles Wade, would come with their large family and there would be kids all over the place."

Strawberry Ranch

North First Street was the dividing line between the Malovoses' "Lighthouse Farm" and the "Strawberry Ranch" of Charles and Estefana Alviso Wade. Estefana, like her sister, received the land, part of Rancho Rincón de los Esteros, as a gift from her grandfather. A picture in the 1875 Thompson & West Atlas shows the Wades' ninety-acre Strawberry Ranch with a long, tree-bordered drive leading back to the house. Chinese in coolie hats can be seen working in the strawberry fields in front of the house. This was said to be the largest strawberry farm in the world at that time.

Charles, who crossed the plains as a boy with his family and had a harrowing experience in Death Valley—many didn't make it—grew up in Alviso in the prefab house his father, Harry Wade, had shipped around the Horn. He met and fell in love with the comely daughter of Domingo Alviso. The course of true love, as sometimes happens, didn't run smoothly. Estefana's parents didn't approve, because Charles was not a Catholic, or even a Christian. But that got straightened out.

William, Charles and Estefana's son, married Mary Margaret Taylor in St. Joseph's. William and Mary's son, Walter, was married in the same church to Clara Gorman by Father Culligan in 1934. Walter and Clara's son is Rev. Gerald Wade, S.J., president of Bellarmine Preparatory School.

William's younger brother, Walter, was also married in St. Joseph's, in 1910 to Loretta Irene Edwards. Their daughter Jeannette Wildhofer lives in Campbell; another daughter, Loretta Erhart, in Sacramento; and a son, James Wade, in Monterey. Walter attended St. Joseph's grammar school and high school. An altar boy, he served with Jerry Chargin and still remembers that "he got to ring the bells." Walter Wade has warm memories of his grandmother Estefana and, especially, of his grandfather Charles. He said, "I had such good times with him . . . he showed me his rifle and pointed out the notches on the handle. 'These are for the Indians I shot coming across,' he used to tell me."

Wade has an old newspaper clipping in which his grandfather was interviewed. He told of riding out to see the old rancho at the wild speed of twelve miles per hour. "When we passed the Richard place with its modern gray bungalow and caught a glimpse of the white adobe I thought to myself, I ought to know this place, because I was married there."

This was quite an eventful adobe. Rancher Henry Richard and his son, Henry, Jr., who now lives in Santa Cruz, were born in that adobe. Kenneth Malovos remembers visiting the Alviso family rancho when a small boy and being told that his grandmother María Jesús Alviso was born in that adobe. Coming full circle, when Mrs. Henry Richard, Sr., died in 1983 at the age of 105, Charles Wade's great-grandson Rev. Gerald Wade, S.J., presided over the services.

George Nicholsons

Not far from the Richard ranch lived the George Nicholsons, another family in the Alviso area who came into St. Joseph's to mass on Sundays. Nicholson, a native of Ireland who brought his family West in the late 1850s, like the Richards planted pears and apples on his property on the San Jose–Alviso Road. His son, George Nicholson, Jr., married Minnie Lorigan in St. Joseph's remodeled second adobe church. After her death he married Anna Baumgartner, mother of the building contractor Wilmot (Bill) Nicholson.

The Strawberry Ranch of Charles Wade and Estefana Alviso Wade on Rancho de los Esteros.

Bill Nicholson, who now lives in Carmel Valley, built the former baptismal room in St. Joseph's, donated by Alice Turel. The Turels, a highly esteemed French family, had a large market on Market Street called "The City Store" that carried choice foodstuffs as well as hardware, farm implements, and wines. It was a place where you went to see everyone you knew. They were active parishioners and generous to the church, and there is a stained-glass window of "Our Lord at Prayer" in memory of Jean and Eugenie Turel in the cathedral. In R.V. Garrod's book *Saratoga Story* he tells of the Turels:

"It was one of those old-time stores; when you had their confidence, you had it. Many a hard-up rancher was carried on their books until better times returned. It was in a way headquarters for many old-time families. There was the manager, Al Col, Pat Carroll, the bookkeeper, Dan Thornton, Frank Quement and others. These men were your friends . . . there you met and passed the time of day with the Mirassous, Kellys, Murphys, Clem Barnett, Pfaus, Cottles, Hasslers, McKiernans . . . and most of the wealthy French families. Henry Lefrance made the store his headquarters."

CHAPTER FOURTEEN

The Second Adobe Church Renovated

After surviving a series of earthquakes, the second adobe church was in a weakened state, and Father Anthony Goetz decided it needed reinforcement and a facelift. With the sanction of the archbishop and the support of the newcomers as well as the Californios, the adobe building was encased in brick and two towers were added. The work was completed in 1856. No longer could it be said, as a visiting writer once wrote, that it looked like a Dutch barn.

During the reconstruction of the church, St. Joseph's priests also got an upgrading of their living quarters. Father Goetz and his assistant, Father Peter de Vos, had been living in a little house on the Peralta property north of Santa Clara Street. The accommodations were poor and the location inconvenient. A piece of property became available next to the church, for which they scraped up a thousand pilasters to purchase and put up a house. The new location made it much easier for them to supervise the construction work.

Father de Vos, a native of Belgium, joined the Society of Jesus in Avignon, France, and, after an assignment to Grand Coteau, Louisiana, was recruited for the Indian Missions. He was among the Jesuit priests who joined the famous frontier priest Father Peter De Smet on the Oregon Trail. He spent ten years in the northwest mission stations. It was Peter de Vos whom Peter Burnett came to see when, after intensive study, he decided to join the Catholic Church. The two men renewed their warm friendship when de Vos came to San Jose.

At his death, Father de Vos, the Jesuit, was buried inside the Santa Clara Mission Church in the tomb with the Franciscan priest Father Catalá, both saintly men. Many years later a plaque to his memory by parishioners of St. Joseph's was found under the church. It is now in the mission church at Santa Clara.

One of St. Joseph's more colorful priests was Father Joseph Bixio, who came in 1857. A native of Genoa, Italy, he completed his studies at Georgetown University. Eager to join some of his fellow Jesuits in the West, he prodded his superiors until they finally consented.

To paraphrase an old saying, "Have horse, will travel" applied to Father Bixio. It was his only means of travel. He visited the flock in San Martin, Los Gatos, and Mountain View. He said the first mass in Los Gatos at the home of a Mr. McCormick. On one or more occasions he said mass in a saloon. For his pastoral work in San Jose, Father Bixio visited the people of the parish. He was always on foot and could be spotted in his long black coat and broad-brimmed hat. He made it his special mission to seek out in the alleys and back streets those who he knew had missed their Easter Duty or hadn't been attending mass regularly.

He especially loved the children and could always reach in his pocket and pull out a gumdrop or two from his endless supply. The sick and elderly also had a high priority. Word got around fast when he was coming, and groups would assemble at one of the houses for a short visit.

It could never be said that Father Bixio's life was dull. When the Civil War broke out he returned to Washington. His dual role of passing between the lines to say mass for both Confederate and Union soldiers brought him a court-martial sentence to be hung. In the nick of time a Union general relented and intervened on his behalf. He sailed back to California in 1866, where he did stints at St. Ignatius Church in San Francisco, St. Claire Church in Santa Clara, and St. Joseph's before getting restless and sailing to Australia. When he returned he spent his last ministry at St. Joseph's from 1884 to 1887.

During this time he performed the marriage ceremony for James (Jimmy) Dunne, son of James F. Dunne, to Viola Lowry at the home of her parents, the Washington Lowrys, at the corner of Market and Divine streets. The Dunnes built a fine home at Rancho San Felipe in Southern Santa Clara County, which Jimmy inherited from his father.

Father Joseph Bixio, one of St. Joseph's more colorful Jesuits. During the Civil War he crossed lines to say mass for both the Confederate and Union soldiers. (ARCHIVES CALIFORNIA PROVINCE + SOCIETY OF JESUS)

Saratoga was then known as McCarthysville for Martin McCarthy, who laid the first plot plan of the village and, as was his privilege, named it for himself. Mass was said in Hannah McCarthy's parlor before moving to larger quarters in the dining room of the spacious Congress Springs Hotel. Swiss, French, and Italian residents, who first were charcoal burners before planting orchards, settled in the mountains and built a chapel of redwoods across from the present Saratoga Springs resort, which they named for St. John the Baptist.

The Saratoga people found it difficult during the winter months to navigate by horse and buggy the narrow mountain road called Lumber Street, now known as Big Basin Way. Pooling their energy and resources, they bought a piece of property at Sixth and Big Basin Way and, after many fundraisers, were able to raise $1,000 to build their church. Named for the Sacred Heart of Jesus, it opened in 1895 as a mission of St. Joseph's in San Jose.

The Jesuit priests came by horse and buggy for the first ten years until the interurban Electic Car line opened. Even then it was a long trip. On Sundays the priests would take the 5 A.M. train from town to say mass, and the Notre Dame sisters would come to teach catechism.

In 1910 Sacred Heart became a parish. The St. Joseph's Boy's Band played to celebrate the day. In 1961 Sacred Heart moved to its present location on Saratoga Avenue. The picturesque little frame church, a victim of the woodpeckers, with a steeple that creaked when the wind blew, was taken down—but not without protest from its loyal followers. Parishioner and insurance man A. A. Dempsey offered refuge for it on his property across Big Basin Way, but Father Gerald Geary thought better of the idea. Saratogans still mourn its loss.

John Tully and John Ashworth

A year or so after the remodeling of the second adobe church of St. Joseph's was completed, Rose Tully married John Ashworth. Rose had come by ship from New York, crossing the Isthmus on the first train, to visit her brother, John Tully. She wasn't here long before she met and fell in love with her brother's neighbor, John

Sacred Heart Church, Saratoga, was founded as a mission in 1895 by a small group of dedicated parishioners. When the mission became a parish in 1911, there was a big celebration at which the St. Joseph's Band played. (MELITA ODEN COLLECTION)

The interior of Sacred Heart Church, Saratoga
(MELITA ODEN COLLECTION)

Ashworth, who lived with his family across Coyote Creek. Although Appleton's 1870 *Handbook of American Travel, Western Tour* speaks well of St. Joseph's Church, describing it as having some fine paintings, including a superb copy of Murillo's *Repentant Peter* and one of Raphael's *Madonna del Seggiola*, according to Rose's great-granddaughter Dorynda Johnston, "My grandmother used to say to me, 'My mother was married in that church with the mud floor.'"

An early-day San Jose orchardist, Tully had arrived by ship and settled in San Jose in 1850. He purchased several thousand acres of land — some of which were on Rancho Pala in the Evergreen area. In 1854 when fences began to appear, Tully and his neighbors, including Peter Quivey and William and Barton McClay, concerned about being cut off from a route to San Jose, petitioned for a road. When completed, it was named Tully Road and was the boundry line between the Tullys and the Ashworths.

The little adobe church of San José de Guadalupe has come a long way. Less than a century later Rose Tully's great-granddaughter, Dorynda Wine (Johnston), at the

age of seventeen, took instructions to become a Catholic in the grand St. Joseph's Church that has just become the cathedral of San Jose.

The Ashworths, who had migrated to the U.S. from England in 1783 and helped Daniel Boone settle Kentucky, bought their farming land on Story Road from C. T. Ryland in 1854 for $1,200. In the early 1890s the Ashworths sold 160 acres to Peter Remillard, a gold rush pioneer, for a branch factory of the Remillard Brick Co. After Remillard's death his daughter, Countess Lillian Dandini, whose palatial estate, "Carolands," in Hillsborough was a showplace, ran the business and used the ranch as a summer home

Dorynda Johnston's husband, attorney Faber Johnston, has even deeper roots in San Jose. His great-great-grandfather Thomas Henry Lane came from Missouri with the Donner Party in 1846. Lane's daughter, Cora, married a lawyer, William Allen Johnston, whose father, Silas Newton Johnston, came by sea in 1860. Their son, Faber Lane Johnston, a lawyer, married Ilma Koch, member of St. Joseph's Church and daughter of Valentin Koch, mayor of San Jose in the late 1890s.

Army review on Market Street in the early 1860s (SAN JOSE MERCURY NEWS)

Horse car on The Alameda (COURTESY CARL ZINK)

CHAPTER FIFTEEN

The Sixties

The sixties got off to a good start when the first gaslights appeared on the San Jose streets in 1861. The San Francisco & San Jose Railroad, after over ten years in the planning, was completed in 1864, followed two years later by the transcontinental railroad. Horse-drawn trolleys started carrying passengers along The Alameda; the San Jose Water Co. was organized in 1866, providing piped water to the town; and in 1867 the city council purchased a block of land on Santa Clara Street on which to build the first public high school.

Society in the Sixties

Social life in the sixties gained momentum, although not yet on the grand scale that was to come. Mrs. S. O. Houghton, social arbiter of San Jose in her time, answered a query from Mary Bowden Carroll for her book *Ten Years in Paradise*. She wrote that in the years from 1861 to 1865, San Jose had its social code and exclusive circles, but was not hedged with formalities. She said that the social events were not yet chronicled in the newspapers and that the brides in those days were not "enriched with wedding presents."

Judging from an account by Mrs. Adolph Fitzgerald, the double wedding of Gov. Peter Burnett's daughter Sallie to Francis Poe of Maryland and of their son Armstead to Flora Johnson would have provided society reporters of today with plenty of ammunition, and the brides would have reaped a harvest of crystal and silver.

"There was a large party on the night of the wedding in Govenor Burnett's old home," she wrote, "and an elaborate supper was served in an unfinished house which Mrs. C. T. Ryland was then building in her father's yard. Flora Johnson's parents gave a dinner the next evening and the night following Col. and Mrs. Younger gave a large party in their honor."

After a week of festivities in San Jose the wedding party, with parents and friends, moved to San Francisco. "There was no railroad then," she said, "and we were driven in carriages to Alviso where we took the boat to the city." There they continued a round of parties. The happy wedding story took a sad turn for the Burnetts. Sallie lived only six months after her wedding; Armstead, a year and a half. Francis Poe was killed in the Civil War.

On the lighter side, Camilla Price honored Mrs. Phoebe Hearst (mother of William Randolph Hearst), with an elegant soiree. Among other standout parties was the dance given by E. C. Singletary at the Music Hall, one of the "swell" affairs of the period. "Mr. Singletary proved himself to be a prince at entertaining. The brilliant parlor and club rooms were open to all who did wish to dance; colored servants in livery attended to every want; carriages were at the disposal of guests, and the sumptuous supper would have done credit to royalty."

Auzerais House

It didn't take long for Auzerais House on Santa Clara Street between First and Market streets to become known as the grandest hotel in California. Edward and John Auzerais had come to San Jose from France in the early 1850s by way of Valparaiso. They started out by opening the Mariposa store on South Market Street before making a fortune in real estate. Their plans to build a business block changed when a fire destroyed one of San Jose's two leading hotels. They decided to change horses midstream and build a truly fine hotel instead.

They did just that. Architect Theodore Lenzen designed a three-story marble and brick showplace with parklike gardens that cost $150,000. On the first floor were located the dining room, shops, hotel offices, a large parlor, and a bridal suite, where newlyweds from San Francisco and surrounding villages stayed. Across the

Agricultural Park, built in the 1860s at The Alameda and Race Street, served as the city's fairgrounds. (SAN JOSE HISTORICAL MUSEUM)

Rates of Toll
ON THE SAN JOSE AND ALVISO
TURNPIKE ROAD!

All the way from San Jose to Alviso, or from Alviso to San Jose:

Loaded Wagons, drawn by Two horses, oxen or mules, - - $1 00
"   "   "   "   Four   "   "   "   - - 1 50
"   "   "   "   Six   "   "   "   - - 2 00
Empty Wagons, one-half the above rates.
Every additional horse in team, - - - - - - 12½
Stages, Omnibusses, and other vehicles carrying freight or passengers, same as Wagons.
One horse Buggy or Carriage, - - - - - - - 37½
Two   "   "   "   - - - - - - - 50
Single Horse with rider, - - - - - - - - 25
Loose Horses, any number less than ten, each, - - - - 5
Ten, or more than ten, for each ten and the fraction over, - - 40
Single Cow, with or without sucking calf, - - - - 5
Loose Cattle, more than one and less than ten, each, - - 4
Ten or more, for each ten and the fraction over, - - - 30
Single Sheep or Hog, - - - - - - - - 5
More than one and less than ten, each, - - - - - 3
Ten or more than ten, for each ten and the fraction over, - - 25
☞ Any animals not enumerated above, at the same rates. ☜
From May 14th to October 14th, inclusive, half the above rates.
Wagons or Carts having wheels with more than 2½ inches tread, the toll to be reduced at the rate of 12½ per cent. for every ½ inch over 2½ inches.
Between the Milpitas road and Alviso, one-eighth the above rates.
Between the Milpitas road and San Jose, three-fourths the above rates.
Between the Milpitas road and Lick's Mill, one-fourth the above rates.
Between the road at Lick's Mill and either Alviso or San Jose, one-half the full rates first above named.
WM. DANIELS, President S. J. & A. T. R. Co.

The Law Regulating Tolls and Toll Gates.

SEC. 29. Each toll-gatherer may detain and prevent from passing through his gate, the person leading or driving animals or carriages subject to toll, until they shall have paid respectively the tolls authorized by law.
SEC. 31. Every toll-gatherer who, at any gate, shall unreasonable hinder or delay any traveler or passenger liable to the payment of toll, or shall demand and receive from any person more than by law he is authorized to collect, shall, for each offence, forfeit the sum of $10 to the person aggrieved.
SEC. 33. Every person who, to avoid the payment of the legal toll, shall, with his team, carriage or horse, turn out of a turnpike road, or plank road, or pass any gate thereon on ground adjacent thereto, and again enter upon such road, shall, for each offence, forfeit the sum of $5 to the corporation injured.—*Wood's Digest.*

Owen & Cottle, Printers, San Jose Mercury.

Poster announcing the toll rates for the turnpike road that ran on The Alameda from San Jose to Alviso (SAN JOSE HISTORICAL MUSEUM)

100-foot frontage of the hotel was a balcony that became known as the Balcony of Presidents. It was from this balcony that Gov. Rutherford B. Hayes and Gen. Ulysses S. Grant (both men became president) and other notables spoke during their stays.

President Benjamin Harrison made little more than a whistle-stop when he came to town; he delivered a little speech at the train station and, after a short drive around town, was off. In 1894 he taught constitutional law at Stanford. One of his students, Herbert Hoover, went on to become president. A lifelong friend of the university, Hoover gave the school his home on San Juan Hill that serves as the "President's House."

John Auzerais married Louise Provost, grandniece of Archbishop Blanchet of Oregon, in St. Joseph's Church in 1855. Louise was twelve years old when, while crossing the Isthmus of Panama, her mother died of fever. Her uncle put her in the care of Notre Dame nuns in San Jose, and she became quite a favorite of theirs. John E. Auzerais, Louise and John's son, married Minnie McLaughlin in the chapel at the home of her parents, Edward and Adelia McLaughlin.

Louise and John were buried at St. Joseph's Church. Dedicated to him is a stained-glass window depicting "St. John, the Baptism of Our Lord." Next to it is "St. Edward the confessor," honoring his brother, commissioned by his friends in the French community.

Agricultural Park

A big boost in entertainment for San Joseans in the sixties was the development of Agricultural Park at The Alameda and Race Street. The Santa Clara County Agricultural Society purchased seventy-six acres of land from Gen. Henry Morris Naglee for $6,000—part of the Rancho Los Coches parcel he had bought from Don Antonio Suñol. The society built the fairgrounds with grandstands to watch the horse racing, a velodrome for bicycle racing, the Pink Pavilion where fancy dress balls took place, buildings for displays, and even a place for circus tents. The crowds cheered when Barney Oldfield broke the world's record speed of sixty miles per hour.

Horse racing was big in this town. Such horses as "Alfarata," "Palo Alto," "Electioneer," and the trotting horse "Goldsmith Maid," who broke the world's trotting record, created wide attention in the racing world. In 1879 ex-President Ulysses S. Grant was in the grandstands to watch Leland Stanford's horse, "Occidental," race.

San Jose pulled out all the stops for President and Mrs. Grant's visit. The couple was greeted with great fanfare

Alum Rock Park in the early 1900s (SAN JOSE MERCURY NEWS)

—all the military organizations marched for them. As the parade approached the courthouse, 500 children in red, white, and blue, each carrying a flag and a bouquet of flowers, sang "America," after which they gave cheers and showered the president with their bouquets. That night the Grants were honored with a banquet at the Auzerais House, where they were staying.

The turn of the century brought a turn in the fate of the Agricultural Park. The state had cut off its appropriation in the eighties, and with agricultural shows losing some of their luster, the property was sold to the Peninsula Land and Development Company to build a fashionable tract of homes called Hanchett Park.

Alum Rock Park

About the same time Agricultural Park arrived on the scene, plans were under way to develop the 600-acre

Alum Rock Park on the east side. The city claimed the land under a liberal interpretation of Spanish law that determined the boundaries of the Pueblo de San José de Guadalupe. The park was first called "City Reservation" and sometimes "Penitencia Reservation." By the early 1880s, because of an enormous rock containing alum that jutted out near the entrance, the name became officially "Alum Rock Park."

One of the natural beauty sites in the state and a native habitat for birds and animals, Penitencia Creek ran through the base of the canyon, sometimes over enormous rocks, and through narrow gorges with 100-foot-tall waterfalls. Its name comes from the custom of the padres at Mission Santa Clara, who used to hear confessions in an old adobe along its banks.

The govenor's board of commissioners appointed Gen. Henry Naglee, Edward McLaughlin, Dr. A. J. Spencer (great-grandfather of Superior Court Judge Marshall

Alum Rock Park campgrounds. These ladies are about "camped out," judging from the sign, "All that's left after five weeks camping."

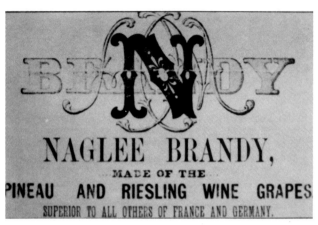

Gen. Henry Naglee made brandy from grapes grown on his Naglee Park estate. (SAN JOSE HISTORICAL MUSEUM)

Hall), Adolph Pfister, D. S. Payne, and B. D. Murphy to superintend the laying out of the park and the construction of a road leading to it. The facilities included campgrounds and a picnic area under spreading oaks on flat ground, a hotel, a plunge filled with sulphur water and roofed with glass, bathhouses, a deer paddock, an aviary, a merry-go-round, and a pavilion where band concerts were given on Sundays. Longtime San Joseans recall happy times there in their youth — riding horseback, hiking to the falls, ferns and wildflowers growing on the walls of the canyon, soda and mineral waters springing out of the rocks.

Alum Rock Avenue (originally called Naglee), an extension of Santa Clara Avenue east of Coyote Creek, paved with red brick to keep horses from slipping on the steeper inclines, was bordered by four rows of trees. On the lower part Andrew Jackson Fowler planted 400 eucalyptus trees from seedlings he had started at his Evergreen nursery, and General Naglee donated the Montery pines that continued past the present San Jose Country Club to the summit. The general's name was given to another street in the Rosegarden section of San Jose.

Localites and residents of neighboring towns came by horse and buggy, by steam train, and later by the more popular electric train, which ran until 1932. Many remember riding on cars similar to the San Francisco trolleys, whose seats faced outwards, pulled behind the train.

Today, the park, which is still popular with hikers and picnickers, is also the home of the Youth Science Institute's Discovery Center (a project developed by Junior League of San Jose, Inc.) which has a live animal room and a library service which lends animals for a week's period to families and schools, giving children a "hands-on" contact with nature. Adults as well as children learn to care for injured animals there.

Naglee Park

After General Naglee sold his Rancho Los Coches acreage to the Agricultural Society's park, he started to develop his 140-acre estate, Naglee Park, that extended from Eleventh Street to Coyote Creek and from Santa Clara Street to Reed Street. He lost his wife after only three years of marriage, and it is believed he threw all his energy into making his estate the showplace of the town. Here he lived like a country squire. A one-and-one-half-mile drive, bordered by trees, led back to his house through magnificent gardens. He planted exotic trees from all over the world, including deodar cedar from the Himalayas, the cedar of Lebanon from Palestine, palms from Mexico, seventeen varieties of acacia, and fifteen of eucalyptus. He had a nutmeg tree, which was one of a kind.

One area he kept for his vineyards (where he grew 150 varieties of grapes), a winery, and a distillery. He produced a potent brandy that became known all over the world. But to the hometown folks it was his military career in the Mexican-American War and the Civil War for which he was most remembered. He graduated at the top of his class from West Point and at the outbreak of the Civil War he was commissioned a brigadier general of the volunteer army. In 1865 he married Antoinette Ringold, daughter of an army officer. Although he had a reputation as a Don Juan and one of his jilted ladies published his love letters, he was deeply affected by the death of Antoinette. After his death, San Jose's major developer, T. S. Montgomery, developed Naglee Park into homesites.

Maj. Samuel Hensley

Montgomery did the same for another military man, Maj. Samuel Hensley. His Southern-style home on North First Street covered four square blocks. Beautifully landscaped, it was surrounded by lawns, fountains, trees, a pond for boating, and extensive pathways. A Kentuckian who became involved in the Mexican War, he went East with military governor Commodore Stockton to testify at the court-martial of Frémont. Besides crossing the continent twice, he managed Captain Sutter's Hock Farm and served as a storekeeper, a navigator on the Sacramento River, and founder and president of the California Steam Navigation Co. Major Hensley's wife, Mary Ellen Crosby, daughter of Elisha Crosby, delegate to the Constitutional Convention in Monterey, and member of the first state senate that met in San Jose, had the honor of carrying to San Francisco on board the *Oregon* the official papers designating California's admission to the Union on September 8, 1850.

In 1990 the San Jose City Council designated the property as Hensley Historical District to encourage restoration of the many Victorian houses still standing.

The Railroad Comes

The most exciting thing to happen to San Jose in the sixties was the completion of the San Francisco & San Jose Railroad. A crowd of 1,000, many of whom had never seen a train, came by foot, horseback, and wagon loads from the surrounding rural areas to cheer the two trains with twenty-nine cars as they chugged into the San Pedro station, decked with flags and evergreen wreaths.

Bands blared, the military gave a thirteen-cannon salute, and Mayor Quinby and Judge Dame gave stir-ring speeches. With the bands leading the way, the military and fire companies, the trains' passengers, carriages, and others on foot paraded the downtown streets. Capping the festivities, everyone returned to the depot for champagne and a free lunch.

This day was the realization of a dream for Judge Davis Divine, who had been promoting a San Francisco & San Jose Railroad since 1851. It had been an uphill battle. First incorporated as the Pacific-Atlantic Railroad, money was raised by conscription and a bond issue floated. With a change of name, the San Francisco & San Jose Railroad became a reality. J. J. Owen, publisher of the *San Jose Mercury*, reported, "The time is not far distant when East shall join the West across the continent and interlock with iron fingers nevermore to be disengaged."

The following year the Southern Pacific was organized. In 1868 with the driving of the golden spike at Promontory, Utah, the transcontinental railroad opened. This proved to be a boon to San Jose's young fruit industry.

The "San Mateo," a diamond-stacked wood burner built in 1863. It later worked the San Jose Railroad yard as SP #5. (SAN JOSE MERCURY NEWS)

By 1876 the Santa Clara Valley was the fruit-shipping capital of the world.

The Courthouse

That grand old 1868 county courthouse on North First Steet opposite St. James Park still stands tall and proud. It survived the 1906 earthquake, and although the Loma Prieta quake in 1989 caused structural damage, plans are, with the help of FEMA funds, to go ahead with the restoration.

The county bought the courthouse property on North First Street from W. H. Hall for $5,000 in gold. This presented a problem because as it turned out the county had no gold. They worked it out by paying $7,535 in currency—the amount of the exchange in greenbacks.

Levi Goodrich, one of the town's outstanding architects, whose credits include Notre Dame College, the University of the Pacific, and San Jose State Normal School, created a Roman-Corinthian design. With its lofty dome (50 feet in diameter and 115 feet high), it was considered the most beautiful building with the purest type of classical architecture in the state. Hopes were high at this point that it might serve to woo the state capital back to San Jose, but that was not to be.

A fire gutted the building in 1931. When it was rebuilt the following year, the dome and the pillars were not replaced, but a third story was added.

It was the scene of many famous trials: the notorious

Santa Clara County Courthouse, completed in 1868. Many famous trials have taken place here, including that of bandit Tiburcio Vásquez. (SAN JOSE MERCURY NEWS)

Robin Hood bandit, Tiburcio Vásquez, was convicted in a trial presided over by Judge David Belden and hung outside the jail. Probably the most notorious trials in the century were the Lamson and Talle trials. Both men were convicted of murdering their wives. Stanford professor David Lamson was convicted for the "bathtub murder" of his wife at their Stanford University home; Tom Talle, an alcoholic whose wife was found shot in the back beside the swimming pool of their Saratoga home, was also found guilty of murder.

CHAPTER SIXTEEN

Early Banking Business

Banks were a long time coming to San Jose. The first bank of any kind was in the 1840s in Don Antonio Suñol's store. What little currency there was in those days he could keep for his customers in a tin box. When gold started coming in during the gold rush period, Josiah Belden guarded it in his safe for his customers. Soon after, the Auzerais brothers and Adolph Pfister followed suit in their merchandise stores. In Clyde Arbuckle's *History of San Jose* he tells of the unique form of check writing. If John Doe owed John Smith five dollars, he would simply write on a piece of paper: "J. Belden, please pay to the bearer, John Smith, five dollars in gold dust and oblige. Signed, John Doe." Belden would handle the transaction and then take a small pinch of dust for his fee. In the case of the Californios, Belden wrote, "The Spanish people coming in from the mines were anxious to trade. Money was a rather new thing to them and having come easy and quickly, they were just as ready to spend it and having a fancy for all kinds of dry goods and dress goods, they spent it quite freely." This, of course, proved profitable to Belden.

It wasn't until 1866 that San Jose had a formal bank. Dr. William J. Knox and his brother-in-law, Thomas Ellard Beans, opened the Knox & Beans Bank on their Knox Block at the corner of First and Santa Clara streets. Knox, who was more interested in medicine and politics, soon dropped out, letting Beans carry on, which he did effectively. In 1868 Knox & Beans incorporated as the Bank of San Jose.

The following year a Pennsylvanian, Edward McLaughlin, and C. T. Ryland, a Missouri lawyer, combined forces to build the Safe Deposit Block on First Street at Santa Clara. In the three-story, ornate structure they opened McLaughlin & Ryland's Bank. Within a few years it became the Commercial and Savings Bank with Ryland president, McLaughlin manager, and Martin Bernard Murphy among the stockholders. After McLaughlin sold his share, Bernard Murphy succeeded

Ryland as president and McLaughlin opened the Safe Deposit Bank in the Safe Deposit Block with Mariano Malarin, member of a prominent old Spanish family, as president, and his son-in-law, John E. Auzerais, as cashier.

In 1874 the Farmer's National Gold Bank, which became The First National Bank of San Jose, was founded to deal with the disparity between gold and silver coin, with John W. Hinds its president. W. S. Tisdale, vice-president, succeeded him, followed by James A. Clayton in 1894. But it was the latter's son, Willis S. Clayton, Sr., who broke all records, serving as president from 1907 to 1940. The Clayton name is even more widely known in San Jose for the real estate business James A. Clayton

Bank of San Jose at the corner of First and Santa Clara streets. It was founded in 1866 by Dr. William J. Knox and Ellard Beans and incorporated two years later as the Bank of San Jose.

& Co., founded in 1867 and carried on for well over a century by his descendants.

A. P. Giannini

While banking was still in its infancy in 1870, Amadeo Pietro Giannini, who was destined to revolutionize the world of banking and become San Jose's most famous native son, was born in the Swiss Hotel on North Market Street just 100 yards from where his first branch bank would be. His parents had come from Northern Italy to New York. His father, Luigi, put his mother, Virginia, on a ship headed for California around the Horn before he took the train across the country and found a job as manager of the Swiss Hotel. A. P., as he was to become known worldwide, and his brothers, Atilio and George, were baptized by Father Bixio in the new St. Joseph's Church completed the year before.

In a few years Luigi Giannini gave up management of the Swiss Hotel to farm at Alviso. They were there only a short time when he was shot by one of his workers in a dispute over a dollar or two in pay. Virginia continued to work the farm. One day, on a trip to market to sell her fruit, she met and soon married Lorenzo Scatena, a fruit broker. A granddaughter of A. P.'s, Virginia Hammerness of San Jose, believes the family moved to San Jose and lived for a time in the Peralta Adobe before moving to San Francisco. Still to be seen on the walls of the adobe are stencils of L. Scatena and Co. The family next moved to San Francisco, where Scatena continued in the fruit brokerage business with an able assistant in the ambitious young teenager, Amadeo, who often went to San Jose on buying trips.

A. P. married Clorinda Cuneo, whose father had done well (he found an enormous gold nugget in the Sierras) and was one of the founders of the Columbus Savings, a small, conservative bank. At his death, A. P. took over his place on the board. But Columbus did business mainly with the rich, which was not A. P.'s cup of tea.

He soon went out on his own to found the Bank of Italy. Instead of just being big city banks, he believed

Commercial and Savings Bank, founded by Edward McLaughlin and C. T. Ryland in the Safe Deposit Block on First Street at Santa Clara.

90

A. P. Giannini, San Jose's most famous native son and the founder of the Bank of Italy, was baptized in St. Joseph's in 1870. His first branch bank was in San Jose. (COURTESY EARL PARISI)

that the banks should go to the people. His first opportunity to found a branch bank came in 1909 when he took over the ailing Commercial and Savings Bank. It was against the law for a bank to buy another's stock outright, so James Baciagalupi, attorney for the bank and later its president, suggested that a group including Scatena, Atilio, and Nicholas Pellerano, a San Jose pharmacist, buy the stock and in turn sell it to Giannini. After the deal went through, Scatena and Dr. Atilio

Giannini, who was more interested in banking than practicing medicine, managed the San Jose branch.

A. P.'s brother George was in the conversion business. His hobby was race horses. He had a state champion named "George Perry" who he raced at Golden Gate fields.

Always a man of vision, after hearing the engineer's story of building Golden Gate Bridge, A. P. agreed to help finance it. A plaque on the bridge is dedicated to him. A strong believer in education, he donated $1,500,000 to U.C. Berkeley for the Giannini Foundation for Agricultural Economics, and Giannini Hall is named for him. A good judge of people, he wouldn't hesitate to loan without colateral. After the 1906 earthquake he immediately set up business on the wharf (he placed planks over barrels) to make loans and played an important part in the rebuilding of San Francisco.

A good friend of the moving picture industry, he could forsee its future and helped with financing in the early days. He recognized the genius of Walt Disney and when Disney was having problems raising money for *Snow White*, Giannini came through.

His son, Mario, apparently was cut out of the same cloth. He became president of Bank of America, president of Transamerica, and took over Occidental Life Insurance Co. when it was much smaller and built it up. His daughter, Virginia Hammerness, remembers how the big men of the motion picture businesses—the Skouras brothers, Samuel Goldwyn, and wartime ship builder Henry Kaiser—used to come to see her father and to pick his brains.

A. P. and Clorinda made their home in San Mateo. A family friend, Mike Paioni, who became vice-president and first manager of the A. P. Giannini branch in San Mateo, not only was born in San Jose but in a hotel just

A. P. Giannini was born in the Swiss Hotel on Market Street.

91

two blocks from A. P.'s birthplace. A. P.'s daughter, Claire Giannini Hoffman, who keeps her interest in Bank of America, serves on its board and lives in the Giannini family home in San Mateo.

A. P. weathered a few storms along the way. Around 1920 a stockholder named Elisha Walker tried to take over the Bank of Italy. He sent proxies to the other stockholders with an invitation to join him. Although Walker had a head start, Giannini put up a good fight. In his inimitable manner, he talked in person to as many stockholders as possible. He enlisted the then assistant manager of the Bank of Italy's San Jose branch, John Boccardo, who spoke several dialects of Italian, to accompany him to the San Joaquin Valley so he could talk one-to-one with the farmers, who were his friends. San Jose attorney James F. Boccardo, who was nine years old at the time, remembers going with the two men in his father's 1917 Buick.

C. T. Ryland

Caius Tacitus Ryland's arrival in San Jose in 1849 was less than auspicious, but makes for a good story. After a fling in the gold fields, he started out to walk from San Francisco to San Jose. When he reached Sunnyvale, Ryland found so many cattle running wild he decided he needed a horse. According to W. T. Rambo in his *History of the Sainte Claire Club*, he stopped at the rancho of Segundino Robles, where, even though Ryland was a complete stranger, Robles, with typical California hospitality, loaned him one of his saddle horses. When Ryland asked him what he was to do with the horse when he reached San Jose, the colorful Californio, with a smile and a wave of the hand, said, "Oh, just turn him loose. He knows the way and everybody knows he's mine. Turn his head toward home, give him a slap on the rump, and he'll do the rest."

C. T. Ryland became one of the most prominent men in town. He practiced law, cofounded the McLaughlin & Ryland Bank, was reelected to the city council in 1861 (he had resigned during Mayor Thomas Fallon's term), and was elected speaker of the state assembly in 1868. Ryland was generous in his support of St. Joseph's Church and of Santa Clara College, where the students called him "Uncle C. T."

Ryland married Letitia Burnett, daughter of Governor Burnett. The handsome brownstone building he built on South First Street and named for her is now a historical monument. After his death his family donated Ryland Park, the family homesite on the west

Lawyer and banker C. T. Ryland was a generous contributor to St. Joseph's. (CLYDE ARBUCKLE COLLECTION)

side of North First Street, to the city. His son, John W. Ryland, a Santa Clara College and Hastings Law School graduate, was the first native San Josean to be appointed the city's postmaster, in 1894 by President Grover Cleveland. He was also president of the San Jose Water Works.

Edward T. McLaughlin

A close friend of C. T. Ryland's, partner in many business ventures, and, like Ryland, a strong supporter of St. Joseph's, Edward T. McLaughlin came to California from Philadelphia by way of New Orleans, where he worked on the docks as a youth of eighteen years. McLaughlin and his wife, Adelia Hickman, a gentle, unassuming southern lady from Kentucky (a kin of Daniel Boone's) went first to Grass Valley. Although he bought the North Star Mine on the steps of the courthouse, he made his fortune with the Union Hardware and Metal Co.

The McLaughlins were low-key, their name seldom appeared on the society pages and their interests focused on St. Joseph's Church and Notre Dame College. While living in Grass Valley they converted to Catholicism. According to their great-granddaughter Winifred Brady Noble of San Francisco, a nursemaid took the children

Edward McLaughlin, businessman and St. Joseph's benefactor, and his wife, Adelia (ARCHIVES CALIFORNIA PROVINCE + SOCIETY OF JESUS)

to mass with her. Adelia started going with them and joined the church. McLaughlin was a holdout. When he finally did go, he stood in the back of the church and, as an act of defiance, kept his hat on. In time he became interested. When he did join the church, he was a devout, involved member.

Winifred Noble told another story about Edward McLaughlin. His daughter Winifred was taken ill with cholera. In desperation he wrote to the Jesuits at the Novitiate in Los Gatos, asking them to pray for her and enclosed a check. Meanwhile, crossing in the mail was a letter from the priests, who were in a financial crisis, asking for help.

The McLaughlins' home at Seventh and Reed streets, covering a city block, had an elegantly decorated chapel where their daughter Minnie was married to John E. Auzerais, son of Louise and John. The young couple became active in the community and in St. Joseph's Church. Veryl Christmas Gassett, a friend of Adelia McLaughlin's, remembers the McLaughlin house well. It was built by her grandfather Thomas Hildreth, a cattleman who had ranches in the valley and a home in San Francisco. He built the San Jose house because he didn't consider San Francisco a good place to raise a family.

Adelia married William Leet. They hired Willis Polk to design their home on The Alameda, and John McLaren, who designed Golden Gate Park, to do the gardens. It was the showplace of San Jose, with a swimming pool (the first in town), a private chapel, a chauffeur, and a butler. The house was taken down in the 1960s to make way for the Garden Alameda complex.

Howard Cunningham, a nephew of Alelia Leet's, who lives in Southern California, remembers the good life at this house. He lived there when he was student at Santa Clara University. His son, Howard, an airline pilot, who lives in San Juan Capistrano, is putting together the family history.

Santa Clara Street looking west from First Street. On the left can be seen the Auzerais House. (SAN JOSE MERCURY NEWS)

CHAPTER SEVENTEEN

Early Churches

By the sixties the Protestant denominations were well represented with churches in San Jose. Trinity Episcopal Church, which became Trinity Cathedral in 1989, is San Jose's oldest church building still in use. Constructed of native redwood in 1863, it stands at the corner of Second and St. John streets, on what had been part of a corral on Maj. Samuel Hensley's property. Its stained-glass windows were brought around the Horn from New York. The organ, first-of-kind in the West, had two manuals and twenty-four stops. Built in Boston, it was carried across the Isthmus of Panama by mule back. By a sad twist of fate, the pastor, Rev. Sylvester Etheridge, who had worked so hard to get the church built, was too ill to participate in the first service in the church on Advent Sunday, 1863. At his death, the following year, complying with his wishes, he was buried under the chancel of the church. Bishop Kip came to San Jose to consecrate Trinity Church in July of 1867. As the church grew, it was enlarged to its present graceful form.

In 1989 Bishop Shannon Mallory selected Trinity Church to be San Jose's Episcopal cathedral—this status to continue until the next bishop takes office, at which time it will be his prerogative as to whether Trinity will continue as the seat of the diocese. At the dedication ceremony Rev. Eugene Doyle, representing Bishop DuMaine, read the Epistle and Temple Emanu-El's senior rabbi, Jonathan V. Plaut, read the Psalms.

The first Protestant service was held at Mission Santa Clara during the Battle of Santa Clara by Rev. Adna Hecox for the child of Joseph Aram who had died. In 1849 three churches were founded: the First Presbyterian Church, organized by eight persons at the home of James Mathers; the Baptists with eight members organized by O. W. Wheeler; and the Methodists, who met at the home of Mrs. Samuel Young with eleven members. Their pastor, William Taylor, who later became a bishop, had just returned from scattering seeds of eucalyptus trees

he had obtained in Australia along the coast. When the *juzgado* was taken down in 1853 the Presbyterians built a frame church mostly of wood from Henry Ward Beecher's old Plymouth Church that had been brought around the Horn.

Temple Emanu-El

Temple Emanu-El owes its origins to the Bicker Cholim Society, whose name, translated from the Hebrew, means "visiting the sick." It was organized by Jacob Rich and Jacob Levy in 1861 with ten men, the required number under the Law of Moses. Their intention was to establish a house of worship, care for the Jewish sick and needy, and provide hallowed ground for the dead. Oak Hill

Trinity Episcopal Cathedral, built in 1863, is the oldest church still standing in San Jose. (SAN JOSE HISTORICAL MUSEUM)

Cemetery had already set aside plots of ground for the Protestants, Catholics, and Jews.

At first, they held services in the city hall on Market Street, then in the Masonic Hall. In 1869 they built their first synagogue, a frame structure at the corner of Third and San Jose streets. Over the entrance door were the words "My House Shall Be A House Of Prayer For All People."

Temple Bicker Cholim survived earthquakes, but finally succumbed to a fire in 1941. A hero in that fire was a refugee from Hitler's Germany, Kurt Opper, winemaster at Paul Masson Winery, who entered the burning building and rescued the Torah. During the forties the congregation held services in churches of other denominations and for holy days in the civic auditorium. In 1948 the church purchased a building site on University Avenue at Myrtle Street, where they built a beautiful temple under the guidance of Rabbi Iser Freund which became known as Temple Emanu-El. With the advent of Pope John XXIII and Vatican II, Catholics were no longer forbidden to attend services in churches of other denominations, and one of the Jesuit priests at Alma College called Rabbi Gitin and asked if they could attend Yom Kippur service. Rabbi Gitin welcomed them and said that twenty or twenty-five arrived in their dark suits and clerical collars and sat in the front row. They included two student priests, Father Daniel Germann, now at Santa Clara University, and Father Thomas Deasy, who is in the Jesuit Community, Hawaii.

During the 1950s Rabbi Joseph Gitin, who has been Rabbi Emeritus of Temple Emanu-El since 1976, Rev. Frank Strayer of Calvary Methodist Church, and St. Joseph's pastor, Rev. Harold Ring, S.J., joined together in the spirit of ecumenism (before Vatican II) to foster brotherhood. According to Rabbi Gitin, "We called ourselves 'The Unholy Trio.' It was really something. We spoke to over 200 different groups." After the deaths of

Bicker Cholim Synagogue was built in 1869 at the corner of Third and San Antonio streets. After a major fire, it was rebuilt on University Avenue with a new name, Temple Emanu-El.

Reverends Strayer and Ring, Rev. Phil Barrett and Father Walter Schmidt of Santa Clara University took their places. Both men are now deceased. Rabbi Gitin is the sole survivor.

Rabbi Gitin told a story of Father Ring visiting the temple. He said that he suggested to the priest that he wait in his study until the time for him to make an appearance. Father Ring would have none of it. "But Harold," protested the rabbi, "it's against your church's rules."

Father Ring said, "So what? The worst they'll do is banish me to Milpitas" (an old vaudeville joke, referring to when Milpitas, now a thriving community, was considered the sticks). Father Ring attended the service, read the prayers, and wasn't sent anywhere.

The third St. Joseph's Church, designed by Theodore Lenzen in 1869, was destroyed by fire in 1875. (ARCHIVES CALIFORNIA PROVINCE + SOCIETY OF JESUS)

CHAPTER EIGHTEEN

A New St. Joseph's

On October 4, 1868, an earthquake lasting forty-two seconds shook not only San Jose but the whole state and continued with smaller tremors until November 4. Following the severe quake of two years before, this was the coup de grace for the second St. Joseph's Church. It was a clear sign to the fathers that St. Joseph's must have a new church. They wanted it to be larger to accommodate the growing community, and to be built on the same site as the two previous adobe St. Joseph's churches, at the corner of Market and San Fernando streets. Father Aloysius Masnata retained Theodore Lenzen, a native of Prussia and the reigning architect from the 1860s to the turn of the century, whose work included city hall, Auzerais House, and the Vendome Hotel.

In December of that same year Archbishop Alemany presided at the laying of the cornerstone, and an American Indian Jesuit, Father James Chrysostom Bouchard, was the speaker for an enthusiastic crowd of San Joseans. The next day the *San Jose Argus* wrote, "While I admit that a dollar is a high price to pay for a lecture in these times, yet we felt as we left the house [St. Joseph's] that we had value received for the investment. We learned that a thousand tickets were sold."

Lenzen, to avoid the fate of the adobe churches, designed a building of wood with brick trim, featuring square twin towers and large enough to seat 500 people. His brother Jacob, a member of St. Joseph's choir, was the contractor, and his brother Mike did the painting and decorating. The parishioners were especially proud of the church's organ, which was built especially for the church, and the paintings by European artists.

For the dedication on December 16, 1869, the Vicar General, Rev. James Croke, came from San Francisco in place of Archbishop Alemany, who was in Rome. The sermon was delivered by Father Bouchard.

The new church cost over $39,000, so it is understandable the parishioners would have problems raising funds for a bell to hang in the belfry in the left tower of the church. The bell they had in mind was to cost $1,500. Father Bouchard gave a lecture that raised $450, but they were still short more than $1,000. St. Joseph's ever-generous Edward McLaughlin and C.T. Ryland solved the problem by donating $1,000 each, stipulating that the money left over would go for vestments.

The bell, four feet in diameter and weighing 3,115 pounds, was cast by the Meneely Bell Co. of Troy, New York, of silver, ingot copper, and tin. The installation in 1871 was such an important occasion that the whole town turned out. It was especially welcomed by townspeople who depended upon the ringing of the bell to tell time.

The American Indian Jesuit

Father James Chrysostom Bouchard was the first American Indian to be ordained as a Catholic priest. Born in a wigwam, the son of a Delaware Indian chief and a French mother, he was trained to be proficient with tomahawk as well as bow and arrow. In a war against the Sioux tribe, Watomika (his Indian name, meaning "Swift Foot") saw his father, Kristalwa, shot by a bow and arrow. Another time, he saw his uncle Whapagong killed in a hand-to-hand conflict with a Sioux.

His mother had come as an infant with her parents from France to Texas. After a raid on the Comanche Indians by the Spaniards, the tribe took revenge by killing Mary Elizabeth Bouchard's parents, burning them at the stake. The chief and his squaw took the little girl and raised her with love as their own child, naming her Manotawan (White Antelope). When she was thirteen years old, she took a trip with her foster parents to visit the Delaware Indians; Kristalwa, the son of the Delaware chief, became enamored with the beautiful young girl and demanded her in marriage. She stayed on with the family, and at the age of fifteen, they were married.

Father James Chrysostom Bouchard. The Delaware Indian Jesuit captivated audiences with his oratory. (ARCHIVES CALIFORNIA PROVINCE + SOCIETY OF JESUS)

A Protestant missionary visited the tribe and asked Watomika and two other young braves to accompany him to Marietta College, in Ohio, to be educated as Presbyterians. Although the other boys left, Watomika, religiously inclined, persevered in his studies and became ordained as a Presbyterian minister, even though he had some doubts about the doctrines of Calvin. He was sent to St. Louis, where, while walking down the street, he saw some children following a priest into a church. He went inside and listened to their catechism lesson. Impressed, he talked to the priest afterwards, pursued further information on Catholicism, and subsequently entered a Jesuit seminary to study for the priesthood.

An impressive figure in the pulpit in his black robes and long flowing white beard, Father James Chrysostom Bouchard captivated the congregations with his silvery voice and persuasive eloquence. His middle name, Chrysostom, appropriately enough, was derived from a fifth-century archbishop in Constantinople who was called "Golden Mouth" because of the eloquence of his oratory. The beard, however, was a point of conflict between him and Archbishop Alemany. Father Bouchard insisted he needed it to keep his chest warm. His Jesuit provincial took the matter to Rome, and the Vatican sided with the priest.

The beloved evangelist and darling of the mining camps preached in the Mother Lode and the Comstock Lode for thirty years, lecturing for the benefit of abandoned orphans, churches heavily in debt, convents, and schools.

Shortly before his death, he received a letter from his brother, Chiwendotah (Black Wolf), which he showed to Father Gleason at St. Ignatius. It was addressed simply to "Watomika, 2014 Hayes St., S.F." He also received a letter from General Beauregard of the Confederate Army, explaining that they were distantly related on his mother's side. Father Bouchard passed away in December of 1890 and is buried in Santa Clara Mission Cemetery.

CHAPTER NINETEEN

The Seventies

San Jose kept abreast of the times as the seventies got underway. Business began to extend over to Second Street, orchards to replace grainfields; the State Normal School moved to San Jose; the town got its first library. The telephone arrived, even though few people took it seriously; and Dr. James Madison Dawson canned the first fruit in a shed in the backyard of his home, giving birth to the canning industry. St. Joseph's suffered a disastrous fire but the grand Bryan Clinch–designed church rose from its ashes.

The Gold Standard

Businessmen, faced with the problem of gold versus silver, organized the Board of Trade and elected George McKee president. They succeeded in getting their business transactions placed on the gold basis. The board ran into problems, disbanded, and regrouped in 1888, with D. B. Moody as president. One of their goals, hard though it is to believe, was to encourage population growth. Their accomplishments included the promotion of the Vendome Hotel. The board went on to greater glory when it became the Chamber of Commerce in 1890.

The Fruit Industry

The first commercial fruit was sold to prospectors en route to the gold fields by enterprising Americans who helped themselves to the Mission Santa Clara orchard's apples, peaches, and pears.

Louis Pellier didn't have much success selling his petit d'Agen prune in his City Garden nursery. It wasn't until the 1870s, after J. Q. A. Ballou grafted it to the domestic plum, that his French prune gained attention. But it was up to John Rock, who recognized its superb drying

qualities, to market it to great success. Thus the Santa Clara Valley became the largest prune-producing area in the world. Meanwhile, although large quantities of fruit were being shipped East after the opening of the transcontinental railroad, orchardists were producing more pears, peaches, apricots, and plums than could be absorbed. It was the ingenuity of a medical doctor, James M. Dawson, that solved that problem in 1870. In doing so, he gave birth to an industry that made San Jose the fruit-canning capital of the world.

Dr. James Dawson, father of the fruit-canning industry.

The Valley of Heart's Delight by E. Standish.

Dawson and his wife set up a canning operation in a woodshed in back of their home at Polhemus and The Alameda, cooking the fruit in a large boiler on a kitchen stove. After Dawson's death, in 1885, his wife and son carried on, and by 1887 they were producing 140,000 cases of canned fruit a year. J. M. Dawson & Co. underwent several name changes and owners. In 1916 it was one of four associations that merged to form the California Fruit Packing Corporation, now known as the Del Monte Corporation.

The Telephone

A year after Alexander Graham Bell's first recognized telephone coversation in 1876, the newly incorporated Bell Telephone Corporation shipped two of its telephones to a man in San Jose named Charles Hensley. It was two years before the town got its first telephone exchange—the third in the state—in the Music Hall Building on North First Street. The new gadget was slow to catch

on with San Joseans. At first there were five subscribers. Even after the Bell Telephone Company came in 1879 and the Sunset Telephone was organized the following years, the town had only 311 subscribers by 1892. Needless to say, the "number, please" girls were not overworked.

The Public Library

San Jose's first library of sorts was started in the State House in 1850. Books, which were in short supply, were provided by volunteers, including Governor Burnett, John Frémont, and William Van Voorhies. Although there had been talk of starting a library in 1856, San Jose's first public library, such as it was, came about ten years later, when E. J. Wilcox and others offered a collection of volumes in the new Young Men's Christian Association reading room on South First Street. The YMCA ran into financial problems, and when it disbanded in 1872, the newly formed San Jose Library

Once a familiar scene in Santa Clara Valley: trays of prunes curing in the sun (SAN JOSE HISTORICAL MUSEUM)

Association purchased the books for a library and reading room in the Knox Block at First and Santa Clara streets. In 1880 a municipal library was established. In 1937 they moved into the old sandstone post office building at Market and San Fernando streets, where they stayed until 1970, when they moved into the multimillion-dollar building on West San Carlos Street. It was renamed the Martin Luther King, Jr., Library in 1990. Since that time the post office building has been the home of the San Jose Museum of Art.

San Jose State University

San Jose State University, founded by George Washington Minns, a Harvard College graduate, had its beginnings in San Francisco in 1857 as Minns' Evening Normal School. On the recommendation of Superintendent of Schools O. P. Fitzgerald, Gov. Henry H. Haight and William Thomas Lucky visited San Jose, one of the locations under consideration. They indicated their preference for Washington Square bounded by San Fernando, San Carlos, Fourth and Seventh streets. In the legislature, Assemblyman B. D. Murphy, according to H. S. Foote in his *Pen Pictures From the Garden of the World*, worked tirelessly to get appropriations and passage of a bill designating San Jose as the site.

Even though the school building was not ready and classes had to be held elsewhere when the Normal School moved to San Jose in 1870, two years later the first graduating class received their diplomas. Among the seventeen graduates was Edwin Markham, who gained fame as a poet; "The Man With a Hoe" was his most

San Jose State University, showing its famous vine-covered Town Hall (SAN JOSE MERCURY NEWS)

famous piece. The school building burned in 1880 and again there was a concerted effort on the part of some of the legislators to move it. Although not a member of the legislature at this time, B. D. Murphy hied himself off to Sacramento and won the fight to keep State Normal in San Jose.

The 1906 earthquake leveled the school buildings, and in 1909 the cornerstone was dedicated for the Tower, the ivy-covered building that today is the hallmark of the university. As San Jose State Teachers College in 1923, it gave its first bachelor of arts degrees. In 1972 it became

B. D. Murphy (standing) and family: His wife, Annie, is holding their son, James (far left). Their daughter Elizabeth (far right) later married Howard Derby.

San Jose State University. In the fall semester, 1989, including its eight graduate schools, the university's enrollment was 29,947. Master's degrees are given in sixty-one fields.

Bernard D. Murphy

Bernard Murphy, who played an important part in getting San Jose Normal School to San Jose, was the son of Martin Murphy, Jr. He came to California in 1844 as a boy before the discovery of gold. According to his obituary in 1911, "His life joined together the romance before the Gringos came . . . his boyhood's memories were full of bailes and fiestas, the click of the castanets and the dancing of dark, inviting eyes." The family first lived along the Cosumnes River eighteen miles from Sutter's Fort and traded with the rancheros, trappers, and Indians. After a few years Martin and Mary Murphy moved to the Santa Clara Valley so their children could get an education. Barney grew up on Rancho Pastoria de las Borregas in the spacious family home that had been precut and shipped around the Horn.

After his graduation from Santa Clara College and

Law School, he practiced law for a time with D. M. Delmas as a partner, but he soon turned his attention to banking and politics. In addition to serving as state senator, he was elected mayor for several terms. He donated his salary to the public library.

Besides his accomplishment in bringing the state college to San Jose, Murphy also served on the board of trustees of Alum Rock Park and is remembered for his part in getting the Lick Observatory built on Mount Hamilton. As a trustee, Murphy was able to persuade Lick to donate $700,000 for the observatory—and to convince him that Mount Hamilton would be the perfect site. When Lick objected that there was no road to the summit, Murphy, accompanied by Judge Belden, went before the board of supervisors and succeeded in making a deal for one.

His generosities were legend; he always had his pockets filled with coins for the depressed who met him on the street. His downfall was as president of the Commercial and Savings Bank, which ran into financial problems because it had too many outstanding loans to family and friends. After selling his personal properties, including the ranches in San Luis Obispo and Santa Barbara counties, he paid off all the bank's debts, leaving him

The St. James Hotel

a poor man but with a wealth of friends. The bank was acquired by A. P. Giannini for the first branch of the Bank of Italy, which would become known worldwide as the Bank of America.

A story is told at the Sainte Claire Club, where he was staying on the night of the earthquake of 1906, that as members scrambled for shelter in the early morning hours, he broke the tension by calling out to them, "Ride 'er out boys! Ride 'er out!" A member of St. Joseph's Church, he and his wife, Annie, always sat in the front pew on the left side of the church.

Patrick Murphy

Bernard Murphy had a brother named Patrick, who also had the Irish propensity for politics and was elected three times to the state senate. He had ranches in San Luis Obispo, Ventura, and Santa Barbara counties. He is said to have lost his share of the Santa Margarita Ranch with the turn of a card. This episode, according to the Murphy family, has been mistakenly credited to his brother, Barney.

A bon vivant, Don Patricio, as he was called, lived lavishly. The late John Burnett, a Murphy cousin and a great-grandson of Gov. Peter Burnett's, used to tell a story he heard from his father. "I was a kid and I didn't believe it then, but later I heard it verified.

"It seems that Pat, a brigadier general in the National Guard, by appointment by Governor Irwin, went back to New York in the middle 1870s, where he attended a banquet. Among the guests was General McDowell, of the Union Army, who was said to have been somewhat of a stuffed shirt. When somebody introduced the two men, 'General McDowell, this is General Murphy,' McDowell immediately asked, 'What division did you

command in the Civil War, General?' Murphy is said to have replied, 'General, I've made many a bull run, but I never ran at Bull Run.'"

When Pat Murphy died, his funeral services at St. Joseph's were attended by an overflow crowd. "My father was asked to be a pallbearer," Burnett said. "Those were the days of eulogies at funerals. It was a solemn High Mass with several priests on the altar. Father Kenna was the orator. 'Pat Murphy,' he said, 'was a man with a heart so filled with generosity that he loved all people and all people loved him. He loved so many that every child between St. Louis and San Jose called him "father."'"

Bronze plaque of B. D. Murphy in the Sainte Claire Club.

103

Market Street. Louis Normandin wrote on the back of this picture, "Y. Bernal, father of S. F. Bernal, driving white horse and our carriage in San Jose." (COURTESY ROBERT BERNAL)

With that everyone broke out laughing. The story made all the papers."

With his extravagent life-style, Murphy dissipated his fortune and died penniless. Years later a nephew found among his effects a savings certificate and book from the Hibernia Bank that was valued at the time of his death at $35,000. Apparently it was an inheritance of his wife's that he had forgotten about.

CHAPTER TWENTY

St. Joseph's in the Seventies

All was well with St. Joseph's active parish as the seventies got under way. Their fine new church, designed by Lenzen, had been completed in 1869, and a new pastor, Father Nicholas Congiato, a native of Sardinia, had arrived. The assignment was intended to be a change of pace for the priest, who had spent ten or more years as Superior of the Missions of California and Oregon, where the Indians were in constant conflict with white settlers. This position required traveling by horseback and ship several months of the year. In California he promoted the growth of St. Ignatius College (now the University of San Francisco) and served as its president. His health suffered, and he apparently was sent to St. Joseph's for rest and recreation. That was not the nature of Father Congiato.

One of his first orders of business was the organizing of the St. Joseph's Benevolent Society for the mutual benefit of the members, the help of the poor, and corporal works of mercy. Banker and financier Edward McLaughlin was appointed president, William O'Donnell (proprietor of O'Donnell's Gardens), vice-president, and Thomas Oakes, secretary. Members included C. T. Ryland, Alexander Yoell, John Devine, J. J. Kell, John Colohan (county recorder), Angel Quevedo (descendant of first settler Valerio Mesa), and ranchers Patrick Martin, John Bulger, and William Quinn (a board member of the Santa Clara County Agricultural Society). Two years later Father Congiato started the Confraternity of the Sacred Heart of Jesus. Judge David Belden, Patrick Naglee, and Thomas Kell were listed among the male members. Louise Lefranc (who became Mrs. Paul Masson), María Jesús Suñol de Saisset, Nellie (Mrs. Charles) White, and Angela and Maggie Kell were listed as members in 1886, and Josephine (Mrs. Peter) Dunne in 1888.

The Coyote Hunt

St. Joseph's parishioners were in for a surprise one Christmas morning in the seventies. As they were coming out of the church from eleven o'clock mass, into the crowd came yipping hounds and galloping horses followed by carriages full of women dressed in their Sunday best. It had all started at Isaac Branham's place, according to Patricia Loomis in her book *Signposts II*. A group of Ike Branham's friends who regularly fox hunted together decided to include their wives in the Christmas hunt. They gathered in a field on Monterey Road about where Oak Hill Cemetery is located. As no fox was available on that day, a coyote was substituted

Father Nicholas Congiato, a native of Sardinia, helped to rebuild St. Joseph's after the fire of 1875. (ARCHIVES CALIFORNIA SOCIETY + PROVINCE OF JESUS)

The Bryan Clinch–designed St. Joseph's of 1877, showing the portico and towers added later

for the scent. Things went awry when the lead horse pulling the coyote scent, apparently on a whim, headed for town and down Market Street followed by the hounds, the hunters on horseback, and the wives in carriages. The incident provided food for conversation for some time to come.

A New Parish

A surprise of a different sort jolted St. Joseph's when, like a bolt out of the blue, came a letter to Father Congiato from Archbishop Alemany explaining that a new parish was to be formed in San Jose, that the boundary line would be Fourth Street, and that the name would be St. Patrick's. Needless to say, this did not sit well with the pastor, who had an enormous debt on his hands. Some of his staunchest parishioners would be within the limits of the new parish; besides that, he commented, the new parish was getting the high, dry part of town and to St. Joseph's remained "the low floodable part of San Jose."

After St. Joseph's survived the arrival of the new parish, twenty years passed before another national church was built. Bishop Riordan granted the request of German residents, who were growing in number, to have their own national church, named St. Mary's; it was located on South Third Street on property donated by Irishman Myles O'Connor, whose wife, Amanda, was German. Other national churches followed. The Italians built their Holy Family Church, a miniature St. Peter's, on the corner of San Fernando and River streets. In 1969, when the property was confiscated for the Guadalupe Parkway, they moved to a garage on Pearl Avenue until a new church could be built on that site. The Portuguese, who farmed on the east side, wanted a church where they could worship in their own language. They first built a small structure, known as the I.E.S. Hall. It was followed, in 1916, by the handsome, twin-towered, European-in-feeling Five Wounds Church on Alum Rock Avenue. It is still a favorite of camera buffs. By 1920 two more parishes had been added: St. Martin of Tours and St. Leo's.

106

The Empire Fire Department with San Jose's first horse-drawn fire engines. (LEONARD McKAY COLLECTION)

The Fire of '75

In the meantime, just when everything seemed to be going well for St. Joseph's, these devoted, loyal people, who so loved their church, saw it go up in flames only five years after its completion. Ironically, it had been built of wood to avoid the susceptibility to earthquakes that plagued the previous adobe churches. The disastrous fire had been started by some small boys smoking in a nearby livery stable. Fanned by a north wind, the flames soon reached St. Joseph's, consuming the frame structure, so that only the two towers remained.

The timing of the fire was unfortunate. The San Jose Fire Department (previously pulled by manpower) had just bought new equipment and switched to horses. For economic reasons the horses were at Coyote Creek hauling gravel. The firemen made a desperate effort to get their equipment to the scene by foot, but it fell to one Patrick McGuire, a drayman, to become St. Joseph's hero. When he learned of the fire, he raced in his wagon to the site, picking up fellow members of the Ancient Order of Hibernians along the way. Pat was the first man to enter the burning building. He emerged carrying the statue of Saint Patrick. Under Pat's expert direction (moving was his trade), his crew saved the pulpit and the altar and rescued the treasured Meneely bell, which is back in place in the cathedral. The statue of Saint Patrick was a gift of Catherine Fitzpatrick in memory of her husband, Patrick. She also honored him with a stained-glass window and gave the Saint Catherine of Sienna window.

Missing none of the excitement was a small boy who managed to make his way among the rescued items stored across the street and climbed up in the pulpit to witness

the demise of the third St. Joseph's Church. The small boy was Charles Sullivan, who was to become a lifelong, dedicated parishioner of St. Joseph's and a good friend to the sisters.

The Curse of Tiburcio Vásquez

An oft-told story about the burning of the church was provided by the famous desperado Tiburcio Vásquez. The jail was located within the parish boundaries, so priests at St. Joseph's visited the inmates at the nearby jail. Although Vásquez was always polite and affable,

Tiburcio Vásquez, the Robin Hood bandit, was tried and convicted of murder in the Santa Clara County Courthouse.

he is said to have told one of the priests—perhaps in jest—that if God condemned him to hell, he would return and burn the church. He was convicted in the 1868 county courthouse in the courtroom of Judge David Belden. The hanging of Vásquez came on Saint Joseph's Day a month before the church burned. Sheriff J. H. Adams issued 400 invitations to the hanging—all that could be accommodated in the small jail courtyard.

The Interim Church

It took more than a fire to get Father Congiato down. Without skipping a beat, he moved the altar, the taber-

Santa Clara County's first superior court judge, David Belden, presided at the trial of bandit Tiburcio Vásquez.

Bryan Clinch, architect for the St. Joseph's Church that is now the cathedral. (COURTESY THOMAS KING)

nacle, and the few pews that were saved to a rented hall at Market and Post streets. So smooth was the transition that a Paulist priest, Father Walter Elliott, who was in the midst of giving a mission to large crowds, was able to resume without missing a session. According to the church bulletin that week, "Pat McGuire was in the first pew, and no one was inclined to deny him this right."

On the following Sunday, masses were said at the usual hours and Sunday School held in the afternoon. The hall was not adequate, however, to serve all the St. Joseph's parishioners. Father Congiato decided that a temporary church should be built at San Pedro and San Fernando streets that could be converted later into St. Joseph's School. Within three months the building was completed and ready for Sunday services.

Although the shock of the fire was still fresh in everyone's mind and the parishioners were in the midst of planning for the new church, the Corpus Christi mass and procession of 1875 came off with all the splendor of previous years. The procession marched down Market Street, the flower girls dressed in white and the little boys in their Sunday best, preceding the Blessed Sacrament. The Sodalites, the St. Joseph's Benevolent Society, the Confraternity of the Sacred Heart, the school children, and the parishioners followed.

Bryan Clinch Design

Father Congiato could now concentrate on plans for the new St. Joseph's. He held a competition with about five architects, including Theodore Lenzen, submitting designs. Bryan Clinch, member of the San Francisco-San Jose architectural firm Hoffman and Clinch, received the commission. Irish-born Clinch, a multitalented, erudite, albeit humble, man, had done a superb job of reconstructing the Santa Clara Mission after the severe earthquake of 1868—a monument to his skill and taste. He designed the Boy's Chapel at Santa Clara that survived the 1906 earthquake better than any other brick building of its size. It is said that he earned more from his writing, including his book *California and Its Missions*, than from his architecture.

His design was in the form of a Greek cross consisting of four cubes, each fifty-one feet in length, interlocked to form a fifth cube in the center of the church. This centrally planned church was based on the 1434 concept of Renaissance artist Alberti. Michelangelo and Bramante designed St. Peter's in Rome with the same Greek cross plan. St. Peter's nave was later lengthened for processions.

Bryan Clinch's design for the 1877 St. Joseph's Church. The church had to settle for a smaller dome. (ARCHIVES CALIFORNIA PROVINCE + SOCIETY OF JESUS)

The fact that there were scarcely more than 12,000 people in all of San Jose at that time did not faze the proud St. Joseph's parishioners. They would have a church unsurpassed for classical beauty.

Work on the new bulding progressed rapidly, and by the feast of Saint Joseph, March 19, 1876, it was ready for the laying of the cornerstone. As told in the *Weekly Mercury*, "At three o'clock, the procession headed by the St. Joseph's Benevolent Society in full regalia, and followed by Right Rev. Bishop Alemany [Archbishop] of San Francisco and members of the Society of Jesus, marched across the platform and halted at the eastern wing, where appropriate devotional exercises were had, after which Bishop Alemany, assisted by Father Masinata, Father Congiato and others, advanced to the stone" (a sixteen-inch cube of sandstone with a receptacle eight inches square and six inches deep).

The contents of the cornerstone included copies of the *San Jose Mercury, San Jose Patriot,* and *San Francisco Monitor* (Clinch was to be its editor in 1891), and catalogues of St. Ignatius and Santa Clara colleges. The box also contained a silver medal of the St. Joseph's Benevolent Society, a few American coins, and a parch-

ment with a Latin inscription giving the day, month, and year and the names of those taking part in the building of the church. After the lid had been placed over the receptacle, the archbishop sealed it in place with his silver trowel, blessed it, and sprinkled holy water over the foundation. In his address Archbishop Alemany compared the little adobe church of 1803, with its tule roof, to the "magnificent temple" under construction.

The residents of San Jose followed the construction of the church with fascination as they watched the rising of the brick and timbered frame. Again quoting the church bulletin, " . . . wonder of the large expanse of the ceiling and the great crown of the dome sustained only by the interdependent trusses anchored to the massive brick walls. No forbidding fence shut off the work from the view of the passerby. Even the vehicle traffic paused to watch the growing wonder of so large a building." By April of the following year, the new church was ready for its first service.

Dedication of St. Joseph's

Two thousand people overflowed St. Joseph's at its dedication ceremony on April 22, 1877. Bishop Alemany celebrated high pontifical mass assisted by twenty Jesuit priests from Santa Clara Mission and College. Father James Chrysostom Bouchard, the renowned American Indian Jesuit, who, according to a story printed the following day in the *San Jose Daily Herald*, "probably has a few if any equals in America as a pulpit orator, preached the sermon which was truly eloquent." Describing the choir under Mrs. Dagenais and the orchestra directed by Professor Manning, the *Herald* continued, "The choir and orchestra accompaniment to the solemn services has never been surpassed in any religious event in this city." At the evening services, officiated by Father Bixio, the archbishop gave the homily.

Father Congiato performed the first baptism in the new church on the day of the dedication—the infant son of Mr. and Mrs. William McEvoy, named Edward. A few days later Father Bixio married Bolum Scresovich and Mary Molinari.

St. Joseph's Art

Outstanding features of St. Joseph's in place for the dedication were the four-by-fourteen-foot stained-glass windows. Some were hand blown by Bavarian artists in Munich, others by Italian craftsmen.

Although Father Congiato realistically knew when the church was planned that the cost was beyond the realm of immediate possibility, he decided that the embellishments could come later. Lest they forget and as a reminder of the ornamentation that would add to the beauty of the church, he hung Clinch's drawing of the church in the entrance. By 1883 the only exterior adornment in front was the medallion over the entrance, carved in wood by San Jose sculptor Edward Power, with Greek letters representing the Holy Name of Jesus and the badge of the Jesuits.

Saint Aloysius altar, a gift from the youth of the church in 1892. (COURTESY MARIE MANN AND GEORGE STRICKLER)

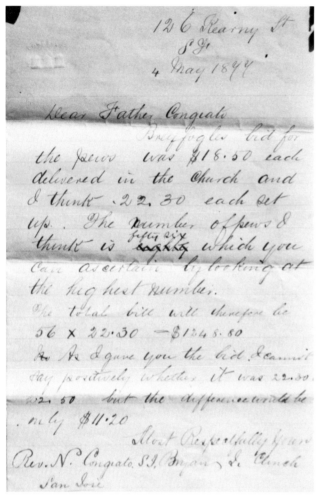

Note from architect Bryan Clinch quoting a bid for pews addressed to Father Congiato and dated May, 1877 (SANTA CLARA UNIVERSITY ARCHIVES)

With the financial backing of Edward McLaughlin and C. T. Ryland, the portico with its four Corinthian columns was completed in 1884. Above the columns in gold letters was inscribed: *Deo Optimo Maximo In Honorem S Josephi* (To the Best and Greatest God in Honor of Saint Joseph). This inspired the parishioners to greater heights. Ryland gave $5,000 to add one of the towers,

and parishioners put on a drive to finance the other.

With the completion of the bell tower came the task of hoisting the 3,115-pound Meneely bell in place. Before a large crowd—just as the bell was being swung into position—the ropes broke and it fell to the roof and was caught in the timbers of the overhanging eaves. As a nervous Father Congiato and Jacob Lenzen watched, the alert workmen, with new ropes, secured it in place. A sigh of relief came from the onlookers.

With the front exterior of the church completed, each year marked additional progress. Unhappy with the size of the dome, the parishioners now focused on it. Unable to afford one so grand as Clinch intended, they compromised and built one smaller than Clinch's design but larger than the existing octagonal copper dome. At the same time they added four small domes to the rounded chapels and cornices to the roof line.

In 1890 Kuchenheiser & Sons Iron Works on South Second Street installed the iron picket fence around the front and south side of the church, with lamps on either side of the front gates. That same year the ever-generous Edward McLaughlin donated the magnificent Carrara marble altar, lavishly decorated with gold leaf. Father Congiato enlisted Bartolome Tortore to do three large paintings for the church. A native of Piedmont, Italy, and a graduate of the Roman Academy of Fine Arts and

A view of Market Street from the plaza, looking north to the light tower and showing the vacant lot in front of St. Joseph's where Chinatown was located

the Roman Faculty of Design, he had become a Jesuit brother. Not only was he responsible for the paintings that decorated many of the churches of San Jose, but he taught painting to, among others, Andrew P. Hill and Ernest de Saisset, both members of St. Joseph's families.

The Altars

Bryan Clinch designed a pair of matching Carrara marble altars: Mary the Immaculate Mother of God for the north transept and the Sacred Heart altar for the south transept. A San Francisco artist, Gregorio Bianchi, made an intensive search for the right hardwood. He found it in the mast of a ship (*Stella Maris*, or *Star of the Sea*) and left its name on the back of the carving. Michael Callahan, donor of the Sacred Heart altar, was so impressed that he commissioned the artist to carve the statues of Saint Michael the Archangel and the Guardian Angel, taken from paintings by Italian artist Guido Reni that hang in the church of the Capuchin Fathers in Rome.

In 1885 Catherine Dunne donated the companion altar of the Sacred Heart. Bianchi carved the statue of the Sacred Heart standing on a globe lettered in Latin: "Come to Me Ye All." On the left side is a statue of Saint Peter and on the right, Saint Paul.

Mrs. Dunne, long a supporter of St. Joseph's, came to the valley from Quebec, Canada, in 1848 as the wife of Bernard Murphy, who died five years later in the explosion of the *Jenny Lind*. She later married James Dunne, a major landowner, who became the father of her three children. She had a home in San Jose and another in Morgan Hill, where she gave land for a Protestant church

as well as the Catholic church named St. Catherine's. Dunne Avenue is also named for her.

The "Our Lady of Guadalupe" altar was a gift in 1891 from the Spanish-speaking people. They enlisted a Mexican artist, Jose M. Obarravan Ponce, to copy the original at the shrine of Our Lady near Mexico City, where the Virgin Mary appeared to Juan Diego in 1531. The artist, who worked three months on the painting, wrote on the back, "painted to the best of my ability, dated 1887." Set in a gold-leaf frame, it is centered over the altar of Italian marble with panels of Mexican onyx. According to Father Jeremiah Helfrich, Juan Diego was

Sacred Heart altar in St. Joseph's Church, now a shrine in the cathedral (COURTESY MARIE MANN AND GEORGE STRICKLER)

111

Catherine Dunne inherited large land holdings from her first husband, Bernard Murphy.

not a simple man but the head of an Indian religion and very proud. He followed the Virgin's instruction, picked the roses (unusual for December), rolled them in his *tilma* (cloak), and took them to the archbishop. When he opened his cloak, the roses fell out; imprinted on the cloak was the vision of the Blessed Virgin.

A year later saw the altar of Saint Aloysius (Patron of Youth) on the gospel side of the church completed. It was made possible from contributions from the youth of the church. At the first mass said at this altar on the Feast of Saint Aloysius on June 21, 1892, there was a parade, a brass band played, and the children sang. The names of the contributors were written on a document placed in the golden heart held on the arm of the statue.

The building that Father Congiato had built immediately after the fire to serve as a temporary church was later raised a story and the lower floor was divided into three classrooms for St. Joseph's High School, with Rev. Thomas Leonard, S.J., the principal. The upper floor served as a hall. In 1898 the Brothers of Mary (Marianists) came to run the high school.

CHAPTER TWENTY-ONE

The Eighties and Nineties

The eighties opened on a bright note—*Mercury* publisher J. J. Owen's dream of an electric light tower became a reality in 1881. Standing eighteen stories high, it straddled the intersection of Santa Clara and Market streets. Underneath ran the horse-drawn trolleys and later the streecars. All this illumination made the sisters at nearby Notre Dame Academy happy. Even though they enjoyed being what they considered "out in the country," they had been unable to have electricity installed and it did save on their gas bill.

This, the largest tower of its kind in the U.S. and the third in the world, gained great fame for San Jose. Constructed of tubular iron with lamps aggregating 24,000 candlepower, it gave the most brilliant light in the country, creating a spectacular effect at night. During the holidays the 237-foot-high cone-shaped frame was strung with colored lights, transforming it into a giant Christmas tree. For thirty-six years the tower illuminated San Jose until one winter day in 1915, weakened by wear and tear and rust, it was felled by a heavy storm. Its demise was witnessed by Phil Jung, uncle of Gene Jung of the Lean & Jung jewelry store family. He was painting the cross on top of St. Joseph's Church that winter morning when, suddenly, to his unbelieving eyes, he saw

the light tower crash to the ground.

It is said that many a duck on a foggy morning "hit the fan" so to speak—providing a free duck dinner for some family that night.

Miles and Amanda C'Connor

In 1883 a couple who were to make an imprint on San Jose and St. Joseph's with their philanthropies and good will, Amanda and Myles T. O'Connor, moved to town. They arrived in time to put much-needed finishing touches on St. Joseph's Church by donating the heating system and fine Odell organ—the only one on the West Coast surviving in its original condition today. It cost $28,000 and it took a man from Troy, New York, a month to install it.

Myles O'Connor, a native of Ireland, as a young man in his middle twenties with a law degree from St. Louis University in his pocket, headed for California with a mule team in 1849. His intention was to open a law office, but when he found everyone digging for gold, he decided to join the crowd.

Only mildly successful at mining, he opened a law

Breaking ground in 1892 for the post office. To the left is St. Joseph's College. (SAN JOSE MERCURY NEWS)

office in Grass Valley and became a justice of the peace and a state legislator. He had a quiet charm, but is said to have had a forceful courtroom manner. His fortunes made a dramatic surge upwards when he and his partners, Edward and John Coleman, discovered gold-laden quartz on the outskirts of Grass Valley. This was to become the famous Idaho-Maryland Mine.

He had struck gold of another kind in 1854 when a young woman named Amanda Butler Young came to

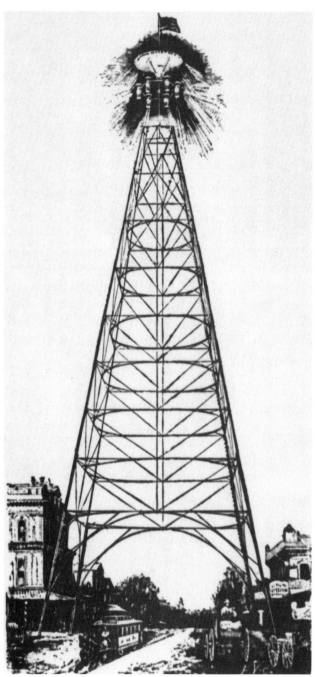

San Jose's electric light tower stood at the intersection of Market and Santa Clara streets from 1881 to 1915. It was a dream realized by San Jose Mercury *publisher J. J. Owens.*

Grass Valley from Ohio to join her brother. Her husband and small son had been victims of lightning. They were married by Father Dalton, a popular Grass Valley Catholic priest. An ecumenical couple, Amanda, who was a Methodist at that time, attended mass with Myles, and he in turn sang in her church choir. They shared a mutual interest in helping the poor, which they did with magnanimity. After their best friends in Grass Valley, Edward and Adelia McLaughlin, moved to San Jose, they visited them and decided to move there, too. On their arrival, Annie Murphy (Mrs. B. D.) showed them around town. Until they found a home to their liking at Second and Reed streets, they moved into the fashionable Auzerais House.

Baltimore, where their good friend Cardinal Gibbons presided, became a second home for the O'Connors during the eighties. It was during this time that Amanda joined the Catholic Church. In 1887 Cardinal Gibbons visited the O'Connors in San Jose and spoke from the pulpit at St. Joseph's.

The O'Connors' contributions to San Jose were many. The most noteworthy was probably the red brick O'Connor Sanitarium for the aged and needy at San Carlos and Race streets. Edward M. McLaughlin supervised the building of the hospital while the O'Connors were in Europe. Archbishop Riordan brought the Daughters of Charity from Maryland to staff the hospital. Edward McLaughlin put one of his carriages at the service of the sisters. They must have caused heads to turn when they went to mass in their distinctive habits with the foot-wide white coronet headpieces. When the O'Connors' health declined, they had a suite built for themselves at the sanitarium and gave their mansion on Second and Reed streets to the Sisters of Notre Dame de Namur for an orphanage. In 1954 the O'Connor Hospital (sanitarium) moved into a new modern facility on Forest Drive.

On their travels to Europe, Myles and Amanda acquired an exceptional collection of art works, which they offered to San Jose. When the city procrastinated over a home for the art Amanda became impatient. They not only sent the priceless collection to Trinity College in Washington, D.C., but also built a gallery to show the collection properly.

The funeral of Myles O'Connor in 1909 at St. Joseph's Church brought mourners from throughout California—the famous and the not-so-famous, representatives of colleges, orphans he had helped, and members of agencies that had benefited from his philanthropy. In Archbishop Riordan's eulogy he said, "He was a man neither bought or led. He stood for the highest

Amanda (Mrs. Myles) O'Connor shared an interest in her husband's philanthropies

Myles O'Connor was a benefactor of schools, orphanages, and St. Joseph's Church.

in morality, law and order. All that he had he held in sacred trust."

His best friend, Edward McLaughlin, commented, "He always listened to the call of the unfortunate and the distressed. He was particularly interested in orphans and was always planning on their behalf." O'Connor was

buried in Santa Clara Mission Cemetery, where Amanda commissioned an elaborate archway. Unfortunately, it was destroyed in the earthquake of 1989. In St. Joseph's Cathedral is a stained-glass window, "The Crucifixion," gift of Mrs. Myles O'Connor in her husband's memory. The Notre Dame sisters honored Mrs. O'Connor with

A sea of white coronets on the Daughters of Charity attending mass in St. Matthew's Chapel at the O'Connor Sanitarium. Myles O'Connor built the chapel in 1892 as a memorial to his brother, who died in the war with Mexico.

The Winchester Mystery House from the air
(WINCHESTER MYSTERY HOUSE)

a confirmation memorial, "Suffer Little Children to Come Unto Me." She survived her husband by seventeen years.

Sarah Winchester

A woman with quite a different personality from the O'Connors was Sarah Winchester, the "buildingest"

Crowd gathered in front of San Jose Mercury-Herald *building in September of 1881 for a memorial for President Garfield.* (SAN JOSE MERCURY NEWS)

woman in history. She did her building right here in San Jose. Standing only four-feet-eight-inches high and always dressed in her "widow weeds," she came from Connecticut in 1881. From her late husband, William Wirt Winchester of the repeating rifle family, she had inherited an immense fortune, reputed to be $20,000,000 plus a sizable monthly income.

Bereft over the death of her husband and her one-month-old baby girl, Mrs. Winchester was urged by her doctor and friends to leave the East, to seek a milder climate, and to find an all-consuming hobby. One physician even suggested that she build a house "and don't employ an architect."

Mrs. Winchester took his advice seriously. She bought an eight-room house in the country on what is now Winchester Boulvard, across from the present Town and Country shopping center and, without any architectural knowledge, started building. If something didn't work, she'd tear it out and try something else. She added on until she had 160 rooms. It was the largest private residence, with the most perks of any in the country. The statistics are mind-boggling: 10,000 windows, 2,000 doors, nine kitchens, forty-seven fireplaces of Italian marble and others hand-carved of rosewood, cherry, mahogany—each one different. The front door key was made of solid gold and the rest of the keys would fill two water buckets. There were steps leading nowhere, a door opened to a twenty-foot drop below, a spiral staircase with forty-two steps two inches high, a skylight placed in the middle of the room on the floor—and other eccentricities too numerous to mention, All this and elegant appointments, too: Tiffany light fixtures, gold and silver trim.

The late writer-artist Ralph Rambo of Palo Alto knew more about Sarah Winchester than any other living person. His father worked as a landscaper on the estate, and his uncle, who was West Coast agent for the Winchester Repeating Arms Co., was her business advisor. Rambo debunked many of the tall tales about Mrs. Winchester in his book *Pen and Inkings*, published by the San Jose Historical Museum. He wrote that she was overcome by the loss of her baby girl and the sudden death of her husband. He believed as did many that she had a guilt complex about the Winchester rifle that had the dubious distinction of "killing more game, more Indians and more U.S. soldiers than any other weapon in this nation's history."

Rambo said that her longtime companion always denied that Mrs. Winchester was a spiritualist—that the "ghostly music" late at night was Mrs. Winchester, an accomplished musician, playing her organ. The bell in the belfry was not to call "a ghostly assembly" but rather to use as a fire alarm and a start-and-stop signal to the workers in the apricot and prune orchards. She suffered from arthritis, which explains the two-inch-high steps in the spiral staircase. The reports that after the 1906 earthquake she left for six years were highly exaggerated. It was more like six months. She stayed on "The Ark," her elegant houseboat at Redwood city.

As to the story of Theodore Roosevelt supposedly going to her front door and being refused entrance, Rambo said he was across the street during the time of the alleged incident and that the president did not personally seek admittance to the house. He was driven past it. The San Jose Chamber of Commerce did ask permission to show off her house to the president. They received her sharp "No."

In her early years in San Jose, she entertained in the lovely gardens of her Queen Anne, Westlake-style home. She was neither cold nor distant and was always concerned for children. But as cruel rumors and idle gossip reached her sensitive ears she became reclusive. The late Edgar Thrift, who grew up across the street and sometimes played in Mrs. Winchester's gardens, said she was always kind and gave him cookies.

Regardless of whether she was eccentric, her building gave work to a lot of people. She was generous and good to her help, including the sixteen carpenters that she kept working every day. All received pensions of full-time pay for life and frequently gifts for their families. Her donations were never made public, but it is known that she contributed freely to charities of all faiths. Today hundreds of thousands visit the Winchester Mystery House, and Sarah Winchester still remains a mystery.

City Hall

In 1887, after voters had twice turned it down, San Jose's city hall became a reality. The ornate red brick building on Market Street facing the plaza was designed by Theodore Lenzen. One of the stipulations the city council made was that no bricks made by Chinese be used—purely from a point of prejudice. For the first time the plaza was attractively landscaped with trees and shrubs. The rococo red brick building in its garden setting was a symbol of San Jose for seventy years. In the 1950s, to the dismay of many and against strong protests of the citizenry, the city hall was torn down. A new, modern edifice was built on North First Street.

San Jose City Hall was built in 1887 and torn down in 1956.

Chinatown

The same year the showy city hall was built, San Jose's nearby Chinatown on the plaza where the Museum of Art and Fairmont now stand was destroyed by fire. Arson was suspected. The Chinese, who fled the famine, wars, and political unrest in their own country, came to California during the gold rush and gradually started moving to San Jose in 1850. They helped build railroads and worked as laborers in the fields, houseboys, cooks, and laundrymen. All the while, they were treated with disdain and distrust by the Americans and the Mexicans, not only in San Jose but in all of California. One of the issues in the county election of 1879 concerned Chinese immigration. The vote count was 36 in favor of the Chinese and 5,581 against.

In a description of the people of San Jose, from the *Springfield Republican*, the writer said, "There is another quarter occupied entirely by Chinese; one-story brick

Chinatown, which burned in 1887, was located at the corner of San Fernando and Market streets.

buildings, crowded and poor, but quaint with Chinese pottery, and brightened by what are called 'Chinese lilies,' bulbs grown in dishes filled with pebbles and water. They are the narcissus of the spring borders in New England and every Chinaman tries to have one blossom for his New Year's."

Faced with a language barrier and sensing the antipathy of the people, the Chinese kept to themselves. St. Joseph's Church members weren't happy over having Chinatown across the street, even though the Chinese had made most of the bricks for their beautiful new church. One of the few people with whom they could communicate outside their enclave was Father Benito Piccard at St. Joseph's. Scion of a prominent Italian family that produced fine papers, he was fluent in many languages, including Chinese. The press,

however, wrote of their opium dens, slave girls, gambling parlors, and tong wars. Even the eloquent Bayard Taylor, on passing through town, had a disparaging word to say. "The shrewd celestials," he wrote, "had already planted themselves here and summoned men to their meals by the sound of their barbaric gongs." In keeping with their religious beliefs, the Chinese joined burial societies to ensure the safety of the ashes of their deceased when sent to their homeland. There was also a Chinese section at Oak Hill Cemetery where some of the departed were taken, led by the municipal band and professional mourners.

With their homes destroyed by the fire, the Chinese people moved to "Heinlenville" at Sixth and Taylor streets—named for John Heinlen, who owned the property. It became the largest Chinatown in the state out-

The Hotel Vendome opened in 1887.

118

Celebration of the first electric streetcar service west of the Rocky Mountains, in 1888. The large building is the Bank of San Jose at the corner of First and Santa Clara streets. (SAN JOSE MERCURY NEWS)

side of San Francisco. By 1900 there were 4,000 Chinese in San Jose. Gradually, as the prejudice eased, the Chinese moved to other areas. Today the role of the Chinese in California is reversed. The hospital orderly is now the doctor; the houseboy and cook are owners of the mansions. They are building industrial complexes on the land they once tilled; they don't ride on the railroad they helped to build, they travel by jet planes (sometimes their own). The American dream comes full circle.

Vendome Hotel

San Joseans had been talking about the need for a swank new hotel to entertain out-of-town people. They got just that in 1887 with the Vendome Hotel. Set in the parklike acreage of the old Josiah Belden estate on North First Street, the handsome Queen Anne-style four-story building had it all—electric lights, hot running water, a billiard room, barbershop, ladies parlors, and an elevator. The ballroom was to become the scene of many an elegant social affair, starting with a grand ball to celebrate its opening, of which society reporter Mary Carroll wrote, "A swell ball where the elite and the creme de la creme of San Jose Society here and in San Francisco gathered at the spacious caravansary." Listed among the ball's committee members were Charles M. Shortridge, the Hon. B. D. Murphy, and E. W. Newhall; included on the floor committee were James

D. Phelan, W. S. Clayton, and James T. Rucker.

Another "social triumph," as the press called it, was the ball given at the Vendome by the Catholic Ladies' Aid Society, whose patronesses included Mesdames. Lawrence Archer, W. B. Hill, Coleman Younger, Nellie G. Arques, Catherine Dunne, and Edward McLaughlin—all members of St. Joseph's.

San Jose had its spinsters and its bachelors. Mrs. Carroll wrote, "The schoolmarms, the gay society butterflies and the grave spinsters... with the dear smiling mothers beaming their approval upon them... the Social Temperance Club was formed." On New Year's Day, 1882, the young women gave their first reception and ball. The young men of the early eighties were not without social graces either. A year later they gave their ball at the Music Hall.

Lick Observatory

James Lick never made a stir socially in San Jose nor did he care to. But his benefactions are legend. A recluse with a penchant for making money—namely in the sandhills of San Francisco real estate—he was regarded as a miser until three years before his death, in 1876, when he started giving his money away. His gifts to San Jose included $25,000 for an orphan asylum known as the Home of Benevolence, which became Eastfield Children's Center. In 1875, with the final deed executed

Cars arriving for a 4th of July celebration in the 1890s

by trustees Bernard D. Murphy, Richard S. Floyd, Faxon D. Atherton (for whom the town on the Peninsula was named), John H. Lick (his son), and John Nightengale, he left $700,000 for the purpose of establishing an astronomical observatory atop Mount Hamilton with the finest equipment, lenses, telescopes, disks of glass, and other important pieces of equipment to be obtained. A winding road named Mount Hamilton for a Presbyterian minister, who climbed to the top with William H. Brewer's Geological Survey Party in 1861, was built, and in 1888 the observatory was completed. Lick Observatory, carrying its benefactor's name, was later transferred to the jurisdiction of the University of California.

A scientific achievement, the observatory attracted visitors worldwide, who were not only impressed with its sophisticated equipment but were also awed by the view of the valley below planted with orchards. Today's visitors look down on a valley covered with homes, accented by the skyscrapers of downtown San Jose.

Lick built a mansion at Santa Clara and, at the time of his death, had laid out plans for another estate with extensive gardens on the road to New Almaden.

The Victory Theater

February 2, 1899, marked the opening of San Jose's finest theater, the Victory, named by its builder, James D. Phelan, for Admiral Dewey's victory at Manila. A packed house enoyed the modern appointments, a two-tier balcony, superb acoustics, and a stage large enough

to accommodate teams of horses for the Ben Hur chariot races in one of its productions. The leading actors of the New York stage came to the Victory, including David Warfield, Otis Skinner, Billie Burke, Ethel Barrymore, George M. Cohan, Sarah Bernhardt, Anna Held, and an actor named Harry Langdon, who was to become famous as a comedian in the movies.

On the society pages the day after the opening, San Joseans read that beauty, fashion, and chivalry of the valley were present and that Mayor Phelan (later U.S. Senator), who had inherited his father's business interests in San Jose, including the Phelan Building and a ranch adjoining Kelley Park, gave a talk.

Villa Montalvo

In 1912 Senator Phelan built his Mediterranean-style mansion in the Saratoga foothills, surrounded by parklike grounds and called Villa Montalvo, then and now a showplace of the valley. There he entertained the famous and not-so-famous from the Grand Duchess Marie of Russia to Chief Snow of the Mountain of the Pueblo Indian tribe; Franklin Delano Roosevelt when he was assistant secretary of the Navy (his only appearance ever in the Santa Clara Valley); actresses Mary Pickford and Ethel Barrymore; poet Edwin Markham; singers John McCormack and Lawrence Tibbet.

In his will Senator Phelan, whose business was politics but whose first love was the arts, requested that the grounds of Villa Montalvo be "used as a public park under reasonable restrictions" and that "the buildings

Senator Phelan's Villa Montalvo

and grounds immediately surrounding same be used as far as possible for the development of art, literature and music and architecture by promising students." The Montalvo Association provides for the upkeep of the buildings.

In the Lillian Fontaine Garden Theater (named for the mother of Academy Award–winning actresses Olivia de Havilland and Joan Fontaine, who produced and directed plays at Montalvo), classical and jazz concerts are presented. The Claire Loftus Carriage House, named for Lillian Fontaine's good friend who co-produced and directed with her, provides a setting for plays and dance presentations, including plays by the Valley Institute of Theater Arts.

In 1987 Olivia de Havilland, accompanied by her daughter, Gisele Galante, came from her home in Paris for a celebration of the reopening of the newly renovated garden theater honoring her mother. At dinner afterwards she recalled that when she and her sister first came to San Jose with their mother as small children, they stayed at the Vendome Hotel before moving to Saratoga.

CHAPTER TWENTY-TWO

Doctors, Lawyers, Merchants

When Dr. Benjamin Cory arrived in Yerba Buena in 1847 and found two other doctors already practicing there, it was San Francisco's loss and the pueblo's gain. He not only cared for the sick of the pueblo but also became its first health officer and helped found the county hospital, now the Valley Medical Center. He contributed to the building of the first statehouse, was elected to the assembly in the meeting of the first legislature, served four terms on the San Jose City Council, was a school trustee (a school and a subdivision were named for him), and served on the San Jose State Normal School Board.

Son of an Ohio doctor, Dr. Cory had come West over the Oregon Trail with an ox team in 1847. Discouraged by the northwest rains, he lost no time in taking a ship to Yerba Buena. He didn't tarry there either when he

Santa Clara County Hospital, or Infirmary as it was called when it was built in 1875 on San Jose–Los Gatos Road. It is now known as the Valley Medical Center.

learned they already had two doctors and that the pueblo of San Jose to the south had none. He quickly took a sailboat to Alviso. There he made a deal with a Mexican cart driver to take him with his medical books and baggage to the pueblo. Little did he suspect that he would spend the rest of his life here.

Less than two years after he opened his medical office in a little adobe on the plaza, the news broke of Marshall's discovery of gold near Sutter's Fort. Although he made only a couple of forays to the gold fields with modest success, he was forever infected with the mining bug and later invested in a silver mine in Durango, Mexico, that proved to be a fiasco.

A warm, caring man, he visited his patients on horseback wherever they might be. His voice could be heard singing hymns as he rode across the countryside to make night calls. After Cory and Sarah Braly, the minister's daughter, married, the couple settled in a large house on South Second Street and had eight children. A grandson, Dr. Benjamin Cory Ledyard, practiced dentistry in San Jose for fifty years, followed by his great-grandson, another dentist, Dr. Benjamin C. Ledyard, Jr., now a resident of Solvang.

Henry Hulme Warburton, M.D.

Dr. Henry Hulme Warburton arrived in the valley from England about the same time as Dr. Cory. He was the son of a Staffordshire doctor and had five brothers who were doctors and two who were lawyers. He left his sailing ship, *Corea*, at Half Moon Bay and made his way to Santa Clara, where he practiced for fifty-six years. San Jose attorney Austen Warburton, his grandson, says he always wore a skull cap when visiting patients and was on a sick call the day he died.

One night he was making a call out in the country and stumbled into the camp of the bandito Joaquín

Dr. Benjamin Cory found his way to San Jose in 1847 after discovering that Yerba Buena already had two doctors. He was the city's first health officer and helped found the county hospital that is now the Valley Medical Center. (SAN JOSE HISTORICAL MUSEUM)

Murieta. They were about to kill him when one of the men recognized Dr. Warburton as having saved his sick child. He vouched for the doctor's honesty, saying that he always kept his word. They released him, with his promise that he would never tell their hiding place. He kept his secret, but family members think it was probably in San Benito County.

Among Dr. Warburton's patients were members of the family of the notorious Robin Hood bandit, Tiburcio Vásquez. After his hanging outside the court house, the body was given to the family. They urgently summoned Dr. Warburton to come to their home on Washington Street. Austen Warburton's father, who went along, told him the Vásquez family implored Dr. Warburton, who had taken care of broken arms for them, to repair Tiburcio's broken neck.

At Dr. Warburton's death the flags flew at half-mast at Santa Clara College, where he had been the school's physician for many years. His grandson Austen Warburton, who taught at the Santa Clara law school at one time, gave his grandfather's medical office to the San Jose Historical Museum and has loaned old medical books and records for display.

Warburton is steeped in California history, with ties that go back to José Francisco Ortega, Portolá's scout, the discoverer of San Francisco Bay. His father, Henry

Luke Warburton, a banker, married Mary Den of the old Santa Barbara family, who had come up to San Jose to study to be a nurse at O'Connor Hospital. His grandmother was Ysabel Argüello and his great-grandmother was Ysabel Alviso, who married José Ramón Argüello, son of the last Mexican governor of California. They had a mansion in Santa Clara on former Mission Santa Clara land.

George Washington Fowler, M.D.

Dr. George Washington Fowler was a rare breed of doctor. He never sent a bill. He said the people would pay if they could, and they always did. Fortunately for his patients, he practiced for sixty-one years — longer than any other doctor in the county. His grandson, Leland Prussia, Jr., retired Bank of America board chairman, speaks with affection about his grandfather, who he says never owned a home and used a horse and buggy up until World War I. He converted to the automobile then because the influenza epidemic was taking a heavy toll. The late Doris Fowler Prussia, his daughter, drove the car for her father while he rode on the running board from house to house to care for the sick.

Dr. Fowler, a native San Josean, was born and raised in the Evergreen area. His father, Andrew Jackson Fowler, had come from Missouri in 1851 in search of gold. He didn't find gold, but he did all right financially by putting to work his skill as a hunter, shooting game and selling it to the miners. He decided he wanted to live in California, and on the way to the Santa Clara Valley

Dr. George Washington Fowler practiced medicine in Santa Clara County for sixty-one years, longer than any other doctor.

123

Dr. Frederick Gerlach taking a Jesuit brother for a ride in his new automobile (COURTESY DAN HRUBY)

was one of the first Anglos to visit Yosemite Valley. An avid abolitionist, he vowed he would return one day to the family farm and buy their slaves so that he could free them. Ten years passed before he was able to carry out his promise, but when he did, the released slaves insisted on staying with him in California. Prussia says they are buried with the Fowlers in the family plot at Oak Hill Cemetery and that their grave stones can still be seen. At his Evergreen farm Fowler planted beautiful gardens and trees. He loved trees so much that he planted several hundred eucalyptus that he had started from seedlings along Alum Rock Avenue and other country roads.

Leland Prussia, Jr., said that his great-grandfather was an avowed atheist and that the first property he bought on Alum Rock Avenue was next to a Catholic cemetery. That was too close to the Catholics, so he sold it. When the young George Fowler converted to Catholicism while a student at Santa Clara College, his father was furious.

Following his graduation from Santa Clara, George Fowler went East to study medicine at the University of Pennsylvania. After his graduation, to the utter amazement of the school authorities, he turned down a full professorship to return to the valley and settle in Santa Clara. In 1892 he opened a practice with Dr. George Seifert, son of Dr. William Seifert, of Germany. One of the first native-born doctors to practice in the valley, Dr. George Seifert was a lifelong bachelor and generous member of St. Joseph's Church. In St. Joseph's Cathedral is a stained-glass window he gave in memory of his parents.

Dr. Fowler brought many babies into the world, but little did he suspect when he delivered the Prussias' baby boy Leland, that that baby would one day marry his daughter Doris. Leland and Doris operated Prussia's, a woman's ready-to-wear store on South First Street that closed in 1953.

Although the Prussias were technically in St. Leo's parish, Leland, Jr., says the family, including his brother, George Washington Fowler II (a San Jose resident), and his sister, the late Mary Prussia Daley, attended Sunday mass at St. Joseph's. Leland Prussia, Sr., later joined the church.

Frederick G. Gerlach, M.D.

Not only was Dr. Frederick G. Gerlach regarded as a fine physician, he was also considered one of the most colorful. Son of the head tailor at Spring's clothing store, he was born in Los Gatos in 1873. After graduating from Santa Clara College he attended the University of Pennsylvania, where he was a classmate of Dr. Fowler's. According to Dick McDonald of Monte Serano, his grandson, Gerlach first visited his patients on horseback and then advanced to horse and buggy, but when he turned his horse in for an autombile, he became an avid car buff—the sportier the better. He had every kind of car you can think of, including a Stutz Bear Cat and a Stanley Steamer.

He was brusque and outspoken. McDonald recalled a time when he was seven or eight years old and was in O'Connor Hospital with pneumonia. "They didn't have penicillin in those days—and sulfa didn't do much for pneumonia. I could hear my grandfather coming down the hall yelling, 'Where is that little ——? We've got to get him well and out of here.'" At Notre Dame convent he was well liked by the nuns, but he had one habit they found distracting. When he arrived to take care of a patient, he would plop his hat on the head of the Blessed Virgin Mary statue in the entrance hall.

McDonald says that during the flu epidemic his grandfather lost two of his nurses as he worked around the clock. Considered by many to be the best surgeon of his time, he performed a double mastectomy on his sister, a Carmelite nun in Santa Clara, when she was thirty-five years old. She lived to be eighty-nine.

A devout member of St. Joseph's Church and known for having a heart of gold, he took care of the clergy without charge. The *San Jose Herald* of 1904 reported that "Dr. F. G. Gerlach was grand marshall in the golden jubilee of the Immaculate Conception procession— followed by 8,000 people in line."

For most of his career Dr. Gerlach was the physician for Santa Clara College, where he was popular with the students. The priests would ring the mission bell to signal that Dr. Gerlach was on his way for those students that might want to see him. An athlete himself, he enjoyed going on trips with the football team—especially to the Sugar Bowl in the late thirties when Santa Clara had championship teams. "He was a nonconformist," his grandson said, "but he cared about people. He had a surgery room at his ranch so that if someone needed attention over the weekend he could take care of them there and," he added, "most likely without charge. After he died they found $25,000 outstanding on his books."

The Peckham Family of Lawyers

The story of Federal District Judge Robert Peckham has a cast of lawyers and judges. "My great-grandfather Robert Peckham sailed in 1846 as a ship's carpenter from Rhode Island on a whaler bound for the Indian Ocean," he says. "After making the trip around the Cape he was disappointed at not finding whales and decided the attraction of California was stronger than the exotic places he was planning to see. He left the ship at Sausalito (my family always said he 'skipped') and started on foot across the hills to the Mission District and continued his walk to the pueblo."

According to histories of the Mexican War, he served with Frémont's California Battalion, then read law in San Jose before going to Branciforte, where he became district attorney and judge. He is credited, along with a partner, Isaac Williams, with planting the first commercial apple orchards in Watsonville in Santa Cruz County, in 1858. A road there is named for him. He returned to San Jose to practice law and had a store at

Market and San Antonio streets. Politically a strong supporter of Abraham Lincoln, he gave a speech in 1864 supporting his re-election.

One of the few Peckhams not to study law was Federal Judge Peckham's grandfather James Albert Peckham. He opted for railroading and was an official with the Southern Pacific. Judge Peckham says, "He had his home at Thirteenth and Santa Clara streets where my father, another Robert, grew up. He practiced law in San Francisco—was a hail-fellow-well-met." Continuing the litany of family lawyers, he says, "My uncle, I. M. Peckham, was U.S. attorney; my grandfather's brother was James Benjamin Peckham, a Stanford graduate and a colorful trial lawyer who died in the early 1940s."

After graduating Phi Beta Kappa from Stanford, Judge Peckham attended Yale Law School. He then came back to San Jose and served as assistant U.S. attorney. In 1958 Gov. Edmund "Pat" Brown appointed him to the Santa Clara County Superior Court. He received the first federal judgeship in Santa Clara County, in 1966, and was later appointed chief judge of the U.S. District Court for California. In the late eighties he gave up the administrative duties to just practice as judge.

Superior Court Judge Marshall Hall

Retired Superior Court Judge Marshall Hall's distinguished background is a mixed bag of medicine and law. His great-grandfather Dr. Alexander Josephus Spencer, who arrived by wagon train from New York, not only practiced medicine, but was also active in San Jose civic affairs, including serving on the board of Alum Rock Park.

One of Dr. Spencer's most unusual medical cases was installing a silver plate in the head of Montain Charley McKiernan. Also known as "Silver Skull Charley" or "Hair-Brained Charley," he obviously was a man who attracted excitement. After being run off the road in his wagon by Indians, McKiernan had gone to Santa Cruz Mountains, only to be mauled by a bear. A doctor sewed up a severe skull wound. But after he suffered from headaches, he went some months later to Dr. Spencer, who removed a wad of hair and inserted a plate made of Mexican silver coins. He became a successful San Jose businessman and lived forty-eight more eventful years that included a shoot-out and the capturing of a pair of bandits in the mountains.

Judge Hall's grandfather Francis E. Spencer practiced law in San Jose before his appointment to the superior court. He was the first chairman of the board of trustees

Attorney Delphine Delmas's winery at Mountain View (SAN JOSE HISTORICAL MUSEUM)

of Stanford University. Judge Hall's father, Joseph Underwood Hall, was personal physician to Myles O'Connor and his wife, Amanda. He was also the first resident physician and first chief of staff at O'Connor Hospital. Marshall Hall was born in the same house at 216 Autumn Street as his mother, Grace Spencer Hall.

Judge Hall's grandfather the senior Dr. J. Underwood Hall, a Kentuckian lured by the promise of gold, came to California in 1852. He combined mining with medicine (his first fee was paid with an ounce of gold), returning East to get his medical degree from Jefferson Medical College in Philadelphia. During the Civil War, as a doctor for the Union Army, he was taken prisoner but was safely returned in an exchange. He and his Kentucky-born wife settled in Gold Hill, Nevada, where they became parents of nine children. After twenty years they moved to California.

Judge Marshall Hall attended Stanford University as an undergraduate and went on to the university's law school. He was a member of the law firm Rankin, Oneal, Luckhardt and Hall until 1957, when he was appointed to the Santa Clara County Superior Court. His son, Clayton Underwood Hall, practices law in San Luis Obispo.

A Silver-tongued Orator

Trial attorney extraordinaire Delphin M. Delmas was the son of early-day vintner Antoine Delmas, who came from France to California to dig for gold. After settling in San Jose he sent for his wife, Coralie, and son, Delphin.

An early bloomer, Delphin graduated with honors from Santa Clara College (Santa Clara University) at nineteen years of age, went East to attend Yale Law School, and at the age of twenty-two, was elected district attorney. Entering private practice, Delmas became partners with Mayor Bernard D. Murphy. But Murphy, more interested in politics and banking, soon gave up his law practice.

He was called the "Napoleon of the State Bar" for his likeness to the French emperor and dubbed "the silver-tongued spell-binder of the Pacific Coast" for his dramatic oratory. This was before fellow Democrat William Jennings Bryant earned the title "silver-tongued orator." Like his former law partner, Murphy, he was attracted to politics. In 1904 he nominated William Randolph Hearst for president at the democratic National Convention.

With a reputation as the best in the West, he was associated for twenty years with the outstanding trials before the state courts. One of his most notorious cases took place in New York in 1907. He defended Harry K. Thaw, who shot and killed popular architect Stanford White in Madison Square Garden, which, ironically, had been designed by White. Thaw had married a young actress, Evelyn Nesbit, who was previously involved with White. By introducing the phrase "dementia Americana" as a defense, he succeeded in having Thaw declared not guilty by reason of insanity.

One of Delmas's cases that titillated the press and a standing-room only courtroom of spectators was *Dixon v. Allen*. Delmas represented nineteen-year-old Anna Dixon, a San Jose Normal School student who had been dismissed by the defendant, the school's principal, Professor Charles Allen, for her unseemly and loud disrupting manners, including loud sneezing in class. Although Allen's attorneys, Thomas Laine and W. A. Johnston, were smooth and considered the best in San Jose, Delmas, who had come up from Los Angeles, where he was then practicing, succeeded in getting a plaintiff verdict and $1,000 for his client.

No less eloquent, although lacking in notoriety, was the courtroom appearance of Delmas before the state legislature, at the request of Santa Clara College president Father Robert Kenna, for Andrew P. Hill in his fight to save the redwoods. Even after the impassioned plea of Delphin Delmas—reported in the *San Jose Mercury* as "one of the most powerful ever delivered on a public project and created a strong sentiment for the bill"—the vote was not assured, and at adjournment time Senator Shortridge, upon the request of Mr. Hill, asked that the legislators remain to hear Father Kenna speak. "His plea for the bill was simple, beautifully worded, but determined." When the vote was taken thirty-three senators voted for the bill—the opposition vote came from the chairman of the finance committee, who said

L. Hart & Son delivery truck. Leopold Hart opened his first store in 1866 at the corner of Market and Santa Clara streets. The store remained in the family for 100 years. (SAN JOSE HISTORICAL MUSEUM)

he hoped it would pass, but that it would not be consistent for him to vote for it. Hill now needed $50,000 for the restoration of the redwoods. Father Kenna solved that problem by securing it from Sen. James Phelan, his cousin.

Delmas bought 400 acres of Mountain View property on which he built a country residence for his wife, Pauline, and four children. In keeping with his French heritage, he planted grapes. He watered his vineyard, said to be the largest in the state at that time, via the D. M. Delmas Dam across Steven's Creek.

Great-nephew Emery Delmas, who died in 1977, like his uncle, attended Santa Clara University and its law school and followed him in the practice of law. He served as president of the Santa Clara County Bar Association, as president of San Jose Country Club, and as a member of the San Jose City Council. His son, Dana, who chose not to follow the family profession, lives in Tuscon, Arizona.

The Merchant Princes

Leopold Hart left his native France to come to California at the suggestion of his half brother, Lazard Lion (L. Lion & Sons furniture). The Alsace-Lorraine was not the best of places to be living in the 1850s because of the political unrest and invasions by the Germans. He settled in San Jose—a move he never regretted. By 1866 he bought the Cash Corner Store at Market and Santa Clara streets—a small, windowless, fifty-by-sixty-foot store, the kind that had wrought-iron grates across the front and some of the merchandise displayed outside. Within a short time he changed the name to L. Hart. When his son, Alexander J. Hart, came into the business, the name became L. Hart and Son; later the name

changed to A. J. Hart, then A. J. Hart & Son, and later simply Hart's. In the meantime he made a trip to France to see his fiancee, Hortense Cahen. She followed soon after with a companion. Their marriage took place in 1863 in the Lions' home in Santa Clara.

After Leopold's death in 1904, Alexander, who had married Nettie Lakeland Brooke in Long Island, New York, not only took over the family business but also became active in civic affairs. The family-owned business grew to become one of the largest department stores in the state in 1941.

He built one of the fine homes on The Alameda. His son, Alex, Jr., recalls happy times growing up in that home with his sisters, Elise and Miriam, and his brother, Brooke. Alex Hart says his father had a group of friends who would come to play poker on the breakfast-room table. They included Jay McCabe, for whom McCabe Hall at the civic auditorium is named; his good friend Father Collins, pastor of St. Patrick's Church; Tom Killmartin; and vintner Paul Masson. "I was allowed to come in to serve hors d'oeuvres, and then I had to leave," says Alex.

Father Genaro, president of the University of Santa Clara, was a dear family friend. Alex and his brother, Brooke, attended Santa Clara as did Alex's sons, A. J. and Brooke. "We always had lots of friends around," he said. "Jackie Coogan, the child star who became famous in *The Kid* with Charles Chaplin, used to come by when he was at Santa Clara; Leslie Peterson, who was the youngest Mason in the state, started as an usher at the Fox California theater and impressed L. B. Mayer, head of M.G.M., who brought him down to Hollywood to become a member of the publicity department; actor Edmund Lowe—his biggest hit was *What Price Glory?*—had attended Santa Clara, where he received a bachelor and a master's degree, and, for a short time, taught.

When he came up to see his aunt Kate Murphy and some of the fathers at Santa Clara, he would come over with Clorinda Bisceglia Geoffroy and Mary Monahan Lane."

With the happy times came sad times for the respected and much-loved Hart family: Brooke died in 1937 at the hands of kidnappers. Adding to the tragedy, an aroused

An early O. A. Hale & Co. store.

crowd of San Joseans broke into the jail and lynched the kidnappers in St. James Park.

At the death of Alex J. Hart, in 1943, his wife became president, but she lived only six weeks. Alex Hart, Jr., then took over the family business. He opened branch stores in Sunnyvale and Mayfield Mall, Mountain View. In 1968, with the decline in downtown business, he moved the store from Santa Clara and Market streets to Westgate Shopping Center. In the face of the competition of large chain stores with their superior purchasing power, Hart's closed in 1982.

L. Lion & Sons

Lazard Lion, a native of Forbach, France, in the Alsace-Lorraine, came to San Jose by a circuitous route: first to New Orleans and then via the Isthmus to San Francisco, where he was one of the founders of the City of Paris Department Store. He moved down to San Jose in 1856, opening a merchandising business at Post and Market streets. According to Paul Lion, Jr., his great-grandfather, who was Jewish, married Zulema Mart, a Catholic. Zulema attended St. Joseph's Church and their children were baptized there.

Diversifed in his business interest, Lazard Lion started

a glove factory in 1872; by the mid-1880s he was president of the Commerce and Savings Bank and had a carpet factory in the Knox building. In the 1920s L. Lion & Sons furniture store moved to Second and San Fernando streets in a building they later purchased and where they remained until the business closed in the

1960s. Lazard's son Gustave, after attending Santa Clara College, became active in the family business and ran the 5,000-acre Paradise Valley ranch near San Martin as well as succeeding his father as president of the business. He married May Johnson in 1880, and their daughter Clara married William Blauer, manager of the San Jose branch of the Bank of Italy.

Gus's brother, Ernest Pierre Lion, succeeded him as president of Lion's. In the thirties Paul L. Lion (Ernest's son) became president of the store, followed, when he retired in 1956, by his cousin Morrell Lion (Gus's son). After Morrell's death, in the late 1950s, Paul Lion, Jr., served as president until the store closed in 1967.

Bloom's Shore Store

Meyer Bloom, a native of Lotz, Poland, set up a combination clothing and shoe store in San Jose in 1867. "I believe he got his stuff on consignment from Levi Strauss," says Maxwell Bloom of San Jose, his grandson. He later settled on just shoes. In 1913 Meyer bought the Star Shoe Store, which became Bloom's. After changing locations several times, he settled permanently on South First Street.

Max Bloom tells a story about another man who had

a shoe store in San Jose named Jesse Lasky, who went on to fame as a major film producer in Hollywood. He gave up the shoe business to go on the road playing trumpet with a band. In New York he became interested in the new nickelodeon. Filled with enthusiasm, he returned to San Jose to raise money to go into the business. He approached a friend from childhood, Manny Michaels, a cousin of Bloom's. Michael and some others couldn't see any future in it—a decision they were to regret as Lasky became a famous moving picture producer for Paramount Studios.

On a visit to San Jose, Lasky was being shown around by Jay McCabe, who brought him to see Meyer Bloom. Unfortunately, the Lasky Shoe Store sign had been painted over just two weeks before. Maxwell Bloom, who inherited the family business, sold the women's shoe section to Florsheim in 1965 and two years later the men's store to the same company. He became a stockbroker.

Meyer Bloom was a friend of the priests at St. Joseph's, and they were frequently guests at his house on Park Avenue. If one of the priests brought in a needy child for shoes, Bloom would fit him without charge. No doubt as a thank-you, the priest gave him a silver goblet. Mr. Bloom used it for the kiddush cup for the blessing of the wine at the traditional eve of the Sabbath ceremony. He apparently never knew that the Greek letters "IHS" on the cup signify "Jesus."

There wasn't much to do for excitement in San Jose in those days. Max Bloom's aunt Hilda, who was a student at Notre Dame Academy, used to go with a girlfriend to St. Joseph's Church to watch the weddings.

Herold's Shoe Store

Phil Herold was one of the few men to come to California in the forties who didn't get bitten by the gold bug. He learned about shoe repairing as an apprentice in what became Yuba County in 1846. On a visit to San Jose in 1864, he stayed in the old Pacific Hotel adjacent to St. Joseph's Church and was so impressed he decided he would return to San Jose. First he went East, bought a stock of leather and findings, and led a wagon train across the country. "He must have liked that sort of thing," says his grandson and namesake, Phil Herold of Pebble Beach, "because he went East and did the same thing again."

A cobbler, he opened his business in 1869 and at first made the boots himself until he was able to have them shipped across the country. He advertised "a splendid line of new shoes for $3.50, $4 and $5." Phil Herold says

that his grandfather was crossing a creek near his home at South First Street and Alma Avenue when his wagon lost a wheel. As a result of the accident he became blind. Phil Herold's father, Chester, and his brothers, Harvey and Fred, took over the business. Chester and Harvey (Fred left the business) moved the store to the Unique Theater building on Santa Clara Street. Besides a legitimate theater featuring variety shows, it was here that Sid Grauman introduced "flickers," as moving pictures were first called, to San Jose. A circus performer and saloon singer named Al Jolson made his first appearances on the legitimate stage here. A local boy, Roscoe "Fatty" Arbuckle, who went on to become a Mack Sennett comedy star in Hollywood, worked as a "mop boy," occasionally filling in as a singer. He was a half brother of Clyde Arbuckle, San Jose's official historian. Grauman moved to Hollywood to bigger things. He built Grauman's Chinese, still noted for its movie stars' hand- and footprints in concrete.

In 1923 Herold's Shoe Store bought out the Bacon Shoe Store and moved into the building at 74 South First. Phil Herold worked in the business, which included a men's shoe store on First Street. He took over in 1957, opened a second store in Town and Country Village in 1961, and sold the business to Craddock Terry Shoe Company of Lynchburg, Virginia, in 1969.

O. A. Hale

An extension of covered wagon days: riding the "iron horse" in a freightcar O. A. Hale came to California with his furniture and household goods, cooking his meals on board along the way. He opened a business in a seventeen-by-forty-foot store where Maurice O'Brien (later O'Brien's Candy) had a "Yankee Notion," or as it was sometimes called a "racket" store—translated to mean a variety store. The entrance sidewalk consisted of two planks from Santa Clara Street. As O. A. Hale & Co. grew, his four brothers each opened a dry goods store in different parts of California. The Hale stores remained in the family until they merged with Broadway Stores. O. A., a strong believer in advertising, used "Good Goods" as his slogan. He is credited with originating the quip "I don't care what they say about me, so long as they talk about me at all."

The dry goods business was going so well that in 1900 Mr. Hale hired a store manager from out of town. After meeting the newcomer at the station in his old phaeton drawn by a gray mare, he took him by St. Joseph's, stopped, and asked the man to go inside the church.

Residence of O. A. Hale, founder of the Hale's chain of stores

Somewhat mystified, he followed orders. When he returned Hale said, "Young man, that is the only place in Santa Clara County that does more business than I do; and I want you to get some of it away from them."

Hale was a director and stockholder of Farmer's Union, was on the board of Agnews State Hospital, and acted as agent in the acquisition of the Peninsula Railway and of rights-of-way to Los Gatos and Saratoga.

Five Generations of Sterns

Five generations of Sterns have been in the leather business. Marcus Stern, a native of Germany and a master craftsman in leather, opened his first shop in San Jose at 40 East Santa Clara Street in 1852, selling saddles and harnesses. His son, Fred who took over at Marcus's death, in 1905, started carrying Stetson hats, western gear, and other cowboy-related items. Outgoing and friendly with all the movers and shakers, Fred was elected to both the Santa Clara County Board of Supervisors and the San Jose City Council.

A favorite family story is told about Marcus and his cousin, Shoen, whom he brought over from Germany. The two men belonged to rival volunteer fire departments—Marcus to Torrent volunteer company and his cousin to the Empire company. They arrived at a fire simultaneously, and while the building burned, they fought over who had jurisdiction.

Next in line after Fred was his son, Harold, a visionary who, after his father's death, in 1937, opened stores in Fresno and Modesto and moved the San Jose store from South First Street to San Antonio. He changed the line from saddles and harnesses and trunks to leather goods and luggage.

He had a warm friendship with Father Laherty, the popular pastor of St. Joseph's Church. Knowing the priest's fondness for horse racing, he would invite him to go to the track. Stern's widow, now Mrs. Howard Miller of Pebble Beach, says, "Although Harold was not a Catholic, he had a custom when he won at the track of slipping by St. Joseph's, unknown to Father Laherty, and dropping part of his winnings in the poor box. One time he bet on a horse called 'Saint Ignatius' [founder of the Jesuit order], which won. On his way home he stopped by the church, and just as he was dropping the money into the box, Father Laherty walked in. 'Aha!' said the priest, 'so you're the one.'"

His son, Howard, opened the Town and Country store, which is now in the Valley Fair, with another branch in the Oakridge Mall. Since his death, in 1988, his wife, Gloria, and son, Clayton, have carried on the business.

130

CHAPTER TWENTY-THREE

Dawn of a New Century

As the twentieth century arrived, the two "A"'s that would dominate transportation—automobiles and airplanes—were still in their infancy. Technology, which was to became the byword of the last half of the century, was just beginning to rear its inquisitive head.

Newspapers

San Jose's first newspaper was the short-lived *State Journal*, a weekly started in 1850 by James B. Devoe. It was

Advertisement for the Montgomery aeroplane demonstration, May 21, 1905.

followed by a succession of weeklies, including the *Santa Clara Register*, whose name was changed to the *San Jose Telegraph*. When the *Telegraph* was sold to Neil Slocum he changed the name to *Mercury* and announced his intentions to publish it as a daily. However, that didn't become a reality until 1869, after J. J. Owen took over. Newspapers made a major advance in 1901, when E. A. and J. O. Hayes bought the *San Jose Herald*, an evening paper; a year later they took over the *San Jose Mercury*, and in 1913 they merged the two papers into the *San Jose Mercury-Herald*.

The Hayes brothers were to purchase yet another newspaper, the *San Jose News*, which had started out in 1883 with the provocative name *City Item*. It was published by Hyland Baggerly for ten years, between 1916 and 1927, before selling to G. Logan Payne. In 1936 Payne sold to the Hayes brothers. Five years later the brothers retired from newspaper publishing when they sold to Ridder Publications. The latest chapter in this chain of newspaper events took place in 1974, when the *Mercury News* became a Knight-Ridder publication, with headquarters in Miami, Florida.

The Father of Flight

In 1883 Santa Clara College science professor John Joseph Montgomery became the first human to fly in a heavier-than-air glider. Although best known for his glider flights, his most significant discovery was that a cambered wing surface would provide maximum lift and stability in flight. After graduating from college, the Yuba City native joined the faculty as a science professor so he could have time to experiment in aviation. His first controlled flight in 1905 was from the Santa Clara campus. The glider was lifted by hot air balloon to an altitude of 4,000 feet, where it was cut loose. Pilot Dan Maloney executed every free-flight maneuver, landing at the pre-arranged destination at Poplar and Alviso streets.

The world's first radio broadcasting station was established by Professor Charles David Herrold on top of the Garden City Bank Building in San Jose in 1903. This picture was taken in 1912.
(SAN JOSE MERCURY NEWS)

Montgomery drew world attention to San Jose and Santa Clara College with his advances in aviation, but it was all to end abruptly at Evergreen in 1911. He was piloting his glider and had just become airborne when it was hit by a freak blast of wind. The glider turned to its side and a bolt protruding from the wing penetrated his head. At the site of his final takeoff, a California Historical Marker is inscribed "Montgomery Hill" in his honor. He is remembered as the "The Father of Flight." His uncle, Rev. George Montgomery, is remembered as co-adjutor to Archbishop Riordan in San Francisco, who took charge during the earthquake of 1906.

The Big Race

The big event of the year of 1908 for automobile enthusiasts was the New York–to–Paris race, which included San Jose on its itinerary. As related by Jack Douglas in the San Jose Historical Museum's *Association News*, the race, sponsored by the *New York Times* and a Paris newspaper, *Le Matin*, started from Times Square in February, headed for Chicago, then moved across the Midwest and West via Wyoming and Nevada.

After five weeks on the road, the American entry, *Thomas Flyer*, was in the lead by 800 miles over the cars from France, Italy, and Germany. When they reached the Pacheco Pass, without a pilot car to guide them, they lost their way but still arrived in San Jose on March 24,

ahead of the others. Greeted by an excited crowd, they circled the downtown and, after a dinner given by the Santa Clara County Automobile Club, spent the night at LaMolle House at Santa Clara and San Pedro streets. When the French and Italian cars eventually arrived, they received equally enthusiastic receptions as thousands of people cheered along the roadside all the way from Gilroy to San Jose. The Germans ran into problems and completely missed San Jose.

Behind on their schedule, the race officials arranged for the cars to be shipped from Seattle to Vladivostok. From there they drove to Paris, where the Americans won first prize. The movie called *The Great Race*, starring Jack Lemmon and Tony Curtis, was based on this race.

The Birth of Radio

Significant experiments were being made in wireless transmission in 1902 by Santa Clara College (University) professor of science Richard H. Bell, S.J. The Jesuit priest, who had studied Marconi's experiments with great interest, fascinated the college students in 1902 with his wireless aerials slung on hammock line between tall masts on the campus.

Three years later Lee De Forest developed the audion, or electron tube, at a house on Emerson Street in Palo Alto. More commonly called the radio tube, it controlled the flow of electrons through a vacuum which had

132

the ability to amplify and generate continuous air waves. This made possible the long distance telephone and led the way for commercial radio broadcasting.

While De Forest was doing his work in Palo Alto, in San Jose Charles Herrold was establishing the world's first broadcasting station. In 1894 he had transmitted California's first wireless message (sixty feet). He operated with a spark gap rather than the De Forest tube. Professor Herrold, who studied astronomy at Stanford, was considered a harmless eccentric when he hauled thousands of feet of wires into the Santa Cruz Mountains and stretched them out over trees. In 1909 he developed what he called "the oldest active radio-telephone station in the United States," which operated from the top floor of the Garden City Bank Building. It was the first to broadcast regularly with scheduled musical programs and speeches. They were published in the *San Jose Mercury*. His call letters, FN, became KQW in 1921 and when Columbia Broadcasting Company took over the station in 1949, KCBS. In the San Jose Historical Museum can be seen the first broadcast microphone and his transmitter, thanks to Clyde Arbuckle, who received them from Charles Herrold.

The Padre of the Rains

If Montgomery was the "Father of Flight," another Santa Clara College professor, Jerome Sextus Ricard, S.J., a meteorologist son of an Avignon, France, farmer, was the "The Padre of the Rains." Ricard started making his weather predictions in 1907. He advanced the study of sunspots and based his weather predictions, which appeared in the daily newspapers, on their intensity. In his campus observatory were an eight-inch telescope, an astronomical camera, a complete 120-foot-high radio receiver and a seismographic laboratory with instruments for recording earthquakes.

Farmers and orchardists paid heed to Father Ricard's predictions. Although some scientists may have argued with Father Ricard's theory, he was widely acclaimed. In 1929, as the golden jubilee mass celebrating his fifty years in the Jesuit order was about to commence, the Santa Clara Mission bell tolled, as did the bells at fourteen of the missions throughout California. On the altar were the bishops from Los Angeles, Salt Lake, and Sacramento; San Francisco's Archbishop Edward J. Hanna preached the sermon. According to Eugene Sawyer in his *History of Santa Clara County*, a gathering of 10,000 members of the clergy, alumni, and friends attended the mass in the mission gardens. The padre

of the rains accurately predicted that the day would be bright.

At a banquet that night, Olympic Club president William F. Humphrey introduced the speakers, who included the university's president, Timothy Murphy, S.J., alumni president Chauncey Tramutolo, celebrated attorneys Joseph Scott of Los Angeles and Delphin Delmas, James Bacigalupi of Bank of America, former U.S. Senator James Phelan of Saratoga, and James Flood of Atherton. As the speeches ended, there was an aerial parade during which the name "Ricard" was spelled out in the sky.

San Francisco's newspaper, *The Call*, did something out of the usual when they sent a delegation down by airplane from San Francisco. Father Ricard sent back a message of his appreciation to all his friends in astronomy. They include Mare Island Observatory, the students' observatory at the University of California, to Dr. W. W. Campbell of the Lick Observatory, to the heads of observatories at Mt. Wilson and Harvard, the weather bureau at San Francisco, and the Canadian Meteorological Service.

Sing Kee

Another weather prognosticator during the period of Father Ricard, but one whose methods were less scientific, was Sing Kee, a Santa Clara laundryman. His predictions, based on the reactions of his pet toad, were also featured in the daily newspapers. He distributed lottery tickets in the back room of his laundry.

The Farmer's Market

Even though San Jose showed every sign of keeping on top of the times, it still retained its rural flavor. French writer Amaury Mars, who visited in 1900, wrote in his book *Reminiscences of Santa Clara Valley, San Jose, California*, "There is a local custom of improvising a fruit and vegetable market every morning, which is not lacking in originality." He described the people coming in from the country to North Market Street between five and seven in the morning and arranging their teams of horses on either side of the street, facing each other, leaving a passageway down the middle. One side was lined with thirty vehicles belonging to the wholesale dealers—usually a Portuguese or a Chinese. On the other side were the retailers, who were nearly all Italians.

"It is an odd and picturesque sight," Mars continued,

Emancipation was the theme of Lincoln Grammar School's float in San Jose's 1901 Tournament of Roses parade. Note the spelling of "grammer."

"watching all those dealers and peddlers (with queer foreign accent) buying and selling." He bought a box of sweet, white grapes for thirty-five cents and thought the price exceptionally cheap and the grapes extremely tasty. "Land of the blest!" he said.

The Visit of President McKinley

In contrast to the country fruit market scene, San Jose outdid itself for the visit of President and Mrs. William McKinley and his cabinet in 1901. The schools, various organizations, and businesses staged a Tournament of Roses parade that would have rivaled Pasadena's. The president addressed a crowd in St. James Park on First Street facing the courthouse. That night an elegant ball was given at the Vendome Hotel. Mayor Charles Martin headed the committee, which included prominent names in the town: Henry and Ernest Lion and their sister, Estelle Lion (furniture store family), who married Charles Fay, Jr., O. A. Hale of O. A. Hale's Department Store, Henry Booksin (orchardist for whom Booksin Avenue was named), J. O. Hayes, publisher of the *San Jose Mercury-Herald*, attorney S. F. Leib, Mrs. Nicholas Bowden, and Mrs. A. H. Marten (the Marten descendants still own property in downtown San Jose). Unfortunately, after charming everyone during the day, Mrs. McKinley took ill, so neither she nor the president could attend, but the party went on. Secretary Hays acted as the president's representative, assisted by cabinet members.

Just four months later, newspaper headlines announced the assassination of President McKinley in Buffalo, New York, shocking the community. Father Robert Kenna, president of Santa Clara College (Pastor of St. Joseph's

The Ladies' Brass Band called their float "Harmony"

Charles Martin, mayor in 1901 when President McKinley visited

134

1897–99), proposed that the $3,600 the Committee for 100 had collected to build a gallery to house the Myles and Amanda O'Connor art collection (offered to the city but not accepted) be used for a monument in memory of the late president's visit.

Two years later a bronze statue of the president, mounted on a granite base, was unveiled in St. James Park on the spot where he had stood to address the people. Seated on a platform, were *Mercury* publisher E. A. Hayes, University of the Pacific president Rev. Eli McClish, Rev. W. C. Evans, who said the opening prayer, St. Joseph's pastor, Father R. A. Gleeson, Judge R. A. Lewis, and Father Kenna, who delivered an eloquent speech on "The Significance of the Monument." The University of Pacific Quartet sang "America," after which the Santa Clara College band closed the ceremonies.

Rockefeller and Roosevelt

John D. Rockefeller preceded President Theodore Roosevelt by a month when he visited the valley in April of 1903. So great was the enthusiasm of the multimillionaire, who was famous for handing out dimes, that he wrote, "It is a picture such as I have never seen. Why! it is even worth the expense of a trip across the continent to look upon the wonderful Santa Clara Valley."

A warm spring day greeted the arrival of President Roosevelt, who was enthusiastically welcomed, first at Gilroy, where he addressed a gathering, then San Jose, where he spoke to thousands of people. He was taken on a drive with a mounted escort that included Clem R. Arques, Ralph W. Hersey, Sheriff R. J. Langford, attorney Leo Archer, Thomas McGeoghegan, and Joseph Rucker of the well-known real estate firm. His cabinet followed in carriages. Along the way they stopped at Notre Dame College, where the students greeted the president, and on behalf of the school, Bertrande Cauhape (daughter of Mr. and Mrs. Victor Cauhape) presented the president with a bouquet of rosebuds.

At Santa Clara College, the school's president, Rev. Robert E. Kenna, welcomed Roosevelt. At another stop he received a bouquet of blossoms from a young boy representing the public school children. As the party moved along Third Street they stopped so a little girl could present him with a basket of flowers. His eyes moistened as he saw that she was wearing a medal around her neck inscribed "for chivalrous service in Cuba." Roosevelt had sent it to her in memory of her father, who was one of "Colonel Roosevelt's Rough Riders." At a stop in Campbell the president participated in a tree-

President Theodore Roosevelt and entourage on his visit to San Jose in 1903. The photo was taken by San Jose's best-known photographer, Andrew P. Hill. (SOURISSEAU ACADEMY)

planting ceremony before continuing on to Palo Alto, where he was received by Stanford University president David Star Jordan.

The Earthquake of 1906

The 1906 earthquake struck the Bay Area at 5:12 A.M. on April 18. Hardest hit was San Francisco because of the fire that followed. San Jose had enough to contend with in just the quake. Totally destroyed were St. Patrick's Church, the Phelan Building at First and Post streets, the Hall of Records, and the Native Sons Hall at Third and San Fernando. Suffering heavy damage were the Doherty Building, Grant and Horace Mann schools, and San Jose High School. At first it appeared that San Jose Normal had come through with only losing a few bricks and some small cracks, but after closer investigation, it was declared unsafe. The post office lost its tower, which was never replaced.

Most severely damaged by the disaster was Agnews State Hospital for the Insane, where the floors of the four-story, two-block-long asylum, which housed 1,080 patients, collapsed, leaving only walls standing. The death toll, including patients and hospital personnel, was 119.

A strange twist to the tragedy, as told by Dan Hruby in his book *Mines to Medicine*, concerned Dr. James Curnow, a man who had done so much for both mental and public health, including designing San Jose's sewer system. Curnow had become mentally ill and was a patient at Agnews. In the midst of the upheaval after the quake, he was discovered administering to the injured. Apparently the severe jolt had snapped him back to reality. Sadly, it was only a remission. He died at Agnews in 1909.

In a state of panic after the quake and concerned over

The Phelan Building the day after the 1906 earthquake (SAN JOSE HISTORICAL MUSEUM)

The post office after the 1906 earthquake (SAN JOSE HISTORICAL MUSEUM)

possible looting, San Jose's Mayor Worswick declared martial law and called in the state militia. Company B camped in St. James Park during the emergency. Those residents unable to stay in their homes were put up in temporary housing at the racetrack at Agricultural Park.

The *San Jose Mercury-Herald* reported that all the Catholic societies of the town organized under one head and worked in conjunction with the main relief society. Under the chairman of the Catholic Relief, David M. Burnett, grandson of the first governor, and his co-chairs, Mrs. John E. Auzerais and Mrs. J. M. McCabe, the societies set up temporary headquarters in tents at Y.M.I. Hall and at the railway depot.

Although St. Joseph's had no structural problems, there was considerable interior damage. Masses were said in a tent on the grounds of Notre Dame College until the damage could be repaired. On the day of the earthquake, the pastor, Father John Walshe, wrote, "The upper story of the Father's residence was badly wrecked and it is declared unsafe. There was no school today. There can be no school til the buildings are declared safe by competent judges."

The priests stayed with the Brothers of Mary or in private homes. The building inspectors reported the church safe but recommended repairs on the north and south gables down to the cornices. St. Joseph's Academy moved its classes to the Y.M.I. Hall. Property was purchased and a new school constructed at Park Avenue between Locust and River streets. The following year the new school opened with the Brothers of Mary teaching the older boys and the Sisters of Notre Dame teaching the girls and younger boys.

136

In view of the parish's need for costly repairs, John R. Ryland (son of C. T. and grandson of Governor Burnett), chaired the restoration project. As they always did, the St. Joseph's people came forward to help. Volunteers included Catherine Dunne of Morgan Hill and her son-in-law, Joseph H. Rucker (of the real estate firm), Mrs. Nicholas Pellerano, Louise Auzerais, Elizabeth Enright, Pedro de Saisset (French consul), Dr. Fred Gerlach, Peter Concannon, Mrs. Albio Berryessa (descendant of the Anza party family), John O'Rourke, Mrs. J. M. McCabe, and Peter Malovos.

By December of that year St. Joseph's parishioners were ready for a pickup. They got one when the Spanish-speaking people celebrated their patron saint's day with their Fiesta de Nuestra Señora de Guadalupe. The day started with solemn High Mass celebrated by Archbishop Riordan and assisted by six priests, including Father Walshe and master of ceremonies Father Jeremiah Collins. In the afternoon the "Blessing of the Roses" took place with a procession of the children to Our Lady of Guadalupe altar. That evening there was a rosary and the Offering of Roses by the little Mexican girls. Father C. M. Heredia, S.J., preached, and the services ended with solemn benediction of the Blessed Sacrament. At the bottom of the program was a notice, "Immediate after the blessing of the roses there will be a drawing of holy pictures in St. Joseph's Hall."

Father Walshe worked mightily to pay off the $90,000 debt for the restoration of earthquake damage, but fell far short. Discouraged and on the verge of collapse, he was transferred to a less taxing assignment in 1907.

The Saintly Father Traverso

St. Joseph's lost another priest that same year. Father Traverso, who for twenty-seven years tended the spiritual needs of the parish, died at the age of eighty-two. Many stories are told about the priest whose given name, Sanctus, meaning "holy," fitted the man. George Strickler, member of an old family that dates back to pueblo days in St. Joseph's Church, says his grandmother Lydia Higuera (of Rancho Pala) told him that after Father Traverso paid a sick call to someone he thought was poor, the sick person would find money under the scarf on the bedside table. "She was sure he must be a saint," Strickler said, "because he would come into her home on E Street [now Montgomery] on a rainy day from walking the muddy streets and there would never be a trace of mud on his shoes."

In Rev. Walter Thornton, S.J.'s series "Fragments from the History of St. Joseph's Church," published in the 1925 parish bulletins, he tells of Father Traverso being called to pray over a sick boy who had a collar button lodged in his lung, which the surgeon was unable to remove. His life was ebbing. After praying over him, he gave the boy some of his favorite St. Ignatius water to drink. Hardly had the boy taken a sip than he began to cough and the button was dislodged.

Father Thornton relates another experience Father Traverso personally told him. He said he was on his way to make a sick call when he came to a house of spiritists that had an unsavory reputation. He was moved by an interior spirit to make the sign of the cross. Instantly the house "shook and swayed like a ship in an angry sea."

The Unique Theater after the 1906 earthquake. The Unique was the first theatrical venture of showman Sid Grauman, in 1903. He went on to build Grauman's Chinese Theater. (SAN JOSE HISTORICAL MUSEUM)

A deafening noise came from within the walls like a crash of thunder. A window was thrown open and the crash was heard in the whole neighborhood. The people in the house rushed out and vented their fury at the priest. No other house in the neighborhood was affected.

Father Henry Whittle

A vigorous younger Father Henry Whittle, S.J., replaced Father Walshe as pastor of St. Joseph's. Whittle, member of a prominent San Francisco family, was a lawyer who, after graduating from St. Ignatius College (University of San Francisco) and Hastings Law School and passing the bar, decided to become a priest. One month after he took over at St. Joseph's, the debt grew larger. A fire broke out in an arcade next to the church that destroyed the second and third floors of the college and 3,000 books.

Spurred on by the increased deficit, Father Whittle conceived some imaginative forms of fund-raising, including his "mighty public fair." In these times before the age of radio and movies when theatricals and "entertainments" were big, he put on plenty of both. The fair was held in a large hall with multicolored booths, many representing ethnic groups. The parish's 100-boy cadet band played, and the theaters presented talent by the "prize graduates" of the musical academy of Notre Dame. The press reported, "Its like had never before been staged in San Jose." The fair became an annual event, from October 14 to 24.

In 1911 a new Jesuit provincial tapped Father Whittle to be his executive secretary. William Culligan, S.J., who served as Whittle's assistant pastor for two years, was assigned to take over the pastorship.

Father William Culligan

Father Culligan, who possessed endless energy, plunged in headfirst to solve the many problems of a multiethnic parish, such as the pastoral issues of both financial and religious nature and, the big one, liquidating the parish debt. He carried on with the "showtimes"; he organized parish-sponsored operettas, which were big fund-raising events; and he staged concerts and entertainments that involved all ages of the parish. The *Mercury* society pages reported, "The costuming was spectacular, and the repertoire of high quality and enthusiasm."

The accomplishments of Father Culligan are exhausting to even think about. He established St. Edward

Chapel, which became St. Leo's parish; he created a special ministry to work with the growing Italian community that led to the building of Holy Family Church; he raised funds to build the Newman Center at San Jose State College; and he upgraded Catholic education by installing chemistry and physics laboratories at St. Joseph High School (through his efforts it was accredited to the University of California). He built a residence for the Brothers of Mary (Marianists) who taught at the school. Ahead of his time, seeing the need for a day-care center for working mothers, he brought in the Holy Family Sisters and built them a convent. That center is now known as St. Elizabeth's Day Care Center.

Strong on religious tolerance, he sponsored talks on bigotry at Newman Center, was one of the leaders in the campaign for the United Jewish Relief Fund for Poland in 1915, and promoted the church as a neutral site in local politics with nonpartisan debates for candidates for city council. He is especially remembered for the St. Joseph Band, which he directed. The band played at festivals and parades, and often on Sunday afternoons for Myles and Amanda O'Connor in their apartment at O'Connor Sanitarium, where they spent their later days.

When Sacred Heart Church in Saratoga, a mission of St. Joseph's, became a parish in 1911 they played for the big event. Father Culligan said mass. St. Joseph's parish gave a great celebration for the twenty-fifth anniversary of his ordination. A month later Father Culligan was transferred to Seattle, Washington. He returned to the valley in 1927 for his last assignments, as pastor of St. Clare's Church in Santa Clara.

Judging from the church's scrapbooks containing *San Jose Mercury* clips, 1915 was a big year. The St. Joseph's Players produced a musical, *Billy*, with Roy Emerson (served as tax collector from 1934 to 1975) singing the lead; a Maypole Social took place in the Knights of Columbus Hall; the Pavlowka folk dancers performed; there was a minstrel show; people had a chance to hear Hawaiian music from the Hui Lei Ilima Sextette.

The Ladies of St. Joseph's gave their annual Easter Ball at the Vendome Hotel. The list of patrons and patronesses included Mrs. W. P. Dougherty (widow of the Lumber King), Mrs. John W. Twohy (the railroad family), Maud Frasse (granddaughter of Martin Murphy, Jr.), Nell O'Brien (candy family), Mrs. W. H. Pabst (wife of the banker), and Mrs. William Leet (whose estate on The Alameda was the town's most elegant residence).

The Knights of Columbus had their day in the sun. Councils from San Francisco to Los Angeles were represented at the 1915 services at St. Joseph's. The

Armistice Day, 1919. The O'Connor Hospital nurses are part of the parade. (SAN JOSE HISTORICAL MUSEUM)

Mercury-Herald reported, "Fully a thousand Knights paraded the streets behind the St. Joseph's Club Band." The newspaper listed those receiving second and third degree in the Knights of Columbus: Archer Bowden, L. D. Cauhape, Victor Chargin, P. J. Foley, and Frank A. Marten.

The *Mecury-Herald* also reported that St. Joseph's had a new moving picture projector: "The movie machine just installed in St. Joseph's school auditorium was tried out most successfully yesterday in the presence of the town electrician, the Liberty movie operator and the brother in charge of St. Joseph's physics department." The film featured the Grand Jubilee celebration of Notre Dame Academy, and the Easter services of Mission Dolores and St. Joseph's.

World War I

In 1916 a popular song was "I Didn't Raise My Boy to Be a Soldier," but by 1917 everyone was singing a new song written by George M. Cohan called "Over There." President Woodrow Wilson, prompted by the sinking of the *Lusitania*, which caused the death of 124 Americans, severed diplomatic relations with Germany. The Senate and the Congress immediately passed a declaration of war. Patriotic posters popped up everywhere. A memorable one showed Uncle Sam with his pointed white beard, dressed in red, white, and blue and top hat, index finger pointed. The caption read, "Uncle Sam Needs You."

The war had to be financed. That meant Liberty Bond drives and the selling of thrift stamps. Dr. W. C. Bailey chaired the local War Work Council, with Arthur D.

Curtner as secretary and A. D. Foster as executive secretary. Representing the Women's Mobilized Army were Mrs. L. T. Smith as colonel and Mrs. L. D. Beattie as lieutenant colonel. The combined four drives for war bonds went over the top. The 14,000-strong Women's Mobilized Army carried through the Red Cross membership drives. The women's organizations and Red Cross circles gathered together to make surgical bandages, to knit, and to sew. War gardens were planted and cared for by the service clubs and high school students.

Anti-German sentiment was high. The Kaiser was regularly hung in effigy, "hamburger" was a dirty word, and as for sauerkraut—well, the Germans were called "Krauts." If you happened to have been born with a German name, that was unfortunate. It was a time of patriotic parades—ten thousand marched in the Loyalty Day parade. Nurses marched in uniforms, even little girls played Red Cross nurses with their dolls, wearing white bands on their heads with a red cross improvised with ribbon.

Along with the Salvation Army, the Jewish Welfare, and others, St. Joseph's did its part. Charles O'Brien (O'Brien's Candy) chaired its drive to raise $50,000 for the needs of the soldiers. Serving on his committee were D. M. Burnett, Jay McCabe, "The Hatter," attorney Robert Bressani, prominent druggist and banker Nicholas Pellerano, Joseph Solari, and C. O. Wendt, who had a popular butcher shop on Market Street.

Bastille Day

The large French colony turned out on July 15, 1918, for the celebration of Fall of the Bastille. The festivities started in the morning with a mass at St. Joseph's. Dainty white-robed children paid homage to the French and American flags, and young Miss Celine Combatalade sang appropriate hymns. Father Fayolle, who celebrated the mass, spoke of their homeland and the glories of its flag. "If you will look across the ocean and gaze upon the battlefields of Northern France," he said, "you will see it drenched in blood and tears; you will see it torn and tattered by the bullets of the enemy, you will see it struggling for victory supported by the strong and fearless American flag."

In the afternoon a happy throng came by streetcars and automobiles to Cedar Brook Park for sports activities and dancing. The American flag and the tricolor of France were the theme of the elaborate decorations by committee chairman J. D. Lazier. A popular booth featured the Kaiser in effigy. For a small fee one could "swat the Kaiser."

The Flu Epidemic

While the American boys were still fighting in France an influenza epidemic hit the country. One-fifth of the population was affected and 200 died. The board of health closed the schools and churches. Gauze masks were required. St. Joseph's set up an altar in front of the church. Morris Dailey, president of the Normal School, offered part of his school buildings to be turned into hospital wards for sick children.

The *Mercury-Herald* ran a tearjerker of a story with the caption "Will You Help The Children Of A Soldier?" saying that the Social Service Agency, with Miss Elizabeth Porter in charge, had sent out pleas for food, clothes, and money, particularly nighties for little girls. In one home, they said, a father died, leaving a mother with two small children who were ill and needed clothes. They wanted their "Daddy" and the mother was too ill to comfort them. In another home, where the father was

A pair of fashionable buildings at the entrance to Fountain Alley
(SAN JOSE MERCURY NEWS)

overseas fighting, the mother died and a six-year-old girl tried to comfort her four-year-old brother, who cried and cried.

The writer praised the work of the Sisters of the Holy Family, "who go from stricken home to home on their errands of service and cheer." They would come home to the convent at night exhausted and throw their clothes in a tank of boiling water and stir them with a brown stick. Peter Dunne offered the nuns his car; Edward McLaughlin told them to charge all their surgical supplies to him. In addition to nursing the sick, the sisters opened a soup kitchen at their Vine Street convent. Mrs. Henrietta Filipello, whose husband, a doctor, was tending the sick, and her sister, Isabel de Saisset, staffed the kitchen.

CHAPTER TWENTY-FOUR

St. Joseph's Families

S t. Joseph's parishioners have always included prominent citizens who were devoted not only to their church but also to the community's welfare. Fitting this description were Maurice O'Brien, a native of Manhattan-on-the-Hudson, and his Savannah-born wife, Margaret Byrne, who came to San Jose in 1860. They had been married in San Francisco, where he learned the confectionary business. That same year he moved to San Jose with, as his grandson, the late Russell O'Brien, said, "a bride, courage, and $500." He opened his first confectionary store in the Pacific Hotel next door to St. Joseph's Church. The store and the hotel live on in replica in the San Jose Historical Museum at Kelley Park.

O'Brien bought a buckskin horse for delivery purposes,

The Pacific Hotel, adjacent to St. Joseph's on Market Street (SAN JOSE HISTORICAL MUSEUM)

decided it was a good image for the candy business, and from then on always had buckskin horses. When his son Charles replaced the horses with horseless carriage delivery wagons, he had them painted the same color. In 1928 he had five buckskin-colored trucks.

About ten years after coming to town, O'Brien moved his candy business to the Ryland Block. In 1903 his son Charles bought the business, and his other son, Walter, was a partner for a short time. After several moves, they settled permanently on South First Street between San Carlos and San Antonio. In the middle twenties O'Brien opened a restaurant in conjunction with the candy store that became a popular eating place.

Harry Farrell, retired *Mercury* political writer, in his book *San Jose and Other Famous Places*, best illustrates O'Brien's fame in an interview he did with former President Richard Nixon at San Clemente following his four-year reclusive period. At the close of the interview Nixon asked Farrell, "Does San Jose still have that great restaurant, the one that sold ice cream and candy?"

Farrell said he hesitated a moment and then asked, "O'Brien's?"

"O'Brien's," Nixon exclaimed. "That's right. That was one of the best restaurants in California."

Not only was it a successful restaurant, but it was famous for its ice-cream sodas and was an after-school hangout for generations of high school and college students. "Meet me at O'Brien's" was the byword. Unfortunately, in the middle 1950s, with the exodus of retail business from downtown San Jose, the ninety-year-old landmark closed its doors.

In 1910 Charles married May Russell of an old San Jose family in St. Joseph's Church. They lived first in the home of his parents at Second and Virginia streets before building their own home on South Thirteenth Street. Charles and May had three children: Charles, Jr., who is retired and lives in Bend, Oregon, with his wife, Madelyn, and Betty O'Brien Walsh and Russell

President Harry S. Truman in San Francisco during his 1948 whistle-stop campaign. Seated at his left is William F. Malone; on his right, John McEnery, state democratic chairman who influenced Truman to stop at San Jose.

O'Brien, both deceased. Although the O'Briens had moved into St. Patrick's parish, Russ O'Brien remembered going to early mass at St. Joseph's on Sundays with his father and opening up the store afterwards.

Charles O'Brien, who was a leader in St. Joseph's affairs, led a fund drive to help liquidate the debt with committee members Angel Berryessa, Studebaker dealer Robert Benson, and Mrs. T. Monahan, wife of mayor and mortician Thomas Monahan, who led another drive for St. Joseph's to help the soldiers in World War I.

Nell and Edith O'Brien, Charles's sisters, were school teachers. Nell, principal of Woodrow Wilson Junior High School, was active in St. Joseph's, and Edith taught at the old Normal School. Neither married.

Pascual Bisceglia, owner of canneries and wineries, bought the O'Briens' Second Street house, where he raised his family of five children. They also attended St. Joseph's Church. The house later became the Chapel of the Flowers and was owned by the late William Geoffroy, who married Clorinda Bisceglia.

The McEnerys

Newspaperman Patrick McEnery, who later became editor of the *San Jose Mercury-Herald*, came to San Jose with his wife, Catherine, at the turn of the century. Their son, John, married Margaret Sellers, whose father, Ben Sellers, served on the city council. Her grandfather Patrick Condon came on the first transcontinental train

in 1869. He built the road to Mount Hamilton.

John McEnery was not only a businessman and founder of the Farmer's Union, but a politician "to the manner born." Serving as chairman of the Democratic party, he greeted all the visiting Democratic bigwigs, such as Eleanor Roosevelt. A Harry Farrell anecdote concerns John McEnery traveling on President Truman's train in 1948. When he learned that no stop was scheduled for San Jose, he maneuvered his way into the presidential suite at the Fairmont Hotel in San Francisco and asked the president why the train couldn't stop in San Jose for a few minutes. Truman wanted to know how many people he could get out. McEnery promised 1,500. "I'll stop anywhere for 1,500 people," the president said. When they got to the San Jose depot, they found a crowd of 4,000 waiting. As they stood on the rear platform of the train, Truman turned to McEnery and said, "You're so conservative, you ought to be a Republican."

It was not surprising that Tom McEnery, John's son, would go into politics, first as a member of the San Jose City Council. He was then elected mayor for the limit of two terms, serving in the 1980s during the period of the city's most rapid growth.

In a conversation with the mayor, he reminisced, "My family has always been involved with St. Joseph's. My brother, John, and I were altar boys and attended St. Joseph's School (he later taught there for a while). I used to serve 5:15 A.M. mass. If we served a funeral we would get a dollar." He said the family lived on Ayer

Street not far from the church. He still lives on that street with his wife, Jill, and three daughters, and his mother lives nearby. "When we were growing up," he said, "life revolved around St. Joseph's. I was baptized, confirmed and married in St. Joseph's. My children were baptized there. The family has all been buried from the church. My nephew (John McEnry IV) is being married in St. Joseph's in February." He will be the first McEnery to be married in the cathedral.

The Ward Family

Mary Sheridan Ward was a hundred years ahead of her time. Not only did she make San Jose the first city on the West Coast to have a woman embalmer when she graduated from the Clark School of Embalming in San Francisco, but she also made it the first city to have three generations of women embalmers. In 1888 the embalming school was not prepared for a woman graduate. On her diploma the "him" was crossed out and changed to "her." Her daughter, Gertrude, followed the family tradition, as did her granddaughter, Mary Gertrude Gray.

Patrick and Bridget Sheridan came from Illinois in 1863 with their infant daughter, Mary. That same year Mary's future husband, William B. Ward, arrived from New York to join his brother, Bernard, in the landscaping business. Before becoming an undertaker, he also worked in the express business and as a policeman. The horse-drawn hearses of Ward's Funeral Parlor could be seen traveling to all parts of Santa Clara Valley.

Ward had the distinction, along with Joseph Chargin and Dan Ryan, of receiving permission to have his head covered in church. He said his head got cold, so he wore a skull cap. From 1899 to 1904 the family lived in a red brick building that housed the mortuary across the street from St. Joseph's. It was formerly the priests' residence. In 1904 the Wards moved into a twelve-room home at Empire and North Third streets. When the earthquake hit two years later, the two staircases leading upstairs were wrecked, trapping the family A friend, Dan Gray, came to the rescue with ladders. He must have made an impression with Gertrude Ward, because he later became her husband in a ceremony performed by Father Jeremiah Collins, S.J., in the family home.

More dramatic was the rescue during the earthquake at Agnews State Hospital of the Ward's granddaughter Angela Kell, a nurse and daughter of Mary Ward and Martin Kell. She had fallen from the fourth floor to the basement of the administration building. Four bodies landed on top of her, all presumed dead until one of the

William B. and Mary Sheridan Ward. Mrs. Ward was the first woman embalmer in the state. (COURTESY MARY GERTRUDE GRAY)

rescuers saw a hand waving in the debris. Although 119 persons at the hospital died from the quake, he pulled Angie unharmed from the wreckage.

Ralph, son of Dan and Gertrude Gray, attended St. Joseph's school and was an altar boy. St. Joseph's was the headquarters of the Jesuits, so the elaborate religious ceremonies required the assistance of many altar boys.

Popular Santa Clara County Supervisor Ed Levin died just at the time Vatican II changes were coming into effect. A large crowd was expected for his funeral. St. Joseph's was caught short without the newly required altar facing the congregation. Ralph Gray came to the rescue posthaste, borrowing one from St. John Vianney Church.

In 1979 the Ward Funeral Parlor, through a business merger, became the Willow Glen Funeral Chapel: Accinelli-Gray-Taketa-Rose. Ralph and Mary Gertrude Gray continue to be active in the business.

Joseph Bihn

A Carrara marble statue of Saint Joseph holding the infant Jesus was a gift to St. Joseph's Church from

Amelia Bihn in memory of her husband, Joseph. Bishop DuMaine selected this statue to represent Saint Joseph at the entrance to the headquarters of the Diocese of San Jose on Lenzen Avenue. The Bihns, who came West in 1910, went first to Petaluma, where they went into the chicken hatchery business. They next moved to San Jose where they became generous supporters of St. Joseph's Church.

Their son, Alphonse (always called Al), a graduate of Santa Clara College, married Celine Combatalade in the Mission Santa Clara church, even though Celine was born across the street from St. Joseph's and her parents were married there in 1880. Celine, the little girl who sang in the Bastille Day Celebration of 1918, became a member of St. Joseph's choir, which was for many years directed by Carl Fitzgerald. The members always relaxed in the choir room until the prompter would give them their signal. According to Mrs. Bihn, one Sunday the prompter fell asleep. Father Culligan turned around and, seeing the singers were missing, said, "The choir seems to have retired. We will now continue with a low mass." Members of the choir included Frank Towner, Charles Sullivan (the little boy who watched the burning of the Lenzen church in 1875), Warren Scheffield, and a couple, Margaret Trevey and Raymond d'Artenay, who many years later both lost their spouses and married each other.

Celine Bihn's mother, Adeline Derrau (Combatalade), as a young woman was nurse to Diana Murphy, who gained notoriety as a Murphy heiress and from her marriages to Morgan Hill and Sir George Rhodes. For an excursion, Adeline would take little Diana in the pony cart from Morgan Hill to San Francisco, stopping at the home of friends such as the Murphys in Sunnyvale and the Floods in Atherton. Celine remembers that when she was a little girl her mother took her to visit Lady Diana in San Jose.

Mrs. W. P. Dougherty

The name of Anna Fenton Dougherty frequently appeared in St. Joseph's news stories as Mrs. W.P. Dougher-ty. One of her many contributions was the founding of the Catholic Woman's Center at San Jose State College at Fifth and San Fernando streets. At that time young women didn't live in apartments, so it satisfied a need not only for the college women but also for single working women. She not only gave generously to the center herself but solicited funds from such well-known Catholics as Charles O'Brien and Bob Benson. Under the direction of Catholic Charities, it is now the John XXIII Center for senior citizens. It was remodeled in 1987 with Jennifer DiNapoli spearheading the effort. A room is named for her husband, Phil DiNapoli, founder and chairman of the Plaza Bank. Noonday meals are served

Anna Fenton Dougherty, prominent San Jose leader and member of St. Joseph's Church (COURTESY CECILY KYES)

Looking down Market Street from the light tower. St. Joseph's is on the left; city hall is in the center.

five days a week, and there are affordable apartments and volunteer counseling and social activities such as bingo and dancing. Valle Monte League gives a generous share of its annual "Christmas Tree Elegance" benefit to the center.

Mrs. Dougherty's family, the Fentons, dates back to the late 1840s on Rancho Ulistac in the Agnew-Alviso area, which was granted to two Santa Clara Mission Indians, Marcelo Pio and Cristobal. Because of the large number of Indians living on the rancho it was called Fenton's Indian Mound Ranch. These Indians sometimes caused serious trouble. On a visit home for the holidays, a Fenton son, who was studying for the priesthood, in his zeal to do missionary work, went to see them and was killed. Another time they set fire to the grain harvest.

When the Fentons' friends the Martin Murphys learned of this, they sent over wagonloads of grain from their nearby Sunnyvale ranch.

Anna's husband, William Patrick Dougherty, was known as "The Lumber King of Santa Clara Valley." He owned most of the San Lorenzo canyon, in Santa Cruz County, and the Dougherty Lumber Company, and he founded the Santa Clara Valley Mill & Lumber Company. The *Evening News* ran a headline story of Mrs. Dougherty's death in an automobile crash in Capitola in 1931, and the next day the lead story on the editorial page concerned her loss to the community. A large crowd attended her funeral in St. Joseph's and heard Father Laherty give one of the most eloquent eulogies of his career.

The sanctury of St. Joseph's Church (before renovation and conversion to cathedral) showing the Sciocchetti murals

CHAPTER TWENTY-FIVE

The Golden Jubilee

The highlight of the twenties for St. Joseph's was its celebration on March 19, 1926, of the fiftieth anniversary of the laying of the cornerstone. The great church was filled to capacity as the procession, headed by Fourth Degree Knights of Columbus in full regalia, left the San Fernando Street entrance to the rectory at 11 o'clock in the morning. Visiting priests and officiating clergy preceded the Most Reverend Archbishop Edward J. Hanna in mitre and cope, flanked on either side by the deacons of honor, followed by 120 surpliced choir boys. The procession moved along San Fernando Street to Market to the entrance to the church and up the main aisle to the sanctuary.

In his sermon the archbishop paid tribute to the Catholic people of San Jose who had made this great church possible. He reviewed its history from the little tule-thatched adobe church of 1803 to the laying of the cornerstone of the present church in 1876. Twenty-five priests took part in the ceremonies, including the Very Reverend Joseph M. Piet, S.J., Provincial of the California Province of the Society of Jesus, and the pastor, Father Joseph Crowley.

The Sciocchetti Murals

Although not finished in time for the celebration, an important phase of the Golden Jubilee was the mural work by the Italian artist Father Luigi Sciocchetti, who had trained under Ludwig Seitz in Rome. He had met Archbishop Hanna in Rome and received permission to come to the San Francisco diocese to join his brother Msgr. Francesco Sciocchetti, who was pastor of Precious Blood Church in San Jose (later Holy Cross).

His niece Dolores Ibbotson of Belmont, with whom the priest lived the last years of his life, said her uncle first spent five months in his San Francisco studio working on the drawings, which she said was the most dif-

ficult part. He drew them on paper divided into small squares. He then came to San Jose, where he worked in the hall of the empty school building in back of St. Joseph's. With his four assistants he transferred the sketches to large canvases that also were divided into squares. They then spent five months gluing them to the walls, ceiling, and dome.

Around the stained-glass skylight in the dome he painted the Evangelists, Matthew, Mark, Luke, and John, and the fathers of the Eastern and Western Church. He also decorated the four vaulted ceilings in a style in keeping with the baroque feeling of the church. His work blends frescoes and oil paintings on canvas so subtly that it is difficult to detect the difference. Using the trompe l'oeil (fool the eye) technique for many of the column capitals, cornices, and moldings, he achieved a three-dimensional effect.

Mrs. Ibbotson came with family members to see the restoration of their uncle's art in May of 1990. They had pleasant memories of helping their uncle during the period he was doing the murals. Her sister, Teresa Sciocchetti Melchori, described the intricate process of doing the gold leaf. Her brother, Guido, said he came down from San Francisco during two summer vacations and helped his father, who was also named Guido, put up the scaffolding and paint portions of the walls. Mrs. Ibbotson described her uncle as "a small, slight man with delicate hands, grey hair that was probably black like my father's and deep-set brown eyes. He was a friendly, outgoing man."

All three served as models. In fact, they got so tired of it they said they would sometimes hide from him. He used their hands and feet as models. Dolores remembers posing for the Virgin Mary, Teresa was an angel, and Guido says he posed holding his arm up and got awfully tired. He said his uncle used many people for models, including assistant pastor Father Ivancovich for Saint Joseph in the murals behind the marble altar and, go-

A view of St. Joseph's from the plaza, looking north in the early 1900s before the post office (foreground) lost its tower in the 1906 earthquake. (SAN JOSE MERCURY NEWS)

ing from the sublime to the ridiculous, he once brought in a hobo who came walking down the street. He gave him some food and, after his modeling stint, a little money.

Some of Father Sciocchetti's work is in the small but beautiful Immaculate Conception Church in San Francisco, designed by St. Joseph's architect, Bryan Clinch. The murals he painted on the ceiling and walls of St. Jose's Five Wounds Church can still be seen. The Greco family, who were friends of the priest, had a painting he did of a peacock in their home. The family said although the remuneration for his work was small (when he finally was paid, he bought himself a Model A Ford), Father Sciocchetti considered St. Joseph's his most important work.

Armando Marchigani

Father Sciocchetti requested that Armando Marchigani, his protege, be hired to assist him. He had discovered the artist as an eight-year-old boy in Florence, sculpting a horse out of sand in the street. Stuck with his talents, the priest paid for his art education. Because he was considered an important young artist, the Italian government did not want him to leave. A special permit issued by the U.S. government had to guarantee that the work he would be doing was essential and that, upon completion of his art work (1928), he would return to

Italy. Bank of America president James A. Bacigalupi signed a bond.

Miriam Hart Alfaro, of the Hart's Department Store family and wife of the late Panamanian ambassador to Great Britain, Carlos Alfaro, on a trip to San Jose in 1988 visited the studio of Andrzej Bossak to observe his restoration project. Marchigani, she recalled, used to come to their home on The Alameda to give her painting lessons. Her father was so impressed with his talent he commissioned him to do a portrait of Miriam and her sister, Elise Hart Walter of Kentfield. "He was good-looking, and lots of fun," she said. "He didn't speak much English. He would say, 'You Americans use too much slang. I don't understand it.' My sister and I wrote it down for him." She said that when Father Sciocchetti brought Marchigani to California he asked the younger artist to go first to the fishing villages and other places to look for good Renaissance art to bring over. "One of those that he brought," she said, "was called *Goddess of the Night.* It was very Raphael, with oval face and a quarter-moon over her head. They said they would have to attribute it to Raphael. I don't know what became of it, but I made a copy that I still have in my home in Panama."

After Marchigani returned to Italy, Mrs. Alfaro said she used to drive to San Francisco to continue her lessons with Father Sciocchetti. Asked about the story that she and her sister were models in the murals, she said, "If you use binoculars, you can see us as angels."

CHAPTER TWENTY-SIX

St. Joseph's Names

In the thirties St. Joseph's continued to be the center of social life for the parishioners. Banker William Pabst emerged a leader in the fund-raising field, chairing the big Halloween festival in the new gymnasium of St. Joseph's School. Teasers in the newspapers advertised: "Only three more days remain 'till the Palace Gates of the Mystic Fairyland will be thrown open to the public and the longed for Carnival of Fun will have begun."

William and Laura Pabst and their family had the sixth row pew on the right side of the church. Their daughter Helen Pabst Walsh, who taught ballroom dancing to generations of San Jose young people, remembers that the pews had gates and that when they were filled, the ushers closed the gates. Another daughter, Francia Hyland, stopped by the church years later and found their name, faded but still legible, on the family pew. Francia met her husband, Jim Hyland, whose family had their pew a few rows behind the Pabsts, after mass one Sunday. It was a custom for the young men to stand outside the church, watch the girls come out, and decide which one they wanted to take for a soda. Pabst, who started out as a cashier at the swank Del Monte Hotel during its heyday, lived with his wife for sixty years at First and Asbury streets.

Josephine and Peter Dunne (son of Catherine Dunne), lived near the Pabsts. Son Peter, ordained a Jesuit priest in 1921 in Hastings, England, frequently returned to his home parish to celebrate mass. Their daughter, Josephine, married Cedric Richmond of the Richmond-Chase family, and their granddaughter, Marilyn Richmond, married Dr. Edward Nino of Hillsborough.

***

Well-remembered are the James Morrison family, who had a spectacular home called "The Bird's Nest" at Fifth and Julian streets. It was said when they bought the house they were looking ahead to holding wedding receptions for their five daughters. The Paradise Sisters, as they were called because they each wore a different-colored dress to mass on Sundays, never married. They did create considerable attention, however, when they arrived at St. Joseph's on Sundays in their electric automobile.

***

Bob Benson, a staunch St. Joseph's supporter, had the Studebaker dealership on Market Street across from the church. A friend, Bill Scilacci, said that one time Benson took out an insurance policy on himself with the Holy Family nuns as beneficiaries. He left his entire estate to St. Joseph's and to Santa Clara University, where Benson Hall is named for him. He never married, but his steady lady friend of fifteen years was Miss McKiernan, who lived in the Rose Garden area. Benson was a friend in need—on such occasions as when the church needed new carpeting, he took care of the bill.

***

The Nicholas Pellerano family, active members of St. Joseph's, were listed in newspaper accounts dating from 1880. Nick Pellerano, who had a pharmacy in San Jose on South First Street next door to the present location of Woolworth's (later taken over by Nick Molle, a cousin, who was with the Bank of America). The red velvet upholstery remained on the Pellerano pew—after pew rent was discontinued. The sisters used this pew at the children's mass. Pellerano left his estate to his sister, Maria, who, in turn, at her death, in the 1960s, willed a generous sum to St. Joseph's.

***

Another St. Joseph's stalwart, Dr. Eugene Filipello, married Henrietta de Saisset, the daughter of Pedro de Saisset (the French consul) and María Jesús de Palomares Suñol (always called Jesusita). They lived in the de Saisset house, about where the parking lot for the civic auditorium now stands. The doctor, a native of Turin, Italy, was much loved by his patients and first visited them on a bicycle. Later he traveled by horse and buggy and eventually, with the coming of the automobile, was chauffeur driven. Henrietta Filipello's spinster sister, Isabel,

A scene from one of the theatricals put on by St. Joseph's players at the Victory Theater in the early 1920s (ARCHIVES CALIFORNIA PROVINCE + SOCIETY OF JESUS)

lived with them. Many recall seeing Dr. Filipello walking to St. Joseph's for Sunday mass flanked by Henrietta on one side and Isabel on the other.

Dr. Filipello sponsored Dr. Evarist Turco, his nephew, to come over from Italy. John Turco, the doctor's son, recalls going with his mother, Genevieve Turco, to tea at the Filipellos. The first floor, he said, was for cooking and the second floor the living area. Turco, who ushered at St. Joseph's married Terry Polk, great-granddaughter of Bernard Murphy.

After the death of the Filipellos, Isabel de Saisset gave money to the University of Santa Clara to build the de Saisset Museum and Art Gallery to house the paintings of her brother, Ernest. Jesusita's daughters, Dolores and Josefa Suñol, whose father, José Suñol, was murdered at Rancho del Valle by a poacher, willed their large inheritance from their grandfather Don Antonio Suñol to St. Joseph's and Santa Clara University. The sanctuary lamp that hung on the gospel side was dedicated to Josephine Suñol in 1907.

The late Dolores Turek, great-granddaughter of Don Antonio Suñol, used to visit this house and remembered, according to her son, George Strickler, seeing a bronze medal on the wall that had been awarded to Antonio Suñol, who was Napoleon's scribe, for meritorious service in the battle of Waterloo. Its whereabouts are unknown.

Joseph and Josephine Chargin came from Hollister in 1903 and bought a home on Vine Street, where they raised their family of eight children. He had Chargin's Grill on Fountain Alley for over fifty years. Totally a St. Joseph's family, their five sons served as altar boys for Father Grisez, moderator of the John Beacham altar boy society, and attended St. Joseph's Grammar and High School and Santa Clara University. Victor, John Mark (Jack), and Gerald stayed on for law school. Gerald became a superior court judge, Joseph a civil engineer, and Lawrence a farmer. The girls who attended Notre Dame Academy were musical, their names appearing on St. Joseph's programs. Mr. and Mrs. Chargin celebrated their fiftieth and sixtieth wedding anniversaries in St. Joseph's, surrounded by their numerous family and friends.

Not many can equal the marriage record of Marceille and Harold Wehner, who, in 1989, celebrated the sixty-ninth anniversary of their wedding in St. Joseph's. They followed in the steps of the bride's parents, James Gregg and Rose Carroll, natives of Ireland, who were married in St. Joseph's Church before the turn of the century. Gregg, an usher at St. Joseph's (he passed the "box" as they used to say), had a neighborhood grocery store where customers, including Harold Wehner's family, visited with their friends. His uncle, William Wehner, had the Lomas Azules vineyards and winery at what is now The Villages.

150

CHAPTER TWENTY-SEVEN

The Twenties and the Thirties

Business boomed in San Jose in the twenties. The new Bank of America (Bank of Italy until 1930) building towered twelve stories high at First and Santa Clara streets. That same year, 1926, T. S. Montgomery, who built the first high-rise, the Garden City Bank, and helped to shape the face of downtown San Jose, built for $900,000 the impressive five-story Sainte Claire Hotel at San Carlos and Market streets. His $500,000 Fox West Coast Theater was a sign that stage productions were out and the movies in.

The twenties symbolized the "Jazz Age," a time of bobbed-hair flappers in short dresses dancing the Charleston; of bootleg booze, speakeasies, and roadhouses. Payoffs to politicians led to tipoffs to the saloon keepers and frustration for the police officers. The horse was out, the horseless carriage in, and aviation took off. By 1930 one in every three persons in San Jose owned a car. Home from the war, Air Force pilot Johnny Johnston bought some army surplus planes and opened a flying field in a grain field off Alum Rock Avenue. Flying was still a novelty, so for ten dollars a pop he would take people up for rides. He made the first aeroplane delivery for an individual firm when, according to the *Mercury-Herald*, he delivered two hats for Jay McCabe, "the Hatter," to Santa Clara. When Father Timothy Murphy, president of the University of Santa Clara, and Ole Hanson, a visiting former mayor of Seattle, signed the delivery book, "seven motion picture men clicked the scene for the screens of America's thousands of theaters." Johnston piloted the valley's first regular airmail route between San Jose and Oakland, starting in October of 1928.

La Fiesta de las Rosas

The Fiesta de las Rosas was a natural for the "land of sunshine, fruit, and flowers" and a big event in 1926 for

The Fiesta de las Rosas was well promoted, always with a Spanish theme (COURTESY ERNIE RENZEL)

this town of 76,000 people. The invitation, printed courtesy of committee members Normandin-Campen Co. (Hudson-Essex dealers), stated, "The grand floral parade of more than ninety floats and twenty musical units will move down the historic Alameda at promptly 2:30 P.M. Saturday, May 19. BE OUR GUESTS." Other familiar names listed on the committee included California history writer Mrs. Fremont Older, who, with Elizabeth (Mrs. Howard) Derby, started San Jose's Rose Garden, and strongly promoted the fiesta, shoe store owner Chester Herold, jeweler Earl Bothwell, furniture man Ernest Lion, banker Paul Rudolph, M. Blum of

The Chamber of Commerce worked hard to bring new residents to San Jose, the "Garden City of the Pacific." (SAN JOSE MERCURY NEWS)

Blum's women's clothing store on South First Street, and George Fontaine (stepfather of actresses Olivia de Havilland and Joan Fontaine) of Hale's.

Patterned after Pasadena's Rose Parade, the elaborate floats sponsored by schools and businesses had an early California theme. Marshalls Louis Oneal, riding his silver-encrusted western saddle, and Tim Sullivan led the parade and its marching bands from the Santa Clara city limits down The Alameda and Santa Clara Street. There were always a few celebrities riding on the floats, such as film actress Billie Dove, brought up from Hollywood by Ford-Lincoln dealer Harry Canelo, and Bea Benedaret, who became a well-known radio performer on the Burns and Allen show. Canelo, a flamboyant character in contrast to his brother, Dr. Kelly Canelo, once challenged Charlie Chaplin to a race from San Jose to Los Angeles. Reflecting her early-California background, Camila Argüello Fisher, descendant of the first Mexican governor, Luís Argüello, rode on a float dressed in Spanish costume.

It was an occasion for residents on The Alameda to entertain their friends. The Sinnott sisters, Catherine and Delia, always had a crowd, including their Stockton relatives, descendants of Charles and Ellen Murphy Weber, at their home on the corner of Naglee and The Alameda. Ted Bonetti remembers their friends gathering on the second-floor porch of the family home on The Alameda at Emory Street to watch the parade. It is one of the few residences on The Alameda still family-owned. Five motion picture companies photographed the event, and the footage showed in theaters all over the country.

152

The next year the fiesta celebrated the 150th anniversary of the founding of the Pueblo de San José de Guadalupe by adding the Santa Clara County Exposition of Progress in downtown. The committee heads, Frank Mitchell, Alvin Long, and Guy Marshall, put on a giant nationwide advertising promotion for the eight-day event with billboards, 30,000 auto stickers, and 10,000 penny postcards. They advised out-of-towners, of which there were many, to make reservations at one of the town's fine hotels. In 1932, after seven years, the Depression brought an end to the Fiesta de las Rosas.

Christmas in the Park

Today's counterpart of the Fiesta de las Rosas is Christmas in the Park, winner of an award from the California State Parks Commission. The 1989 opening-night parade drew a crowd estimated at 70,000. In the plaza park, once the center of the pueblo life, the crowd enjoyed the spectacle of thousands of lights on the trees and sixty-five animated Christmas exhibits, sponsored by businesses, schools, and clubs. Included were the original exhibits given to the city by the late Don Lima, who had displayed them at his Willow Street Lima Family Mortuaries. St. Joseph's Cathedral was illuminated for the first time to show off its newly coppered dome and towers. As carolers sang on the steps, over 1,300 visitors got a first look at nearly completed art restoration.

Fiesta de las Rosas float from the late 1920s (SAN JOSE HISTORICAL MUSEUM)

The Great Depression

Living was high in the twenties—until that October day in 1929 when the bubble burst as the Dow plummeted to a resounding crash. With that crash came the Great Depression. San Jose, still an agricultural community, was not hit as hard as the industrial areas. Although wages were low, school girls still cut cots as they always had during summer vacation at the local canneries, and the boys picked apricots and prunes. Nevertheless, the Depression was for real. The Unemployment Relief Council, which was similar to the WPA, provided work with a small wage, food, and shelter to 850 people who cleared orchards and planted trees along Park Avenue, East Santa Clara and Keyes streets, and ten miles of median strips. A *San Jose Mercury-Herald* story told of Brother David handing out meal tickets to long lines in front of St. Joseph's.

Sodality Park, the baseball field of the Men's Sodality of St. Joseph's Church, provided an antidote for fathers and sons, who cheered their favorite baseball teams. The field stretched along the Los Gatos Creek between San Carlos, Royal, and Auzerais Avenue. At exhibition matches, they gazed in awe as the likes of Babe Ruth and Lou Gehrig lofted balls over the fence. Here the Pacific Coast League teams played and the Portland Beavers trained for several years. All that good wholesome fun came to an end when the railroad came through Sodality Park's outfield.

More than a few nostalgic tears were shed on April 18, 1938, when seventy years of public transportation that had started with horsecars and then electric cars, came to an end with the employment of busses. As a farewell gesture, the railway turned the day into a fun affair by giving free rides from 9 P.M. until midnight.

But the good news for trolley fans is that they are back. Not only do the light-rail cars run out First Street through the modern office and industrial complexes that once were grain fields and pear orchards to Great America, but they will link up with surrounding towns to alleviate traffic problems. Antique streetcars, restored at the San Jose Historical Museum by dedicated

153

volunteers, now run downtown.

The thirties also saw the St. James Hotel torn down and replaced with a new post office. The old brownstone post office building, built in the mid-1890s, became the city library. In 1970 the library moved into a handsome new building on San Carlos Street, and the San Jose Museum of Art took over the brownstone building.

The Airport

The groundwork for San Jose's International Airport was laid in 1937, when Russ Petit, head of the Chamber of Commerce, asked Ernie Renzel, one of the board members, who later became mayor, to talk to Pat Le Deit and some members of the Junior Chamber who were interested in building an airport. Renzel became chairman of the Citizen's Central Airport Committee. The committee had a choice of three parcels of land but preferred the larger and better-located 473-acre Mary Crocker Ives estate, which extended south from Newhall Street to Brokaw Road, and between the Southern Pacific Railroad and the Guadalupe River. Renzel didn't realize that the Southern Pacific Railroad—which, in a sense, owned the town and was a power in the state at that time—didn't want an airport to be built. It had the support of three men who wielded a lot of clout: Southern Pacific attorney Louis Oneal, James Clayton, who handled the comany real estate, and Frazier Reed, of the Clayton office, a background player.

According to Renzel, a representative of the railroad came to him and told him that they wanted the property for a freight yard. Renzel told the man he personally thought it would be ideal for an airport. The S.P. representative assured Renzel, "You'll never get it." But the powerful Southern Pacific was wrong. This was the straw that broke the camel's back—the end of the power of the S.P. After receiving the approval from the Civil Aeronautics Authority (CAA), the proposition was put on the ballot as a tax levy and passed by a narrow margin of 200 votes. Through Renzel's efforts the city was able to buy 615 acres of farm land off Coleman Avenue from the Mary Ives Crocker estate for $300 an acre instead of the asking price of $625. Unfortunately for the CAA man who gave his approval, political power came into play and, within a month, he lost his job.

It wasn't until 1947, after delays due to World War II, with the usual government red tape and many revisions of plans, that it got started. The San Jose Municipal Airport was finally dedicated on February 1, 1949. Southwest Airways regular passenger and freight service were under way.

154

The Naval Air Station

The Navy gave the thirties economy a welcome shot in the arm when, in 1929, it chose Sunnyvale over the front-runner San Diego for its Pacific Coast lighter-than-air station. The offer of 1,000 acres of Rancho Posolmi in the South Bay lowlands was the clincher that swayed Congress' vote. Posolmi was a Mexican land grant to an Indian, Chief Ynigo, in 1844. Part of this land was owned by the Holthouse family. They farmed and marketed their peas under the Ynigo name. Its label was an Indian wearing a war bonnet.

Over five hundred men to work to build the Navy's base and hangar, the largest in the world (1,133 feet long and 308 feet wide) to house the helium-filled dirigible U.S.S. Macon. This monstrous airship, which could hold at least five scout planes in her hull, if stood on one end would equal the height of a seventy-eight-story skyscraper. She carried a crew of seventy-eight men. At first it was just called the Naval Air Station, but when the Macon's sister ship, the Akron, crashed in 1933, the base was named for its skipper, Rear Adm. William A. Moffett. Besides the tragic loss of the man, his death was a blow to the South Bay for another reason. Moffett was an advocate for a project that was never to be realized: the making of Alviso into a deep-water port for naval vessels. In 1935 the Macon suffered the same fate as the Akron when it crashed in the ocean off Point Sur. The only possible "saving grace" was that the Macon lost only two crewmen compared to the seventy-three who died on the Akron.

The empty silver hangar and field stood as an embarrassment to the Navy until four years later, when they were saved by the announcement that the National Advisory Committee on Aeronautics (NACA) had chosen Moffett from among fifty-four sites in the country as the base for its supersonic travel and outer space projects. NACA built a wind tunnel, the largest in the world, that became the foundation of Ames Aeronautical Laboratory.

One good thing begets another. In 1955 when Lockheed was relocating its Missiles Systems Division, it moved next door, leasing twenty-two acres from Stanford University for its laboratory. The Lockheed brothers grew up in the valley and had a sentimental attachment to the area.

Eimac

Signs of things to come in the technology field passed unnoticed in the early thirties when Jack McCullough,

John Bean with the spray pump he invented to rid his Los Gatos orchard of scale. (SAN JOSE HISTORICAL MUSEUM)

World War II

World War I wasn't the war to end all wars after all. When the Japanese Imperial Navy bombed the U.S. Pacific Fleet at Pearl Harbor on December 7, 1941, killing 2,700 U.S. servicemen, President Roosevelt retaliated by declaring war on Japan. Germany and Italy, in turn, declared war on the U.S. We were now into our second world war, fighting the Germans and Italians on one side and a formidable enemy, Japan, on the other.

Inevitably the war put a crimp in San Jose's life-style. The draft, already a fact, escalated. It meant food stamps with rationing of butter, sugar, meat, and, unless you happened to be a farmer or defense worker, gasoline.

The growth of defense industries brought an influx of 500,000 out-of-state workers—most of whom never went back home. Many of the valley housewives, who had never worked before, became "Rosie the Riveters" as they took jobs in such plants as the Josuah Hendy Iron Works, which produced engine and ship fittings. By the end of the war Hendy employed 10,000 men and women. Hendy, whose California career had started out in the gold rush with a mechanism he invented for screening gold, later sold to Westinghouse.

FMC

Food Machinery Corporation had humble beginnings in Los Gatos in the 1880s as the Bean Spray Pump Company. John Bean's orchard, like many others, was plagued by a scale. Determined to do something about it, he invented the spray pump, which he marketed under his name. His son-in-law, D. C. Crummey, and then his grandson, John D. Crummey, carried on the business.

In the mid-1920s the younger John Crummey persuaded Paul L. Davies, his son-in-law, to give up his position as vice-president of American Trust and join the Bean company. According to Faith Crummey Davies, "I was opposed to a family arrangement, but it turned out very well." Davies proved to be the catalyst as the company started buying food-processing companies, including Anderson-Barngrower, which produced prune-dipping equipment. The company changed its name to Food Machinery Corporation, later shortened to FMC. Paul Davies became known as the "Father of Diversification" when the firm moved into the development of military equipment, including tanks and landing craft for use of the Marines in the Pacific.

In the field of communications, Jo Emmett Jennings, who was manufacturing condensers for the Signal Corps,

who played around with radio and built his own crystal set at the age of fourteen, joined forces with another buff, Bill Eitel, a 1926 graduate of Los Gatos High School. They manufactured Lee De Forest's vacuum tubes under the trade name Eimac. De Forest, sometimes called the "father of radio," who started inventing at the age of thirteen, had developed the vacuum tube in his laboratory in a house on Emory Street in Palo Alto. After many efforts, he gained fame for his electron tube, which amplified and generated continuous air waves, making possible long-distance telephone and improved radio broadcasting.

Eimac's growth in the thirties, along with the times, was slow, with only seventeen employees by the end of the decade. With the advent of World War II, Eimac, the only producer of radar transmitting tubes for the Western Alliance, took a giant spurt upward as its work force escalated to 3,000. The company was eventually absorbed by Varian.

made the fortuitous discovery that nickel could be substituted for tantalum — a scarce metal during the war. He and his partners, Calvin Townsend and Arthur Neild, expanded their plant on an orchard at McLaughlin and Story roads. By the time they sold out to International Telephone and Telegraph, in 1961, they employed 450 persons.

USO

Recognizing the inevitability of a war, a group of San Jose men got together to plan a recreation area for the servicemen, who would be passing through town. As former *Mercury News* columnist Wes Peyton tells it in his book *San Jose, A Personal View*, they had an ideal location, the plaza, but neither the city nor the USO had the money. Jay McCabe organized a committee that included Russ Petit of the Chamber of Commerce, merchants Phil Hammer and Leland Prussia, and a future owner of radio stations, Joe Levitt. The men managed to get $4,500 worth of construction materials donated

and 160 volunteer skilled workmen to give their time. Army cooks from Moffett Field served them food from kitchens set up in the plaza. In one day they completed San Jose's USO Hut.

For that first Christmas of 1941, Dr. David Roy and his wife, Rosa, joined by a dozen members from Temple Emanu-El, prepared and served dinner to the servicemen at the USO Hut. They said they wanted their Christian neighbors to be able to celebrate their holiest of days at home with their families. The Jewish community made it a tradition that continued for thirty years.

The USO Hut accommodated the servicemen well. There they could play games, write letters, and dance with the local girls. With the Seventh Army headquarters established in San Jose and Moffett Field returned to Navy control, the city had its share of servicemen. Under the direction of Mrs. Mark Rifenbark, wife of Trinity Episcopal Church's pastor, more than one million servicemen were served coffee, sandwiches, cookies, cake, fruit, and beverages provided by the many women's organizations.

CHAPTER TWENTY-EIGHT

St. Joseph's in the Forties

During the war, San Jose's population surged, and St. Joseph's congregation increased accordingly. The fathers set up a service shrine where they listed the names of 480 members of the parish in the armed service and the names of ten men who died. There was a marked increase in the number of worshipers—businessmen, office workers, and shoppers—at the noonday mass. A patriotic Jesuit priest with a gift for oratory, Father William Laherty, drew such large crowds to the 12:15 P.M. mass on Sundays that they had to put a loudspeaker in front of the church for the overflow. Many St. Joseph's parishioners remember that Sunday, December 7, 1941, when Father Laherty announced to the congregation in a subdued voice, "The Japanese have bombed Pearl Harbor." So great was the enormity of the act that he could say no more.

The stories about Father Laherty are legend. San Jose attorney Herman Mager, whose parents had a residential hotel at First and San Carlos, usually served the 6 A.M. mass. He says it was the "dress rehearsal" for Father Laherty's 12:15 P.M. mass, which he called "The Matinee" and sometimes "the bromo seltzer" mass. The priest, according to Mager, had a different and sometimes dramatic approach to his sermons. "One Easter morning, I guess I was kind of sleepy. Father Laherty pulled out a newspaper and called out, 'Extra! Extra! Christ is risen from the dead.' I thought for a minute he had gone off his rocker. But that's how he was; he'd always make his point."

The late Don Lima loved to tell the story about the Sunday he and John McEnery were ushers. Bob Trevey's hunting dog had gotten out of his car and came into church looking for him. Father Laherty turned and said, "Will the ushers please seat the dog or take him out so they can take up the collection."

His assistant pastor, Father Thomas Donahue, tells another story of the time a drunk came in off Market Street and walked down the aisle throwing something.

St. Joseph's choir boys. On the left, second row, is Leo Ruth; on the left in the front, Herman Mager (COURTESY HERMAN MAGER)

Father Laherty asked the ushers to lead him out. Afterwards, when he learned that the man was throwing money, he said, "If I'd known that, I'd have let him stay."

The Romantic Angle

St. Joseph's seems to have been a fertile ground for romances. Leo Ruth, son of an old St. Joseph's family and founder of the engineering firm Ruth & Going, and his wife, Dorothy, sang in the choir together. They met while Leo was a student at St. Joseph's High School and Dorothy at Notre Dame.

The courtship of Lon Normandin and Peggy Gretz likewise flowered at St. Joseph's. Lon, now the

St. Joseph's High School orchestra (COURTESY HERMAN MAGER)

Normandin-Chrysler-Plymouth dealer, is a great-grandson of Amable "Amos" Normandin's, who came from Montreal in 1870 and started the Pacific Carriage Factory. According to Lon, "Peg came down on the bus from Mountain View every morning to attend Notre Dame High School. I would meet her at the bus and we would attend 7:15 A.M. mass. Afterwards we would go over to Mauers Cafeteria for a doughnut and milk with Pete Chrishman and the girl he was dating at the time, Rosalie Pizzo. From there we'd take the girls over to Notre Dame and we'd go on to Bellarmine." Just before Lon graduated from Santa Clara University, he and Peg were married. There was no wedding, however, for Pete and Rosalie. She became a Notre Dame nun. In 1989 Sister Rosalie was a member of the Provincial Team of the California Province of Notre Dame de Namur.

The People of St. Joseph's

St. Joseph's families of the fifties remember dinner dancing in the gymnasium to Dan Pasetta's five-piece orchestra—all for $5—and barbecues at the Mataschi Ranch south of San Jose that included steak with all the trimmings and doorprizes for $2. The invitations reminded everyone to bring their own utensils.

Jane Carrera Levitt, who was baptized and received her first Holy Communion and the sacraments of confirmation and matrimony in St. Joseph's, remembers those days. The much-loved church probably never had a more dedicated friend than her father, Pat Carrera. He had a key to the church and, at the age of eighty, would still prepare the altar every morning for early mass and then wake up the priest. If the altar boy didn't show up,

St. Joseph's Sodality Cadet Band

The wedding of Patricia Perucci and James Stock Melehan in 1950 in St. Joseph's Church, almost 100 years after the Stocks came to San Jose

he would serve the mass. On Sundays he attended three masses: one to take up the collection, another to sing with the choir, and the third just to attend mass. His daughter says he had a nice tenor voice, and in the early days of silent movies he would sing the accompaniment to the action on the screen at the San Jose Theater.

Carrera was a painter by trade. One day his wife, Marie Louise Klinkert (whose father, William J. Klinkert, was an architect and builder of churches, including St. Patrick's and St. Mary's) was passing St. Joseph's. She looked up and saw him swinging from a rope, painting the dome. Mrs. Carrera promptly put a stop to that. After all, he was the father of five children.

Long identified with St. Joseph's are members of the Kelly family. The late James and Bridget Kelly had Kelly's Market at Fourth and Empire streets and built a home next door, where they raised five children. Their son, Sunnyvale attorney James Kelly, remembers, as a boy, delivering groceries to the St. Joseph's Rectory. He'd make a point of getting there around five o'clock when the cook, B. I. Biagini, was preparing dinner, because he knew he'd give him snacks. Still active in St. Joseph's parish are his sister, Mary Kelly Sheridan, and his nephew, Pat Kelly.

The late attorney Irvin Frasse (great-grandson of Martin Murphy, Jr., and his wife (the former Mary Cribari of the wine family) were active St. Joseph members. Mary belonged to the altar society; their daughter, Ebe, and son, Ben, attended St. Joseph's School. Ben, who was an altar boy, remembers that Father Donahue used to take them to the McEnery ranch behind Mount Hamilton to hike and swim in the lakes. Among the altar boys trained by Father Donahue were Kevin Crist, Nick Livak,

Al Nausche, who became a Jesuit, and his brother, Ted.

Irv Frasse's mother, Maude Arques Frasse, a longtime member of St. Joseph's, was living at the Vendome Hotel when she met his father, Dr. Irvin Frasse, a guest at the hotel on a trip from the East. Later when she was a widow—a life-style that has passed—her lady friends, Adelia (Mrs. William) Leet, Mrs. de Saisset, Mrs. Singletary, and a Murphy cousin, Elizabeth Whittaker, who still lived on the Martin Murphy, Jr., estate in Sunnyvale, would call for her in their chauffeured limousines to go out to lunch.

The Centennial

Nineteen forty-nine marked St. Joseph's centennial as a parish. Father Ring celebrated a solemn high mass at 10 A.M. Bellarmine Preparatory School president Father Thomas Cosgrove, who later became the church's pastor, preached the homily. The following year Father Ring started the much-needed structural work on the church's dome and other restoration work, which included replacing crosses. Ring's successor, Father Raymond Prendiville, an Irishman, painted the crosses green. His successor was reluctant to change the color for fear of hurting his feelings.

A Man for All People

A priest at St. Joseph's in the fifties, Father Frank Franchi is remembered with affection by many San Joseans: by his math students at Bellarmine, for whom he gave

159

a spaghetti and meatball feed every year; by the Boy Scouts (he built a chapel for them at the Big Sur camp and was a role model when he achieved Eagle Scout at the age of forty-five after intensive training to pass the swimming test and received the prestigious Silver Beaver award at a ceremony attended by 2,000); by the indigents living in squalor at the red brick Metropole Hotel across the street from St. Joseph's, whom he bathed and fed and whose wounds he dressed; by the patients at the county hospital (Valley Medical Center), who, when they told him they were worried about their dogs, knew that he would take them and care for them (they say he sometimes had twenty dogs at one time); and by the parishioners at St. Joseph's. According to Dr. Jim Vaudagna, "He had the confessional nearest to the entrance. There would always be fifteen or twenty people waiting. His penance," Vaudagna said, "was always the same whether you committed murder or ate meat on Friday: 'Now for your penance, say three Hail Marys and try to do better.'"

CHAPTER TWENTY-NINE

The Fifties and the Downtown Exodus

In 1950 the personable, sometimes controversial promoter A. P. "Dutch" Hamann replaced the cautious, competent Hump Campbell as city manager. With the population about to explode, Hamann, concerned about the threat of being hemmed in by surrounding incorporated areas, set about aggressively annexing large tracts of land, including Coyote on the south and Alviso on the north. When Hamann took over as city manager, the population was 95,000. A decade later it had grown to 204,196; in 1978, 445,779; and as 1990 arrived, 765,000.

Robert Doerr, who was mayor at the time, says, "Contrary to what many people believed, Dutch didn't always get his way." Such was the case when Ford Motor Company bought the Milpitas property. They wanted to become part of San Jose. Hamann was in favor of it, but the council voted it down. Consequently, Ford incorporated Milpitas. The same was true of Campbell, Doerr says.

The crisis of the fifties was the exodus of business from downtown. According to attorney Al Ruffo, who served on the council and as mayor, the city had Hale's, Hart's, Penney's, and Roos Brothers. Macy's wanted to build an eleven-story building next door to Penney's in the Smout Building and to have parking for 600 cars. The top three floors would be leased to the telephone company. Barrett Brothers had agreed to come down from San Francisco and operate a garage. Sounded like a perfect deal. Unfortunately, the owner of the property, Warren Holmes, refused to sell. When the city was unable to replace O. H. Hale's with another department store, the movement out of the city by retail businesses, restaurants, and theaters was irreversible. Adding insult to injury, city hall was moved to North First and Mission streets.

The owners of the unincorporated land at Stevens Creek and Winchester Boulevard wanted commercial zoning from San Jose. Because San Jose was trying to keep business downtown, the council voted against it.

According to Doerr, what took place was never reported in the press because before the Brown Act reporters were not permitted at council meetings. Santa Clara, in spite of a verbal agreement, using a method called strip annexing, ran Santa Clara's municipal boundary line down the center of Winchester Boulevard and Stevens Creek Road, thereby avoiding public hearings. Stevens Creek Plaza was built and housed the Emporium, Magnin's, and other retail businesses. When Macy's and Valley Fair wanted to build next door, they sought to become part of San Jose. The council realized they had no choice. If they refused, Santa Clara would step in. Valley Fair's opening in 1958 changed the face of downtown and the direction the valley was taking. Many, however, felt that this was the way the whole country was going and that it would have happened anyway. After IBM bought property on Monterey Road, the San Jose Council voted for annexation. If they hadn't, they knew IBM was ready to form a city and to call it South San Jose.

It became apparent to all that downtown was falling into a state of decay. Robert Doerr, who succeeded George Starbird as mayor, appointed an Urban Renewal Agency to apply for federal funds and to plan for a new development. On the board of prominent local men were Roy Butcher, chairman, Frank Mitchell, Alden Campen, Paul Marchese, and Hollis Logue. They called it Park Center Redevelopment and chose a fifty-nine-acre area bordered by Santa Clara Street, the Guadalupe River, San Carlos Street, and the west side of Market Street. The plan was that one developer would come in and clear 220 buildings, half of which were in blighted condition. They met with resistance from three property owners who sued, resulting in a long delay, with property going up in value all the time. Finally, in 1962, after a Supreme Court decision in the agency's favor, the Wolff-Sesnon Corporation (originally called the San Jose Center Corporation) started building. The result was the highly successful Park Center Plaza, which became a model for other cities.

Efforts to build a community theater, in spite of the dedication of people like Alex Hart and the late Virginia Mitchell, and even though over 60 percent of the people voted for the bonds, ran into heavy resistance. Finally, in 1966 City Manager Hamann and the city council put together a successful joint bond deal that did not require a two-thirds majority. The Taliesin Associates of Phoenix provided the design, and construction got under way in 1969. But all was not to run smoothly. Not only did the costs escalate, after the years of delay, but in 1972 the movable ceiling collapsed. Fortunately, it was not during a performance. The theater project, deeper in debt, was rescued by the Redevelopment Agency. The name was changed to the Center for the Performing Arts.

CHAPTER THIRTY

St. Joseph's in the Sixties

Father Joseph Dondero, a giant of a man (at least six-foot-five) and a San Francisco native, became the popular pastor of St. Joseph's in 1964. A University of San Francisco Law School graduate and a musician before he entered the seminary, he was up to the first task that faced him at St. Joseph's: the church's need to be renovated. With support from his good friends Santa Clara County Supervisor Sam Della Maggiore, architect Bud Curtis, and San Jose State art professor John DeVincenzi, the building was painted inside and out, the Odell organ was worked on by Edward Stout of Grace Cathedral, and new carpeting was laid. He gave most of the pews (the names of the pew holders of times past still attached) to the new Holy Spirit Church in Almaden Valley. He laughed as he said, half apologetically, "I sold some of them to the Protestants for $10 a piece. That was before we became ecumenical. But," he added, "they were glad to get them."

When the urban renewal came in, the powers that be wanted to confiscate St. Joseph's School and make it into a restaurant. Father Dondero was adamant. With the support of San Jose attorney Gerald Hansen, who had been his student at St. Ignatius High School in San Francisco, they fought the government for seven years and won. "Fortunately," the priest said, "Jerry never sent us a bill. It would have broken us."

But he said the biggest disappointment of his ten years at St. Joseph's was the eleven-story building he proposed to build next to the church. He felt strongly for the little widows living on social security, who would be out of money towards the end of the month and would come to him for help. He wanted to provide low-income housing for them and use the top floors for the Jesuit priests working with the students at San Jose State during the turbulent sixties. Again his friend Bud Curtis helped by drawing the plans, without charge. He had all sorts of problems with permits, and, for many reasons, it never worked out. Another great friend at St. Joseph's, Father

Dondero said, was Ray McElwaine. "Whenever I needed help, he was right there."

St. Joseph's was an open parish. In the postwar years many of the working mothers would take their children to St. Elizabeth's Day Home on Vine Street to be supervised by the Holy Family Sisters. A school patrol of older students from St. Joseph's School, who had been trained by the San Jose police, would come over when it was

Father Joseph Dondero, pastor of St. Joseph's in the 1960s. On his left is former Santa Clara Supervisor Sam Della Maggiore.

Notre Dame High School students file out of St. Joseph's following their graduation.

time for school and escort the children to St. Joseph's. After school they would take them back to St. Elizabeth's.

The St. Joseph's Mother's Guild and Dad's Club, who later joined to become one organization, were the back bone of the church's fundraising. The parents who helped with the bingo games run by Yano Circo (they were the big money-makers) and the barbecues included Dad's Club president Henry Shiro, Dr. Jim Vaudagna, and his wife, the late Carmel Perrucci, who was a volunteer art teacher in the school as well.

The Mother's Guild put on fashion shows. John DeVincenzi created settings with diverse themes (Circus, Paris, and Bourbon Street) that were spectacular. For the Venice theme they built a movable gondola.

Rosemarie Shiro (Matchak) did the decor. The shows, featuring fashions from Blum's on First Street, took place at the Hotel Sainte Claire, at Alpine Park, and at the newly opened Elk's Club, where they drew a record-breaking crowd of 800 guests. On the ninetieth birthday of Josephine Bruno, mother of former Mothers' Guild president Nina Boyd, Father Dondero stopped by and played "Happy Birthday" on the piano for her.

On his eightieth birthday in November, 1989, Nina Boyd, Lonnie DeVincenzi, and Mary Ann Cellini, second-grade teacher in the school, brought together 120 of his friends for a surprise party in the Diocesan Center on Lenzen Avenue. Bill Scilacci (Smiling Bill's Furniture), his ninety-six-year-old friend, whose wife was ill and

The eighth-grade class of St. Josph's grammar school, 1926: Richard Thrift, left end of row three; Charles Lux (grandson of Charles Lux of Miller & Lux), third from left in front row; Bart Concannon, second from right in second row. (COURTESY RICHARD THRIFT)

St. Joseph's before renovation

couldn't attend, sent a message with his son, Bill, Jr. (chairman of the Bank of Santa Clara), "Tell the kid hello." Among those paying tribute to the priest was Mother's Guild member Rose Olivo. She told of how Father Dondero baptized their first child, Nello, Jr., then a year later, Mary Alice, followed by Christie, then Bill, and so on until she had named all sixteen of her children, including Nancy, a Harvard Law School graduate who practices law in the East.

St. Joseph's High School Reunions

Although St. Joseph's High School, founded by the Jesuits in 1898 and taught by the Marianist brothers (called Brothers of Mary in those days) from 1907, was closed in 1935, the bonding with St. Joseph's was so strong that fifty-five years later the alumni group still holds its barbecue reunion every year. The 1989 gather-

ing at Mitty High School was headed by alumni president Willie Radunich, with Joe Albanese, Jack Chargin, and Bill Dreischmeyer doing the barbecuing. Pat Concannon, who lived just a couple of blocks from St. Joseph's, went through the grammar school and high school, and his wife, Kay, as usual, served on the committee. Among the familiar faces usually spotted at such gatherings were Leo Ruth, founder of the Ruth & Going engineering firm; Norb Mirassou, head of production, with his brother, Ed, of Mirassou Wines; Dr. Emmett Henderson; Armand Heymann; Red Gangi of Gangi Bros. Packing Co.; Leo Solari, whose wife, Agnes, coauthored the book *San Jose's St. Joseph's* with the late Margaret Zaro (her husband, Louis Zaro, also attended); and past alumni presidents Mitch Ucovich, with his wife, Evelyn, and Herman Mager.

Nothing much changes with this group; they still greet each other with the nicknames they had in school, such as "Worms" (William) Cropley and "Flops" Feirrera (he

St. Joseph's School, built in 1907 at Locust and River streets

inherited dairyland from his Portuguese father on Story Road and used to get up at 4 A.M. in the morning to milk cows). A favorite story is about Jim Bailey, now a Pan-Am pilot, who was a cutup. When Brother Dave, who lighted the sacristy and rang the church bell in the steeple, was away, Bailey took his place, even wearing a cassock. One time, instead of letting the rope go up he held onto it. An elderly lady passing by saw him flying through the air and thought something had happened to Brother Dave and hurried to the rectory to tell them.

The stories go on and on. Brother Robert Jueneman of the Marianists recalled the day in 1958 when he called on the late Miss Alice Turel. She told him, "I remember the day the Marianists came. I was standing on this porch and saw them drive up in a horse and buggy." The Brothers of Mary, he said, taught grammar school, with two years of so-called commercial course after eighth grade, from 1898 to 1907. At this point they took over grades eight through twelve at the college prep St. Joseph's High School. Part of that time they also taught elementary school grades four through eight. During the Depression, enrollment dropped and the high school closed. Thirty years later the Marianists returned to open Archbishop Mitty High School. In the fall of 1990 the school changed to all lay faculty.

Many of those attending the reunion had attended St. Joseph's grammar school. Until 1986, when St. Joseph's School closed, there had always been a grammar school. The children were first taught by the Notre Dame nuns (from the early 1850s). Starting in 1878 the fathers at St. Joseph's started teaching all the boys at the school on the corner of San Pedro and San Fernando streets. A new school was built in 1892 adjacent to St. Joseph's. When it suffered severe damage in the 1906 earthquake, still another school had to be built—this time at Locust and River streets. Archbishop Riordan came for the dedication. The last St. Joseph's school was built on the same site in 1948.

CHAPTER THIRTY-ONE

Silicon Valley

Almost overnight the name "Silicon Valley" focused the attention of the world on the Santa Clara Valley and the city of San Jose. It conjured up high-tech images of computer chips, transistors, and personal computers, of young men driving Ferraris, wearing Brioni suits, and living in mansions in the hills of Los Altos and Saratoga. The name came from the ingredient silicon, essentially refined sand, used as the underlying medium of the semiconductor chips.

But the success came at some cost: crowding, pollution, and skyrocketing cost of living. No longer could the valley be called as it once had been, "The Garden of the World."

The beginning of Silicon Valley dates back to the twenties and thirties with a professor of radio engineering, Frederick Terman, at Stanford University. Terman attracted aspiring engineers and scientists like a magnet, and quickly the school became one of the world's foremost centers for research in the field of electronics and electrical engineering.

Terman was a pivotal figure in the creation of Silicon Valley, not only because he trained a generation of engineers, but also because he found them a place to work. He did so by helping to develop Stanford Industrial Park, the world's first high-tech business enclave.

Among the park's first tenants were Russell and Sigurd Varian, who had come from Ireland as small boys. While at Stanford, they became intrigued with the idea of using radio to see through fog and darkness. Sigurd, a pilot, knew well the trouble of landing at night. An added incentive was the unrest in Europe. In April of 1937 the brothers made an agreement with Stanford president Ray Wilbur by which Stanford would provide the pair with the use of the physics laboratory, shop facilities, $100 for materials, and the right to talk with Stanford professors. The result was radar, a crucial advantage of the Allied forces during the war.

The Varian brothers turned out to be a good business investment for Stanford. The return for the $100 the university put up for the cost of experiments has been in the millions. As for the brothers, they went on to found Varian Associates, Inc., in Stanford Industrial Park.

Hewlett-Packard

Professor Terman also was responsible for putting together another pair of Stanford engineering graduates, William Hewlett and David Packard. These two were destined to become achievers in technology, as well as two of the wealthiest men in the world.

The pair started out in 1939 inventing electronic instruments in a garage in Palo Alto. It was an audio-oscillator, based on a Hewlett design, that got the pair on their way when Walt Disney Studios bought eight to use in the soundtrack for the classic movie *Fantasia*. During the war HP, as the company was called, produced devices to measure and control radio and sound frequencies that led, over the next four decades, to computers, calculators, and work stations. Today HP has 95,000 employees worldwide — 18,000 in the Bay Area — producing 10,000 products. They make computing and electronic measuring equipment for people in business, industry, science, engineering, health care, and education.

HP has been a remarkable Valley citizen as well. For example, in 1988 the company contributed more than $41 million of its equipment to high schools, colleges, and universities. The company's total philanthropic contributions that year were $50.4 million. HP takes care of its own people as well. Employees share in HP's success through regular cash profit-sharing.

When Queen Elizabeth II visited California with her husband, Prince Philip, she asked that Silicon Valley be included on their itinerary. It is a measure of HP's prestige that the White House in coordination with the State Department arranged for the royal couple to visit

Hewlett-Packard. David Packard escorted Queen Elizabeth and Prince Philip on a tour of the plant. That evening in San Francisco at a state dinner given by President Reagan, Queen Elizabeth commented on Silicon Valley, "which has brought the world of yesterday's science fiction into today's home, office and classroom and into Buckingham Palace, too." No company more exemplified her words than Hewlett-Packard.

The Second Wave

The Varians and Hewlett-Packard were the first wave of Valley technology. After World War II Lockheed chose to locate its Missiles and Space division in Mountain View. That in turn led to the opening of NASA's Ames Research Laboratory. At the same time, many young servicemen who passed through the area on the way home from the Pacific decided to come back and pursue engineering careers.

William R. Hewlett

In 1947 William Shockley, who had grown up in Palo Alto, helped develop the transitor at Bell Telephone Laboratories in New York. Composed of silicon crystal (that is, solid state), the transistor could do the same job as the fragile vacuum tube without heating up or burning out. It was also a fraction of the size. The key was controlling the conductivity of the silicon through the careful application of impurities, hence the name "semiconductor." In 1956 the King of Sweden awarded Shockley and his two partners the Nobel Prize in physics.

Wanting to create a business from his invention, Shockley came back to California and set up a short-lived company called Shockley Transistor. He then recruited eight of the finest engineering minds in the country, who called themselves the "Corps of Eight," to run the firm. Unfortunately, Shockley didn't have the personality to operate a company, and the "Corps of Eight" quit to create the semiconductor division of Fairchild Camera and Instruments. Shockley was furious and labeled them forever as the "Traitorous Eight."

But the deed was done, and by the early 1960s Fairchild was the world's most important semiconductor company. It was during this time that division head Robert Noyce revamped the transistor to create the first integrated circuit chips. Unfortunately Fairchild headquarters in New Jersey didn't appreciate its California division as much as the world did. Thus, by the late sixties a deep discontentment had set in at the division. The result was a mass defection from Fairchild that eventually would create 100 new, young companies. The most notable of these were Intel, founded by Robert Noyce, Gordon Moore, and Andrew Grove; National Semiconductor, put together by a team led by Charles Sporck; and Advanced Micro Devices, run by Jerry Sanders.

The seventies marked a third wave of new companies and the true beginning of Silicon Valley as we know it today. With the proliferation of chip companies and their products, a new generation of entrepreneurs saw exciting opportunities using these chips. They led to the development of calculators, digital watches, and games. Then in 1974, an Intel team under Ted Hoff developed the microprocessor, the computer on a chip. It was this device that made possible the personal computer.

Apple

In the late seventies, two young men still in their twenties, Steve Jobs and Steve Wozniak, began building personal computers, first for their own amusement, then

Queen Elizabeth was taken on a tour of the Hewlett-Packard Cupertino plant by David Packard (center) during her 1983 trip to California with Prince Philip. (COPYRIGHT DAVID POWERS, COURTESY HEWLETT-PACKARD COMPANY)

to sell. The result was Apple Computer—the first successful personal computer company.

The story of the two Steves is another garage story. They had been friends at U.C. Berkeley and were still in their twenties when they designed and put together their first home computer at a cost of $270. They worked in a garage using some HP manuals—Jobs paid his sister $1 each to plug in the board. Wozniak developed its basic software by hand.

Jobs suggested they start a company. They needed a name, so, off the top of their heads, they chose "Apple." The two set their sights low, but when Jobs, obviously a good talker, landed a $50,000 order, Apple was on its way. Jobs met Mike Markkula, who had made it big at Intel, and asked him to help write a business plan. Markkula, a Valley vet with considerable savvy, decided that the home computer market was going places and became one-third partner. The Apple II, the computer that changed the world soon followed, and Apple set the lead

in personal computers it holds today.

The rise of firms like Intel, National, and Apple was emblematic of a unique sensibility that was being born in Silicon Valley—an appreciation of entrepreneurship and the new companies it created, and the formation of infrastructure to help those new firms in their development.

The result was one of the greatest bursts of new business created in history. By 1990, more than 3,000 companies existed in Silicon Valley, employing more than three-quarters of a million people. Among that multitude were some giants, including in addition to those already named, such firms as Rolm, Amdahl, Memorex, Tandem, Atari, Seagate, Sun, Mips, Conner Peripherals, LSI Logic, and Cypress—all of them dominant players in the world scene in their particular industries. And each, in its own way, changing the nature of everyday life, both at home and in the office.

This extraordinary growth created an explosive counterpart in the service industries that support Silicon Valley, including law firms, real estate agencies, banks, development companies, consulting firms, retailer shops, hotels, restaurants, and print and television media. The area's colleges and universities, including Stanford, San Jose State, and Santa Clara, as well as a host of junior colleges and trade schools, also expanded rapidly to meet the demand for skilled engineers and managers. The result of all this frenzy was to balloon the population of the Valley's cities, beginning in Palo Alto then spreading south to follow the jobs at newly emerging companies.

San Jose downtown was the last area that Silicon Valley reached. Until the early 1980s it had been the bedroom community for the electronics industry. Now, with the opening of the Golden Triangle industrial community north of the city, San Jose became the center of Silicon Valley life. The resulting influx of accountants, advertising people, and lawyers gave impetus to the construction of the high-rise bank buildings that now characterize the downtown. Ultimately, it was the Siicon Valley companies and their tax base that made the redevelopment of downtown San Jose possible.

International Business Machines

There is another company that deserves credit. Here from the beginning of Silicon Valley, crucial to its development, but yet never quite part of it, IBM has long been important to San Jose life. Little did anyone imagine in 1934, when the company rented the old Temple

IBM board chairman Thomas J. Watson, Jr., took Nikita Khrushchev to lunch in the plant's cafeteria during the Soviet leader's 1959 visit to the U.S. Khrushchev was amused to be carrying his own tray and said he was going to take the idea back to his country. (IBM)

Laundry building at Sixteenth and St. John streets in San Jose to manufacture accounting machine cards, what the future had in store.

As IBM became aware of the advantages of San Jose's location and the direction it was taking in technology during the postwar boom, it opened a laboratory in an old printing shop at 99 Notre Dame Avenue. Little atten-

tion was paid by the public to what was going on in that laboratory, so that in 1955, when the company introduced the first computer disk storage system, RAMAC, it came as a complete surprise.

IBM's next move was to acquire 190 acres of orchard land at Cottle and Monterey Road on part of the old Rancho Santa Teresa land grant where Don Joaquín Bernal's cattle once roamed. There it built a plant that would become world renowned. The plant's most exciting day came on September 21, 1959, when IBM chairman Thomas J. Watson, Jr., played host to Nikita Khrushchev and Andrei Gromyko. Instead of preparing a banquet for the visitors, Watson took Khrushchev to lunch in the plant's cafeteria. The Russian leader was highly amused as he carried his own tray.

IBM San Jose continues to play a major role in the IBM success story. On December 13, 1989, IBM scientists and engineers set a world record when they unveiled at the Alamden Research Center IBM's experimental achievement, a "gigabit" memory, a single square inch of disk surface using experimental components capable of storing a billion bits of information—the equivalent to 100,000 double-spaced typewritten pages. A product of IBM San Jose, it is in direct line of descent from that original RAMAC developed in the fifties in San Jose.

CHAPTER THIRTY-TWO

A Cultural Account

In the transformation from a farming community to metropolitan city, San Jose's cultural life kept pace. The San Jose Symphony, the oldest symphony west of the Mississippi and now one of the best, went through hard times during and following the Depression. In the 1950s and 1960s a group of dedicated women, including Lorraine Boccardo, Gerry Witkin, and the late Frances Snyder, served as presidents of the board, followed by Pauline Pace and Rosalie Lincoln, with able assistants such as Stephanie Drozdiak, giving the symphony a much-needed boost.

Around this time Sandor Salgo, professor of music at Stanford, was brought in to conduct, and he stayed on for eighteeen years. In 1972 Maestro George Cleve took over as its conductor and has brought the orchestra to world-class recognition. In 1988 the orchestra performed twelve sets (Friday and Saturday nights) of the Master Series at the Center for the Performing Arts and nine at Flint Center; four Pops each at the civic auditorium and at Flint, besides four Favorite Classics at Flint Sunday afternoons; one *Messiah* at Flint and one at CPA. With demands on his time internationally, Professor Cleve has announced his plans to leave the San Jose Symphony in 1992.

When the symphony was going through a transition period in 1985, Carl Cookson, a strong symphony supporter, a past board president, and a friend in need, stepped in as a volunteer interim director. When the executive director position and the board president were combined into one position, Douglas McLendon, who was already board president, took over. The symphony has 11,500 season ticket holders, and, a rare achievement in these times for any symphony, operates in the black.

Credit must be given, too, to the Symphony Auxiliary, founded in the forties by Steffi Sims and the late Evelyn McGrath. It has been a strong fund-raising arm with its annual "Showcase," featuring designer-decorated homes and mansions. In 1989, with Villa Montalvo as its showcase mansion and chaired by Martha Small, they shared a profit of $300,000. Altogether they have raised close to $1,500,000 for the symphony under the financial leadership of Florence Barker and, for the past eight years, the artistic flair and expertise of Sandra Farris.

San Jose Civic Light Opera (CLO)

San Jose's Civic Light Opera, founded in 1934 by Margaret Trevey d'Artenay, is a success story that was a long time in the making. It was not until the mid-eighties that CLO received a ground swell of support from the public, who suddenly realized what the music theater organization had going and that they didn't have to drive to San Francisco for good entertainment.

Too much credit cannot be given to Ginny and Syd Levin for their consistent and generous backing of CLO in the lean times, and to executive director Stewart Slater, who brought it to the good times. With 32,000 subscribers in the 1989–90 season, it is the largest subscriber musical theater organization in the U.S. In the 1990–91 season another week is being added to the schedule of performances at CPA.

Opera San Jose

Opera San Jose is the realization of a dream by its founder, Irene Dalis. The San Jose–born diva, who rose to the pinnacle of opera success as star of the Metropolitan Opera under Rudolph Bing, returned to her home town and her alma mater when she retired, to become a professor of music at San Jose State. Her goal was to provide a showcase for talented young singers in her opera workshop and good opera for San Jose music lovers. As executive and artistic director she succeeded in both.

Her current concern is an opera house. The Montgomery Theater is small and its availability is limited. Many opera goers have to be turned away. But when Madame Dalis, a woman who, "when she has a will, has a way," says they will get an opera house, people listen.

She made her surprise farewell performance with the San Jose State Choral Group in 1978 from the pulpit of St. Joseph's Church, where she attended mass with her family as a child. As she was walking into the church with her late husband, George Loinaz, she turned to him and said, "This is going to be my farewell performance." He looked at her questioningly. "Yes," she said, "it is. God has been very good to me. This my way of saying 'Thank you.'"

Opera San Jose has a unique Resident Artists program that gives singers who are ready to begin their professional careers an opportunity to perform in principal roles and to be paid a living wage on a twelve-month salary basis. It is their entry into the profession. The only alternative for singers in this country, ready to start their careers, is to sing bit roles or appear in the chorus in San Francisco. The Met offers nothing for young singers. The only alternative for these singers is to go to Europe, and the opportunities there are diminishing.

Opera San Jose's program is being eyed by other opera companies. It is apparent that opera is on the move upward. There are thirty opera companies in California. Fifty years ago there were only two in the United States. Five Opera San Jose artists are currently performing in Germany.

San Jose Repertory Theater

San Jose Rep is riding the same crest of the wave as the other performing arts groups by staging first-rate productions. Founded in 1980 by visionary James Reber, the first season opened with Noel Coward's *Private Lives* to good reviews. The company has grown from 16 performances the first year to 172 in the 1988–89 season.

Rep enjoys a healthy 10,000 subscribership. But like Opera San Jose it is limited in its scheduling time at Montgomery Theater. Past board president Phil Hammer is in charge of the new theater project. He and another past president, Elaine Knoernschild, are the motivating force for the Rep, with a strong supporting board. The Rep draws its actors from auditions all over the country, including New York, Washington, and Los Angeles. With the stature of artistic director Timothy Near, Rep is able to sign top-notch actors, directors, and set designers.

San Jose Cleveland Ballet

As with most of the arts groups, it took one dedicated, determined leader to bring ballet to San Jose. That person was Karen Lowenstern. Joined by her assistant, Anita Del Grande, she traveled all over the states looking for a co-venture company. In Cleveland she found what she was looking for, and that was the beginning of the San Jose Cleveland Ballet. Thus began a "tale of two cities." With the Cleveland partnership, San Jose ballet inherited the highly talented artistic director Dennis Nahat. It also was the beginning of a happy arrangement with the San Jose Symphony.

A ballet company requires large financial resources. A gift of $1 million from Apple Computer cofounder Steve Wozniak helped the ballet get started. The ballet presents five productions annually at the CPA.

San Jose Museum of Art

The San Jose Museum of Art is a child of the sixties that is coming of age in the nineties. Incorporated in 1969 as the San Jose Center for Art, it was the first art museum in the city's history. Although Senator James Phelan offered the building that became the Sainte Claire Club to the city for an art museum, and before that Myles and Amanda O'Connor wanted to donate their extensive art collection if the city would provide a home for it, neither offer was accepted.

In 1968 when a group of concerned art enthusiasts, headed by Barbara Cassin and John DeVincenzi learned that the library was about to be vacated, they lobbied San Jose City Council meetings. When they received approval, a dedicated group of founding members, including Ann Marie Mix and Charlotte Wendel, who are still active, and the board's second president, Virginia Youngblood, now of Pebble Beach, set to work to convert the library into an art museum. The name was changed to San Jose Museum of Art.

The handsome Romanesque building, originally San Jose's post office and first federal building, was made of sandstone from the Levi Goodrich quarry in the Almaden area—the same material used in Stanford University. It faces Plaza Park at Market and San Fernando streets. In good company, its neighbor on one side is the new Fairmont Hotel and, on the other, the plaza's senior citizen, St. Joseph's Cathedral.

In 1976 former mayor and museum president George Starbird persuaded the city council to allocate a parcel of land for an addition. Under the direction of Museum

The San Jose Symphony—the oldest in the West—circa 1892

of Art Building Foundation president Drew Gibson and Facilities Planning chairman Averill Mix, the 45,000-square-foot new building is scheduled for completion in 1991. It will be a harmonious blending of the past, the present, and the future. In 1987 former San Jose Mayor Janet Gray Hayes stepped in to replace retiring president of the board Dean Bartee, senior vice-president of the *Mercury-News*. At the same time Albert Dixon, former museum director, returned until a new director, I. Michael Danoff, took over.

San Jose Historical Museum

If you happen to fly over San Jose at night, that tall lighted pyramid you see below is the electric tower. It's a replica (two-thirds scale) of the tower that lighted San Jose at the corner of Market and Santa Clara streets from the 1880s to 1915. It stands in front of the Pacific Hotel in the San Jose Historical Museum at Kelly Park.

Under the leadership of museum director Mignon Gibson and San Jose Historical Foundation president Kathleen Muller, the museum is effectively recreating old San Jose at the park. Here one can see the Empire Firehouse, the Dashaway Stables, the plaza with its bandstand, the Bank of Italy, the Stevens Ranch fruit barn, and Dr. Henry Warburton's medical office. Poet Edwin Markham's home is among the historic houses. The latest addition is the Gordon House. Restored with taste by San Jose Rotary, it houses their offices, club rooms, and meeting rooms. It is also open to tours conducted by the museum's 200 docents.

With the support of the Chinese American Women's Club and their fund-raising efforts, under the leadership of Lillian GongGuy and Gerrye Wong, ground was broken in June, 1990, for the recreation of Ng Shing Gong Temple, sometimes erroneously called the Joss House. In the late 1940s the temple that stood at Sixth and Taylor streets was demolished to make way for a city project—but not before its original facade, most of the temple's furnishings, and the elaborately carved and gilded main altar were saved. The new building will feature exhibits on Chinese history, art, and culture on the first floor and the altar and religious effects on the second floor.

Kelley Park, which includes Happy Hollow, a children's playground, the Japanese Friendship Garden, and the Leininger Center, owes its existence to the foresight of two men. The late Alden Campen went to Ernie Renzel and told him that twenty-five acres of Arch-Kell, the 160-acre estate built by Judge Lawrence Archer in the early 1860s, were for sale. Archer's daughter, Louise Kelley, who was in her nineties, wanted to dispose of the beautifully landscaped property. Renzel, his wife, Emily, and Campen made a generous offer to the city to finance the purchase of the property and to sell it to them on a six-payment deal.

When Renzel, a man who cares about his native town, San Jose, learned that Trader Lew's priceless collection of historic artifacts, buggies, and antique cars might be sold, he made possible its purchase for the historical museum with another such loan. Renzel says, with some amazement, the last shipment contained three hearses.

Following up the acquisition of the Kelley Park property, it was through the efforts of Theron Fox and the Historic Landmarks Commission that the city of San Jose agreed to set aside sixteen acres for the reconstruction of a historic town to be known as the San Jose Historical Museum.

The Guadalupe River Park

Long in the talking stage and now in the active working stage is the Guadalupe River Park—San Jose's answer

173

On stage at the Met in a performance of Aida *is San Jose and St. Joseph's most famous daughter, Irene Dalis (Yvonne to her family and old friends) at far right. Beside her are Leontyne Price and Richard Tucker.* (OPERA SAN JOSE)

to New York's Central Park and San Francisco's Golden Gate Park. According to plans, it will run along the banks of the Guadalupe River through three miles of downtown San Jose, retaining as much of the natural character of the river as possible with plantings of native trees, shrubs, and flowers. No dams will interfere with the life cycle of the fish, including the salmon which spawn in the river and which, in the early days, the grizzly bears found so tasty. The white heron and other long-legged birds that make the river their home will add to the atmosphere. There will be walking and bicycling paths on both shores between Highways 280 and 880. The long-range planning includes pavilions, fountains, and picnic areas and there is talk of a carousel. A lake is to be built between West Santa Clara and New West Julian Street.

The first segment, already completed, adjoins River Park Towers and was landscaped by the developer, Lincoln Properties. Work on the second segment in front of the Children's Discovery Museum was completed summer 1990.

Children's Discovery Museum

The striking "color me purple" Children's Discovery Museum, which opened in June, 1990, as the name implies, provides children with a learning experience through exhibits—a "hands-on" participation project in the fields of arts, sciences, technology, and humanities. The museum is a success story in which the pieces all seemed to fall into place to create a premier children's

museum on the West Coast without having to run the obstacle course in fund-raising faced by so many other organizations. Much of the credit goes to executive director Sally Osberg, who started out as a volunteer, for her enthusiasm and dedication.

Getting it off to a grand start was Apple computer founder Steve Wozniak's donation of $1.8 million. Devoted to children, his interest has been constant. As a tribute to him, a street that borders the museum was changed to "Woz Way." Other generous people came forward: Lee and Diane Brandenburg, who gave $250,000 for a theater; Allen and Gloria Gilland and the water company gave the same amount; and David Packard and his late wife, Lucile Packard, gave a personal donation of $500,000.

Technology Center of Silicon Valley

The Technology Center of Silicon Valley credits a group of women—members of Junior League of Palo Alto, for conceiving the idea of a science museum. They approached Anthony P. Ridder, then publisher of the *San Jose Mercury*, with their idea in the early 1980s. Ridder was receptive, and it took off from there. By a sequence of events Ed Zschau, the first chairman, after being elected to Congress, was succeeded by Tony Ridder, who in time was transferred to Miami to become president of the newspaper division of Knight-Ridder, Inc. By this time Zschau had returned from Washington, and he is now back where he started as chairman.

174

According to president Peter Giles, the center, which will feature 170,000 square feet of exhibits, learning labs, classrooms, and conference areas, is targeted to open in the mid-1990s. In the meantime, as a sign of things to come, the center plans to open in 1990 its first public exhibit space with a presentation called "The Garage." The name is inspired by the legendary beginnings of Silicon Valley companies. It is to be located in a remodeled McCabe Hall across from the new San Jose Convention Center. Exhibits will feature space exploration with a model of the Hubble space telescope; microelectronics centering on the silicon chip; superconductivity and its uses, including high-speed trains that float on magnetic fields and small superfast computers; biotechnology and the exploration of DNA; robotics; and other highly technical innovations.

The Big Quake

The decade of the eighties will most be remembered for the Loma Prieta earthquake. At 5:04 P.M. on October 17, 1989, baseball fans were in their seats at Candlestick Park ready for the World Series game between the Oakland A's and the San Francisco Giants to begin when the big jolt, registering 7.1 on the Richter Scale, hit. There was no game that night or for more than a week afterwards. Oakland fans were faced with the problem of getting home. A section of the upper deck of the Bay Bridge fell and closed the main artery across the bay. The Cypress approach to the bridge collapsed, presenting a long-term problem. The quake ran a crazy kind of hit-or-miss course. San Francisco's Marina District had structural damage and fires while most other sections had mostly minor damage. On the peninsula, Stanford Memorial Chapel will be closed for three years from the earthquake's effects, while in Los Altos the St. Joseph's College, a seminary, was beyond repair. One workman died as a result of falling debris.

Hardest hit were two areas closest to the epicenter: Watsonville, where a tent city was set up for the hundreds who lost their homes (later replaced with mobile homes), and Santa Cruz, where the historic red brick Cooper House and many buildings on the mall were lost. Most

The Ng Shing Gong temple that stood at Sixth and Taylor streets. The facade was saved when the building was demolished. It is being rebuilt at the San Jose Historical Museum in cooperation with the Chinese American Women's Club. (SAN JOSE MERCURY NEWS)

of those businesses have moved into pavilion tents until new buildings can be constructed. Hollister lost a section of buildings along the Calaveras fault; Los Gatos lost half a block along the main business street, Santa Cruz Avenue, in addition to damage to homes.

Although downtown San Jose seemed to fare better than most places, the venerable Santa Clara County Superior Court building of 1862 was severely damaged. At first believed to be beyond repair, it is, with FEMA funds, on the list for restoration. St. Joseph's escaped unscathed. Project supervisor Terry Barnum was taking his family on a tour of the cathedral, showing them the newly coppered dome and towers that had been put in place just a few days before, when the quake came. Fortunately, the reinforcement of the walls was completed and the church suffered no damage.

Tony Nunez (right) working on the
restoration of St. Joseph's ceiling.
(COURTESY DIOCESE OF SAN JOSE)

Construction work on the exterior
of St. Joseph's

CHAPTER THIRTY-THREE

A New Decade

The dawn of the nineties brought a new day to St. Joseph's Church when in November, 1990, it became St. Joseph's Cathedral. At the same time the city of San Jose had taken on the look of the twenty-first century. Its skyline, dramatic against the backdrop of the eastern foothills, was moving ever upward with such buildings as the Fairmont Plaza, the ultramodern Federal Office Building, Lincoln Properties' River Park Towers on the Guadalupe River, the Ten Almaden office building, and the Commercial Center Bank at the corner of Almaden and Santa Clara streets. Twenty of the nation's largest banks had already moved into the city by 1975.

During the two terms of Mayor Tom McEnery the population surged to 765,000, making San Jose the third-largest city in the state and the twelfth in the United States. On New Year's Eve, 1989, ten thousand people celebrated in the convention center's one million square feet. The sports arena, scheduled to open October, 1992, will accommodate up to 18,000 fans. According to Chamber of Commerce head Steve Tedesco, Guadalupe River Park, expected to be completed before the year 2000, will be the largest urban park in the country since San Francisco's Golden Gate Park and New York's Central Park.

Setting the tone for the city is the Fairmont Hotel. It was a long time coming. After years of multiple problems, the $120 million hotel, built by Richard and Melvin Swig, Kimball Small, and San Jose's Redevelopment Agency, opened in November, 1987. The inaugural event, chaired by Ann Atkinson, was one of the splashiest affairs the city had ever seen. Under way, adjacent to the convention center, is a glitzy new Hilton Hotel.

Structures that add to the rich history of the town are the Scottish Rite Temple at St. James and North Third streets, built in 1925 and now the San Jose Athletic Club; the De Anza Hotel, which was built in 1931, renovated

in 1990, and retains much of its art deco influence (it was once a stopping place for celebrities as varied as Mickey Rooney and Eleanor Roosevelt); the rejuvenated Knox-Goodrich Building of 1889; the Letitia Building on First Street (recently given historical landmark status), built by C. T. Ryland and named for his wife, daughter of the first governor; the New Century Block at the southeast corner of Second and Santa Clara streets, built

The Odell organ, built in 1886

From left, Mayor Tom McEnery, Bishop Pierre DuMaine, and Father Jeremiah Helfrich. The mayor was baptised, confirmed, and married in St. Joseph's. Father Helfrich's roots in San Jose go back to the mid-1840s; his great-grandfather James Ford settled on a farm along Coyote Creek. Bishop DuMaine can claim no California connections; he was born in Paducah, Kentucky. (BOB PIERCE)

in 1889 by Adolph Pfister, a three-time mayor of San Jose; and the Sainte Claire Club on St. James Street, built by Senator James Phelan. The Fairmont's neighbors on the plaza are the San Jose Museum of Art, built in the 1890s, and St. Joseph's Cathedral, which dates to 1877.

The Diocese of San Jose

It was big news for Catholics in the valley in 1981 when word came from the Vatican that San Jose would be separated from the diocese of San Francisco and that the boundaries would cover the Santa Clara Valley from Palo Alto in the north to Gilroy in the south. San Joseans had harbored high hopes in 1962 when the archdiocese of San Francisco was first divided. The dioceses of Stockton, Santa Rosa, and Oakland were created, but

the fast-growing Santa Clara Valley had to wait almost twenty years for a diocese of its own.

St. Joseph's, California's oldest parish, began under the Spanish jurisdiction of the archbishop of Mexico City. After 1840, during the Mexican period, it was under the jurisdiction of the first bishop of Upper and Lower California, Francisco García Diego y Moreno, followed by Father José María Gonzalez, the vicar general. After Upper California became part of the United States and the diocese of Monterey, established in 1850, it came under control of Bishop Joseph Sadoc Alemany, a native of Spain and a naturalized American citizen.

On March 18, 1981, Auxiliary Bishop of San Francisco Pierre DuMaine, a native of Paducah, Kentucky, was formally installed as bishop of San Jose by Archbishop John Quinn of San Francisco at a vesper service in St. Patrick's Cathedral. The following day, March 19, on the solemnity of Saint Joseph, a public celebration was held in the Center for the Performing Arts. Pope John Paul II's representative in the United States, Archbishop Pio Laghi, and Archbishop Quinn celebrated the mass with Bishop DuMaine. Cardinal Timothy Manning of Los Angeles presided. Twenty-nine bishops from California, Mexico, and six western states attended.

Although in the hearts of most San Joseans St. Joseph's has always been the cathedral from the first adobe church (the Spanish-speaking Catholics have long called it "La Catedral"), the Vatican chose St. Patrick's — apparently because of its newer facility, slightly larger seating capacity, and parking. Also under consideration, no doubt, was the deteriorated state of St. Joseph's and the tremendous cost of renovation. Nevertheless, the decision was a deep disappointment to many San Jose Catholics, who felt because of its history, its location, and its architectural beauty, St. Joseph's should be the cathedral.

In 1984, Bishop DuMaine successfully petitioned the Sacred Congregation of Bishops for permission to make St. Joseph's the cathedral church of San Jose. The church itself had already been deeded to St. Joseph's by the diocese of San Francisco, and the land by the Jesuits at the request of Rev. John Clark, Provincial of the California Province of the Society of Jesus in Los Gatos, after petitioning his superior general in Rome. Alcalde Dimmick had originally deeded the land to Vicar General Gonzalez in 1849. Three years later the vicar deeded it to Bishop Alemany, who in 1859 passed it on to the Jesuits. Afterwards, Alemany wrote to the pope, saying that he feared he might have exceeded his authority. The pope answered that he had done the right thing, but that there should be a stipulation that the property would always be a place of worship.

San Jose's Fairmont Hotel

The Cathedral

The pope's request has been complied with. The land that Bishop Alemany deeded to the Jesuits at San Fernando and Market streets has been the place of worship for four St. Joseph's churches, and now the cathedral. The name cathedral is taken from the Greek word *cathedra*, meaning chair, and is the most ancient sign of the bishop's office, more significant than the mitre or crozier. It is in the cathedral that the bishop leads his people in worship and in the celebration of the sacraments, presides over ordinations to the priesthood, and celebrates the annual Chrism Mass, a solemn ceremony at which the sacramental oils are blessed for use by the parishes and other pastoral centers throughout the year. The Rite of Election, an important stage in the adult catechism, traditionally takes place in the cathedral on the first Sunday of Lent.

The Bryan Clinch Church

When the beautiful church designed by Theodore Lenzen was destroyed by fire in 1875, only six years after

it was completed, a lesser man than Father Nicholas Congiato, the pastor, would have despaired. But not this Italian priest. He immediately opened a competition for architects, which Bryan Clinch of the San Francisco and San Jose firm of Hoffman and Clinch won, his classical Greek cruciform design beating out the more traditional design by Theodore Lenzen. Clinch, born in Maryborough, Ireland, in 1842, was both a writer and an architect. Churches Clinch built include Blessed Sacrament Cathedral in Sacramento and St. Mary's and St. Anthony's churches in Oakland. A student of classical and Renaissance art and architecture, Clinch could not have anticipated that almost a hundred years later there would be a Vatican II and that his Greek cross design, as first planned by Michelangelo for St. Peter's in Rome, would lend itself so well to the new liturgical ideals.

The Remaking of St. Joseph's

As the renovation of St. Joseph's got underway, Bishop DuMaine found himself faced with costly structural problems that neither the architect nor the construction firm of Toeniskoetter and Breeding and their co-venture partners, Dinwiddie Construction Co., could have antici-

179

Saint Matthew, one of the Father Sciocchetti murals (PHOTO © JAMES CLARK)

Saint Luke (PHOTO © JAMES CLARK)

pated. All concerned agreed, however, that if the work had not been done, St. Joseph's would never have survived the October 17, 1989, earthquake.

The restoration of the church's art works, which suffered from water infiltration and mold that weakened the plaster under the murals and in some areas destroyed the bond between the canvas and the plaster, proved more complicated and costly than predicted. Bishop DuMaine said, "I found it impossible to cut corners. It would have been easier to sell this valuable piece of property and build somewhere else or to strip the inside, whitewash it, and just save the shell." He said he couldn't do that, that he couldn't compromise with partial measures. He felt that this unique church, a state historical landmark and listed on the National Historical Register, belongs to all Californians and is a link to a rich past. He said he owed it to the diocese's 400,000 Catholics to enable them to experience its beauty. "What we have received," he said, "we want to pass on. It's that simple."

180

The renovation turned out to be more than plastic surgery on a large scale. As the workers moved up and down the scaffolded exterior walls, they forced epoxy into the voids and implanted thousands of steel dowels in the brick, holding them in place with epoxy. To these dowels they attached woven mats of steel bars, over which aggregate concrete was blown from the base of the foundation forty feet up the inside walls. The exterior was then stuccoed and repainted, a job that presented yet another challenge. Four, and sometimes five, coats of paint had to be stripped from the old plaster. The paint was removed by applying liquid nitrogen and then blasting with ground walnut shells. The domes, towers, cupolas, and 12,000-square-foot roof are covered with copper, which in time will turn the soft green color one sees on the cathedrals and town halls in Europe. Ribs of reinforced fiberglass clearly define the octagonal form of the seven domes. The six smaller domes were removed from the roof with giant cranes, reinforced, and returned to their places.

Saint Athanasius and Saint John Chrysostom (PHOTO © JAMES CLARK)

A detail from Father Sciocchetti's mural work in the dome of St. Joseph's (PHOTO © JAMES CLARK)

The Interior

During the renovation, the interior of the church was cloaked in a network of scaffolding, and an elevator, the same one used in Washington, D.C., for the Capitol Rotunda restoration, was installed. A platform was built to enable Polish artist Andrzej Bossak to restore the Father Sciocchetti murals of the Evangelists and the fathers of the Eastern and Western church in the dome and the ornate decorations of the four vaulted ceilings that are in keeping with the baroque style of the interior of the church.

Bossak, a native of Poland, spent several years doing restoration work for Archbishop Karol Wojtyla, who later became Pope John Paul II. His wife, Barbara, who did the delicate gold-leaf work, was confirmed by the pope while he was archbishop. After being active in the Solidarity movement, the Bossaks came to the United States as political refugees in 1982. Bossak's work can be seen in Missions San Juan Bautista, San Jose, and

Carmel. For his giant undertaking and slow process Bossak set up a studio in the old St. Joseph's School building, where he restored the murals, paintings, frescoes, and statues, many of which had suffered severe damage from water, the smoke from candles, and earlier poor attempts at restoration. The layers of dust, grime, and varnish had to be carefully removed and the paintings transferred by an intricate hot-wax procedure to new canvas.

The Complete Circle

The focal point of the church is the new walnut, marble, and bronze altar, which is seventy-two inches in diameter and sits on an octagonal marble base directly under the seventy-foot-tall dome in the center of the church. The congregational seating is in interlocking chairs, which have the appearance of pews and are set in concentric circles around the altar. The bench in which the bishop's chair is fixed is in the same arc, to form a complete circle. This creates an open participation between the celebrant and the congregation. The ambo, which provides a proper place for the book of scriptures, stands immediately behind the altar and is slightly elevated so the reader or preacher can see the congregation.

The altar, ambo, cathedra, and bapistry were created by San Jose artist James A. Bacigalupi III. Bacigalupi, who is Jesuit educated, attended Bellarmine Preparatory, and three generations of Bacigalupis have attended Santa Clara University and St. Joseph's. He said that James Bacigalupi, his grandfather, was born at the corner of The Alameda and Franklin Street and that James, Jr.,

181

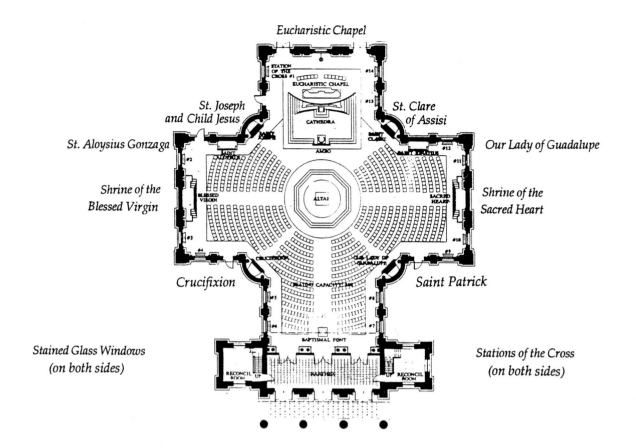

Eucharistic Chapel

St. Joseph
and Child Jesus

St. Clare
of Assisi

St. Aloysius Gonzaga

Our Lady of Guadalupe

Shrine of the
Blessed Virgin

Shrine of the
Sacred Heart

Crucifixion

Saint Patrick

Stained Glass Windows
(on both sides)

Stations of the Cross
(on both sides)

Floor plan of St. Joseph's Cathedral

his father, grew up in the valley. The first James Bacigalupi was president of the Bank of America and signed the bond that allowed artist Armando Marchigani to come from Mussolini's Italy to assist Father Sciocchetti with the murals.

On entering the church, one first sees the walnut baptismal font, which contains living water—an innovation of Vatican II, the water is constantly moving.

To complete the symmetry of the four transepts and make the church a true cruciform, the nave was shortened by moving the vestibule wall forward six feet. This gives additional space to the entry, whose floors have been re-covered with marble to match the stairs.

The Doors

The inner vestibule doors, similar to those one sees in the cathedrals of Europe, are made up of pieces of clear glass and each panel is surrounded by a ribbon of gold-tinted Bohemian glass. In the upper panel of each door is a leaded cross of jeweled glass picked out in gold with red accents. Over the entrance doors are three

semicircular, five-by-seven-foot stained-glass windows Tiffany style.

The copper outer doors at the entrance were beyond repair and discarded, but the hand-carved, solid golden oak doors were in good condition. The only problem was that they opened inward and had to be reversed and given new door jambs. Because of their weight, the three sets of doors, twelve feet tall and three inches thick, had to be fitted with special eight-inch-square hinges made of solid brass; it took several men to lift them. These doors, similar to those in the Stanford Chapel, were hand carved in Europe in the 1870s.

The Eucharistic Chapel

At the suggestion of the bishop, the 100-year-old altar of Carrara marble, decorated with gold leaf, which was no longer functional in the new liturgy, has been relocated to the newly formed eucharistic devotional chapel in the east transept. In it is enshrined the Blessed Sacrament. Hanging on the wall nearby, in its original place, is the restored bronze sanctuary lamp that honors the memory of Josephine Suñol, a member of an early St. Joseph's family. The chapel affords a quiet place to kneel and pray. The moving of the altar, which is set in concrete and brick and weighs twenty-six tons, was an engineering feat; it took twelve hours to turn it around 180 degrees. A freestanding low wall separates the altar from the bishop's chair.

Odell Organ

What was once called the choir loft (the choir now joins the congregation downstairs) now has walnut chairs matching those in the main body of the church. They are set on risers on either side of the famous Odell organ to accommodate the overflow when the main body of the church is filled. Light enters through a pair of eight-foot-in-diameter, rose-colored Tiffany stained-glass windows. The windows are encircled with angel heads.

The organ was built especially for the church in 1886 by the J. H. and C. S. Odell Company of Yonkers, New York, one of the leading organ builders of the nineteenth century. A gift of Myles and Amanda O'Connor, it is the only Odell instrument surviving on the West Coast. Its clocklike mechanism has twenty-seven ranks, each with fifty-eight pipes. A representative of the company came from New York in 1886 and spent a month installing it. On the statement of expenses is noted that the trip to California took seven days by train each way and that his fee was $7.50 a day.

Edward M. Stout, longtime curator of musical instruments for Grace Cathedral and the Palace of the Legion of Honor in San Francisco, did major repair on this same organ in 1968 when Father Joseph Dondero refurbished the church. For the cathedral in 1990 he did a complete restoration. He removed the instrument to the St. Joseph's School, where all 40,000 parts were identified and cleaned. It was a little disarming at first sight to see all those parts lying on the floor. But unlike Humpty-Dumpty, Stout got all the pieces back together again. He cleaned and repaired the action and re-winded the organ, installing five new wind reserves.

Commenting on its 104 years, Stout said that it plays from its original tracker with mechanical key action. Its oak case, which had suffered much abuse, has been completely repaired. He replaced with wood 300 places where there were gouges, digs, and other parts that were broken, cracked, or split. He re-covered the ivory keyboards that had played through to the wood with art-grade ivory (the heart of the tusk), the last available from an existing stock. "It's a wonderful instrument to sing to," said Stout.

The lowering of a newly coppered dome

"Its fine ensemble pervades the church without being overly aggressive."

The Towers

The towers, which now serve as museums of the parish's rich past, are fitted with new wide stairs. Here visitors can see art objects and historical artifacts such as the gilded bronze baldachin that surmounted the tabernacle of the Carrara marble altar, the pulpit that was so dramatically saved from the 1875 fire, and the tabernacle door from the Sacred Heart and Blessed Virgin altars, which are now shrines. In each belltower is a reconciliation room.

The nine stained-glass windows in the towers came from the chapel of Notre Dame College and are the oldest in the church, dating to the 1860s and '70s. One window, a gift of Dr. George Seifert in memory of his parents, features "St. Ignatius," founder of the Society of Jesus. It is a copy of a painting by Rubens in the collection

The stained-glass window of the Holy Family honors the memory of José Suñol, son of Don Antonio Suñol and Doña Dolores Bernal Suñol. (PHOTOGRAPHY BY AL MAGAZU)

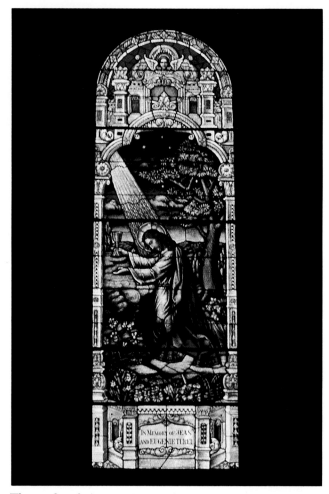

The window depicting "Our Lord at Prayer in the Garden" was given by the family of Jean and Eugenie Turel, well-known members of the French colony. (PHOTOGRAPHY BY AL MAGAZU)

at Warwick Castle. Dr. Seifert, a man much admired by the Notre Dame sisters, restored the sight of one of the older nuns by surgery. One of the first doctors born in the valley, he left his entire estate to his alma mater, Santa Clara. The window on the facing wall features Mother Julie Billiart, who founded the Sisters of Notre Dame de Namur and who has since been canonized. The window that honors Thomas and Annie Flood was a gift from their daughter.

Back in its place in the belltower is St. Joseph's 3,115-pound, four-foot-in-diameter Meneely bell, which survived the 1875 fire and the 1906 earthquake. No longer hand-pulled by a rope, it is installed in a steel carriage with a mechanically controlled ringing mechanism. Its rich D-sharp tones once more serve as a timepiece to the town and to summon the parishioners to mass. Also back in place is the iron picket fence around the front and south side of the church. It was

184

built in 1890 by Kuchenbeiser and Sons Iron Works of San Jose.

Stained-Glass Windows

An outstanding feature of St. Joseph's are the thirty-four stained-glass windows. They honor old St. Joseph's families, including those of Jose Suñol, son of Don Antonio Suñol, who came to the pueblo in 1818 and became one of the church's most generous benefactors; the Stocks, who came in 1852 and opened the first hardware store; John and Edward Auzerais, prominent members of the French colony, who came in the 1840s and built the famous hostelry the Auzerais House; the generous Myles and Amanda O'Connor; C. T. Ryland, banker, state senator, judge, and son-in-law of Gov. Peter Burnett; Margaret Duncan, who came in 1846 and married James Enright, who was destined to become a major land owner; and Jeannie and Eugene Turel, prominent members of St. Joseph's Church, who ran the City Store.

On the side walls of the cathedral are eighteen arched windows (nine on each side), four-by-fourteen-feet in size. Hand-blown in Bavaria, they were shipped to San Francisco, where they were leaded before being sent down to San Jose. When it was decided to complete the continuity and let in light by adding three complementary stained-glass windows to the east wall of the Eucharistic Chapel, the construction people found that space had already been framed with bricks. Apparently windows were part of the church's original plan but never completed because of lack of funds. Mill Valley artist Eleanor Devereaux crafted the new windows, which are contemporary in design and integrated with the 100-year-old windows and architecture of the church while pointing to Vatican II theological concepts.

Alan Dragge, who cleaned and releaded the windows, did a major job of rebuilding of the skylight (twenty feet in diameter) in the dome. Apparently it had been damaged in the 1906 quake and received a poor patch job.

The Lighting

The electronically controlled lighting is subtle and yet effective. Of special interest is the unique system for raising and lowering light in different parts of the church for different liturgical or devotional purposes. Around the circumference of the dome is a fiber-optic tube; hidden in the cornices are fluorescent lights that bathe the vaulted ceiling and the Sciocchetti murals in light. One hundred and fifty spots are recessed in the transept ceiling fixtures. Suspended from the ceiling twenty feet above the floor of the church are sixteen chandeliers, installed in the 1920s, which have been modified to accommodate the sound system. The exterior lights, mounted in fix-

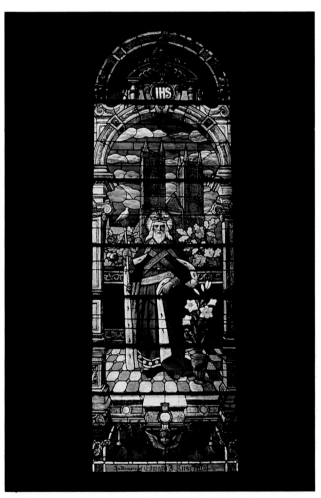

Saint Edward the Confessor, by artist Carl Heineke, was given by friends of Edward Auzerais. (PHOTOGRAPHY BY AL MAGAZU)

Saint Ignatius of Loyola, a gift of Dr. George Seifert to the College of Notre Dame. (PHOTOGRAPHY BY AL MAGAZU)

185

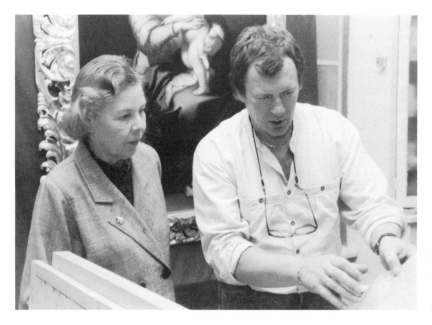

Miriam Hart Alfaro of the Hart's Store family visited Andrzej Bossak during his restoration work. Mrs. Alfaro studied painting under Father Luigi Sciocchetti and his assistant, Armando Marchigani. (BOB PIERCE)

tures on the ground and on surrounding buildings, play on the copper domes for dramatic effects.

Altars Turned Shrines

With the new liturgy, the sacrifice of the mass occurs only at the main altar of a church. Thus the former altars have become shrines, such as the two marble altars in the north and south transept designed by Bryan Clinch. Michael Callahan gave the "Mary the Immaculate Mother of God" altar. The companion piece, the "Sacred Heart" altar, was a gift in 1885 of Catherine Dunne, who first attended St. Joseph's Church in 1848 when she came from Canada as the bride of Bernard Murphy.

The shrine of "Our Lady of Guadalupe" was a gift to St. Joseph's from the Spanish-speaking people of the parish in 1891. Her feast day, December 12, marking her appearance to the Indian Juan Diego in 1531, has always been the occasion for a celebration. A 1908 invitation for the "Fiesta de Nuestra Señora de Guadalupe" tells of a day-into-evening celebration attended by Archbishop Riordan. On Pope John Paul II's visit to Mexico City and the sanctuary in May of 1990, he beatified Juan Diego, the first step towards sainthood for the young Indian man to whom the Blessed Virgin appeared.

"Saint Aloysius, Patron of Youth" is another altar-turned-shrine, given in 1892 by the young people of the parish from the profits of their fund-raising activities. Back in the cathedral is the statue of Saint Patrick that gained so much notoriety when Patrick McGuire saved it from the burning church in 1875 and created an uproar in contemporary times when the local newspaper

reported that it was being given to the diocese of San Francisco, a rumor emphatically denied by everyone from the bishop on down.

In the two most prominent niches in the church are new statues: one of Saint Joseph, patron saint of the city, and the other of Saint Clare of Assisi, patron saint of the Santa Clara Valley, whose terrain is quite similar to the Umbrian countryside where Assisi is located. She founded the Poor Clares, who have a foundation at Immaculate Heart Monastery in Los Altos Hills. The artist, Sandro Lorenzini, used a wood called cirmolo from the region above Venice—a prized wood for religious sculpture since the Middle Ages. He depicts Jesus as a boy of ten or twelve handing Joseph the carpenter a piece of wood, symbolic of what is to be his own incarnation, the cross. The statue of Saint Clare is dressed in the somber Franciscan robe and holds a light in her right hand ("clare" means light), symbolic of the holy sacrament of the eucharist. The name was given to her by her mother, who, after praying for the safe deliverance of her child, was enveloped in light.

The Le Mercier Stations of the Cross were a gift from Mr. and Mrs. Myles O'Connor, who saw the originals on a visit to Rheims Cathedral in France in 1900 and commissioned an artist to reproduce the paintings for St. Joseph's. The cathedral was bombed during World War II, and it is believed St. Joseph's has the only existing copies. They have been restored and set in less ornate frames. When art restorer Bossak noted one of the stations was a replacement by an American artist, he repainted it to conform to the European quality of the others. Bossak also restored other paintings brought back by the O'Connors: one *Madonna and Child* of the

Murillo school (he discovered someone had painted a diaper on the Infant Jesus) and a copy of Mariotto Albertinelli's *The Visitation*.

All Things to All People

Much like the great cathedrals of Europe, St. Joseph's plays both sacred and secular roles in the city. Bishop DuMaine considers it not only a place for Catholic worship but also a public place to be shared by parishioners, tourists, historians, artists, and workers of all faiths for appropriate artistic performances and exhibitions. Brother Joseph Aspell expressed it well when he said, "St. Joseph's is not only an expression of the Catholic church but also of the city of San Jose. It's the centerpiece, a little jewel interwoven into the fabric of the city."

Traditionally, San Jose State University holds its Scholarship Orchestra and Chorus Concerts here every December. The American Guild of organists and the California Bach Society offer concerts on the Odell organ, as does the annual Schweitzer concert that benefits the poor.

St. Joseph's is home to many people, a cosmopolitan center of faith composed of a large Spanish-speaking community (five masses are said in Spanish and four in English every weekend), as well as Filipinos, Vietnamese, and other ethnic groups.

During the week it is a church away from home for Catholics and non-Catholics, as several hundred members of the business community drop in for noonday mass. It is open from dawn to dusk, and people can be seen kneeling in prayer, saying the stations, walking around the church, stopping to study a painting or a statue. Others may be just sitting quietly in contemplation.

When San Jose City Councilman James Beall was running for office the first time, his father, James Beall, Sr., dropped in to St. Joseph's to say a prayer. There, to his surprise, he met his wife, Katherine, who had come in for the same purpose. Her ties to St. Joseph's go back to 1879 and the marriage of her grandparents, the O'Regans, in the church.

The diocese bought the 80 South Market Street building next door — originally built by the Pacific Tel & Tel in 1910 — for a cathedral center. On the first floor are the parish hall, a gift shop, and the sacristy. In the basement are meeting rooms, a small assembly hall (the choir holds its practices here), and offices. On the second floor are diocese offices; on the third floor, a cathedral lounge; and the rectory is on the fourth floor.

St. Joseph's, the Parish

The pastor of St. Joseph's, Rev. Jeremiah Helfrich, S.J., although raised in Los Angeles, has deep roots in San Jose. His antecedents, the Fords, came from Ireland by way of Boston in 1849. His great-grandfather James Ford, for whom the road is named, settled on a farm on Coyote Creek at Edenvale.

The family attended St. Joseph's Church and school. Father Helfrich's grandmother Margaret Ford and her husband, William Tell Aggeler, lived in town at Fifth and San Carlos streets, where Father Helfrich's mother was born. In 1911 Aggeler moved his family to Los Angeles, where he became one of the city's first public defenders and later a superior court judge.

Spanish has always been a first or second language at St. Joseph's. Father Helfrich has four assistants, Jesuits trained in inner-city work who say masses in Spanish. Their works of charity are numerous. On Mondays and Fridays they distribute food vouchers to the poor. In between times they have a service for helping these people find work. Relatively new is the evangelization program that sends people from door to door in poor neighborhoods to see if anyone needs help.

Saturdays are busy days at St. Joseph's. Five teams of parishioners cook breakfast at the Living Family Consortium at Agnews, a building that houses families until they can find a home. Another five teams of parishioners, joined by Santa Clara University students, come in at 5 A.M. on Saturdays and cook breakfast to serve to the street people either at the Julian Street Inn or the Salvation Army. Afterwards they give them a bag lunch. Joe Asunsolo, who created the Morning Ministry, received the Saint Joseph Award at the Schweitzer concert in 1988.

One of the parish's most important works, Father Helfrich feels, is the transitional house, officially the "St. Joseph, the Worker" house but usually called the "Green House." It accommodates eight men for up to three months. Many are Vietnam veterans or men just out of jail. "We set up a bank account for them at Wells Fargo Bank, help them get jobs so they can get their lives together after they leave. Many of them come back to see us." Father Helfrich says, "I've even married some of them."

Pat Kelly, third generation of his family in St. Joseph's, heads the pastoral council. Another active council member and usher for twenty-five years is Tony Maruca.

The diocese of San Jose has yet another project. Within the boundaries of St. Joseph's parish it is cooperating with the Sisters of Mercy to build low-cost housing on the site of the former St. Mary's German National Church.

Summing Up

As the Pueblo de San José de Guadalupe, the state's first civil settlement and the first American capital, grew from a cluster of adobe houses along the Guadalupe River in 1777 to a metropolitan city, so grew its little tule-roofed adobe church, founded in 1803, to the grand Cathedral of St. Joseph on the same site. It is the heart and soul of the city, its stately presence a focus of faith and a monument to the city's past, present, and future.

On October 28, 1990, the transfer of the cathedral from St. Patrick's, proto-cathedral, to St. Joseph's Cathedral took place. The following Sunday, November 4, bishops and archbishops from the Western states and the apostolic pro-nuncio (the pope's ambassador to the U.S. and its Catholic churches) joined Bishop Pierre DuMaine for the dedication of the cathedral. The 120-member diocese choir sang. That evening the San Jose Symphony Orchestra gave a concert in the cathedral, after which the Bishop's Charity Ball took place in the nearby Fairmont Hotel.

One of the two circular, angel-head stained-glass windows at the front of the cathedral (PHOTOGRAPHY BY AL MAGAZU)

View looking northeast of St. Joseph's Cathedral during renovation (PHOTOGRAPH © ROBERT W. CAMERON)

Bibliography

Arbuckle, Clyde. *Clyde Arbuckle's History of San Jose.* San Jose: Smith & McKay Printing Co., Inc., 1986.

———. *Santa Clara County Ranchos.* San Jose: Harlan-Young Press, 1968.

Bancroft, Hubert. *History of California.* San Francisco: The History Company, Publishers, 1886.

Barrett, Dick, editor. *A Century of Service.* San Jose: San Jose Bicentennial Commission, Inc., 1977.

Beilharz, Edwin A. *Felipe de Neve.* San Francisco: California Historical Society, 1971.

———, and Lopez, Carlos U. *We Were 49ers.* Pasadena: Ward Ritchie Press, 1976.

———, and DeMers, Donald, Jr. *San Jose—California's First City.* Tulsa, Okla.: Continental Heritage Press, 1980.

Belden, David, and Thorne, W. S. *Santa Clara County, California.* San Jose: Board of Trade of San Jose, 1887; San Francisco: W. B. Bancroft, 1887. Reprint. San Jose: San Jose Historical Museum Association, 1980.

Brewer, William H. *Up and Down California in 1860–1864.* Edited by Francis P. Farquhar. New Haven: Yale University Press, 1930.

Brunch, George G. *History of Los Gatos.* Fresno: Valley Publishers, 1971.

Bryant, Edwin. *What I Saw in California.* New York: D. Appleton & Co., 1848.

Bulmore, Laurence, and Lanyon, Milton. *Cinnabar Hills.* Los Gatos, Calif.: Village Printers, 1967.

Burnett, Peter. *Recollections and Opinions of an Old Pioneer.* New York: D. Appleton & Co., 1880.

Butler, Phyllis Filiberti. *The Valley of Santa Clara: Historic Buildings, 1792–1920, with Architectural Supplement by the Junior League of San Jose, Inc.* San Jose: Junior League of San Jose, Inc., 1975. 2nd ed. Novato, Calif.: Presidio Press, 1981.

Carroll, Mary Bowden. *Ten Years in Paradise.* San Jose: Press of Popp & Hogan, 1903.

The Country Club of Washington Township Research Committee. *History of Washington Township.* Alameda County, Calif.: Country Club of Washington Township, 1904. 2d ed. Stanford: Stanford University Press, 1950.

Cunningham, Florence. *Saratoga's First Hundred Years.* Edited by Frances Fox. San Jose: Harlan-Young Press, 1967.

Dana, Richard Henry, Jr. *Two Years Before the Mast.* New York: Harper & Brothers, 1840. First expanded edition. Boston: Fields, Osgood, & Co., 1869.

Davis, William Heath. *Sixty Years in California.* San Francisco: A. J. Leary, Publisher, 1889.

Delgado, James P. *Witness to Empire: The Life of Antonio María Suñol.* San Jose: Sourisseau Academy for California State and Local History, San Jose State University, 1970.

DeNevi, Don, and Moholy, Noel Francis. *Junípero Serra.* San Francisco: Harper & Row, 1985.

De Vries, Carolyn. *Grand and Ancient Forest.* Fresno: Valley Publishers, 1978.

Dillon, Richard. *Fool's Gold: A Biography of John A. Sutter.* New York: Coward-McCann, 1967. Reprint. *Captain John Sutter: Sacramento Valley's Sainted Sinner.* Santa Cruz: Western Tanager Press, 1981.

Dwyer, John T. *Condemned to the Mines.* New York: Vantage Press, 1976.

Engelhardt, Zephyrin, Fr. O.F.M. *The Holy Man of Santa Clara.* San Francisco: The James H. Barry Company, 1909.

Farrell, Harry. *San Jose and Other Famous Places.* San Jose: San Jose Historical Museum Association, 1983.

Foote, H. S., ed. *Pen Pictures From the Garden City of the World.* Chicago: Lewis Publishing Co., 1888.

Fox, Frances. *Luís María Peralta and His Adobe.* San Jose: Smith-McKay Printing, 1975.

———. *Land Grant to Landmark.* San Jose: Pied Piper Publishers, 1978.

Garrod, R. V. *Saratoga Story.* N.p., 1962.

Gudde, Erwin G. *California Place Names*. 3rd ed. Berkeley: University of California Press, 1969.

Guinn, J. M. *History of the State of California and the Biographical Record of the Coast Counties of California*. Chicago: The Chapman Publishing Co., 1904.

Hall, Frederic. *History of San Jose*. San Francisco: A. L. Bancroft and Co., 1871.

Hittell, Theodore H. *History of California*. San Francisco: N. J. Stone & Co., 1898.

Hom, Gloria. Ed. *Chinese Argonauts*. Los Altos, Calif.: Foothill Community College, 1971.

Hoover, M. B., and Rensch, H. E. and E. G. *Historic Spots in California*. Revised by Abeloe, William. Stanford, Calif.: Stanford University Press, 1966.

Hruby, Daniel D. *Mines to Medicine*. San Jose: Rosicrucian Press, 1965.

Hyman, Beth. *Hiram Morgan Hill*. Morgan Hill, Calif.: N.p., 1983.

Jacobson, Yvonne. *Passing Farms: Enduring Values*. Los Altos and Cupertino, Calif.: William Kaufmann and California History Center, De Anza College, 1984.

James, William F., and McMurry, George H. *History of San Jose, California*. San Jose: Smith Printing Company, 1933.

A Judicial Odyssey. Edited by Fritz, Christian G., Griffith, Michael, and Hunter, Janet M. San Jose: Advisory Committee, San Jose Federal Court, 1985.

King, Thomas M. *A History of St. Joseph's Catholic Church*. San Jose: Research paper for San Jose State Geography Department, 1973.

Koch, Margaret. *Santa Cruz County, Parade of the Past*. Fresno: Valley Publishers, 1973.

Life in the Mines of New Almaden. San Jose: San Jose Historical Museum Association, 1978.

Loomis, Patricia. *Signposts*. San Jose: San Jose Historical Museum Association, 1982.

———. *Signposts II*. San Jose: San Jose Historical Museum Association, 1985.

Mackey, Margaret. *Early California Costumes*. 2nd ed. Stanford, Calif.: Stanford University Press, 1949.

Malone, Michael. *The Big Score: The Billion-Dollar Story of Silicon Valley*. New York: Doubleday, 1985.

Margolin, Malcolm. *The Ohlone Way*. Berkeley: Heyday Press, 1978.

Mars, Amaury. *Reminiscences of Santa Clara Valley and San Jose*. San Jose: Artistic Publishing Company, 1901.

McEnery, Thomas. *California Cavalier, the Journal of Captain Thomas Fallon*. San Jose: Inishfallen Enterprises, 1978. Reprint. San Jose: San Jose Historical Museum Association, 1986.

McGloin, John G. *Eloquent Indian*. Stanford: Stanford University Press, 1949.

McKevitt, Gerald. *Santa Clara University*. Stanford: Stanford University Press, 1978.

McNamee, Mary Dominica, S.N.D. de N. *Light in the Valley*. Berkeley: Howell-North Books, 1967.

———. *Willamette Interlude*. Palo Alto: Pacific Books, 1959.

Muller, Kathleen. *San Jose, City With a Past*. San Jose: San Jose Historical Museum Association, 1988.

Munro-Fraser, J. P. *History of Santa Clara County, California*. San Franciso: Alley, Bowen & Co., 1881.

Nailen, Richard L. *Guardians of the Garden City*. San Jose: Smith & McKay Printing Co., 1972.

Older, Mrs. Fremont. *California Missions and Their Romances*. New York: Coward-McCann, 1938.

Palou, Francisco, O.F.M. *Life of Ven. Padre Junípero Serra*. San Francisco: P. E. Dougherty & Co., 1884.

Peyton, Wes. *San Jose, a Personal View*. San Jose: San Jose Historical Museum Association, 1989.

Pierce, Marjorie. *East of the Gabilans*. Fresno: Valley Publishers, 1976. Reprint. Santa Cruz: Western Tanager Press, 1981.

Rambo, F. Ralph. *Pen and Inklings*. San Jose: San Jose Historical Museum Association, 1984.

———. *Lady of Mystery*. San Jose: Rosicrucian Press, 1967.

Riordan, Joseph W., S.J. *The First Half Century of St. Ignatius Church and College*. San Francisco: H. S. Crocker Co., 1905.

Robinson, Alfred. *Life in California*. New York: Wiley & Putnam, 1846.

Sawyer, Eugene T. *History of Santa Clara County*. Los Angeles: Historic Record Company, 1922.

Shumate, Dr. Albert. Edited and wrote introduction. *Boyhood Days, Ygnacio Villegas' Reminiscences of California in the 1850s*. San Francisco: California Historical Society, 1983.

Shortridge, Charles M. *Sunshine, Fruit and Flowers*. San Jose Mercury Publishing and Printing Company, 1895. Reprint. San Jose: San Jose Historical Museum Association, 1976.

Solari, Agnes, and Zaro, Margaret. *San Jose's St. Joseph's*. San Jose: N.p., 1975.

Spearman, Arthur. *The Five Franciscan Churches of Mission Santa Clara, 1777–1835*. Palo Alto: National Press, 1963.

Starr, Kevin. *Americans and the California Dream, 1850–1915*. New York: Oxford University Press, 1973.

Sullivan, Sister Gabrielle. *Martin Murphy, Jr., California Pioneer, 1844–1884*. Stockton: Pacific Center for Western Historical Studies, University of the Pacific, 1974.

Taylor, Bayard. *El Dorado*. New York: G. P. Putnam, 1850.

Thompson & West. *Historical Atlas Map of Santa Clara County*. San Francisco: Thompson & West, 1876. Reprint. San Jose: San Jose Historical Museum Association, 1973.

Thornton, Walter, S.J. *Fragments From the History of St. Joseph's Church*. San Jose: St. Joseph Church Bulletin, 1926.

Vancouver, George. *A Voyage of Discovery to the North Pacific Ocean and Round the World*. London: G. G. and J. Robinson and J. Edwards, 1798.

Appendix

The Four Churches of St. Joseph

1803   The cornerstone is laid for the first pueblo church, San José y Nuestra Señora de Guadalupe.

1835   The cornerstone is laid for second adobe church at same location, now the corner of San Fernando and Market Streets.

1850   The second adobe church is encased in brick and two towers are added.

1868   A disastrous earthquake severely damages the second adobe church.

1869   The third St. Joseph's Church, designed by Theodore Lenzen of wood with brick trim, is dedicated at the same location.

1875   The beautiful St. Joseph's Church is leveled by fire.

1877   The fourth St. Joseph's Church, designed by Bryan Clinch, rises on the same location.

1990   St. Joseph's Cathedral is dedicated.

Significant Dates of Spanish Era

1769   Don Gaspar de Portolá and party are the first white men to visit the Santa Clara Valley. They miss their destination, Monterey, but scout Francisco Ortega discovers the Golden Gate. The folowing year they succeed and take possession in the name of King Carlos III.

1770   Capt. Pedro Fages is appointed *comandante*. Accompanied by Padre Crespí, he is the first to enter the Santa Clara Valley from the south.

1775   Capt. Juan Bautista de Anza opens an overland route to Monterey from Tubac, Mexico (now Arizona).

1776   Anza leads a party of 230, including women, children, priests, and soldiers, 165 mules, 340 saddle horses, and 302 beef cattle to Monterey.

1777   Mission Santa Clara is established in January. On November 29, Lt. José Moraga, with sixty-six settlers, founds the Pueblo de San José de Guadalupe.

1822   Mexican rule begins.

1834   Mexico secularizes the missions, confiscates church lands, and makes land grants.

1846   The United States goes to war with Mexico.

1847   The Mexican War ends. Andrés Pico signs an agreement with Capt. John Frémont to accept sovereignty of the United States.

1848   The Treaty of Guadalupe Hidalgo signed.

1849   Constitutional Convention in Monterey votes San Jose California's first capital.

1850   California admitted to the Union.

Glossary of Spanish Terms

acequia	irrigation ditch or channel	*llagas*	wounds
alameda	avenue of trees	*llano*	plain or flat area
alcalde	mayor	*matanza*	killing of cattle for hides
alférez	ensign	*mayordomo*	manager
arroyo	a dry creek	*merienda*	light lunch
ayuntamiento	city council	*mestizo*	half-breed
caballero	gentleman	*metate*	flat stone for grinding corn
Californio	native-born Californian	*padre*	priest
camino	road	*palisado*	fence of logs
capilla	chapel	*plaza*	square, usually parklike, in front
carreta	two-wheel wooden cart		of church
casa	house	*pobladores*	settlers
ciénaga	swamp	*presidio*	military station
comandante	commanding officer	*pueblo*	town
comisionado	commissioner	*ranchería*	Indian village
diseño	map sketched by hand	*ranchero*	rancher
don	title of respect for a man	*rancho*	ranch
doña	title of respect for a woman	*regidor*	town councilman
embarcadero	wharf, dock	*reglamento*	rules, bylaws
encinal	oak grove	*riata*	rope made of horsehair
fandango	Spanish dance	*sala*	living room
gringo	slang term for American	*solar*	house lot
hacienda	large estate or farm	*suerte*	farm lot within pueblo
juez de campo	judge of the field	*vaquero*	cowboy
juez de paz	justice of the peace	*vara*	a measure of distance, approximately
junta	council or assembly		one yard
juzgado	town hall, courthouse		

Index

197